How to Ruin Your Life:
The Daily Grind of a DIY Tour

Sammy Warm Hands

Foreword by Carnage The Executioner

How to Ruin Your Life
© 2020 by Take 92 Music
Edited by Sammy Warm Hands & Brady O'Rourke

All rights reserved. No part of this book may be reproduced or transmitted in any form unless you want a punch in the dick. You'll never see it coming.

Printed in USA by 48HrBooks (www.48HrBooks.com)

Dedication

For George Carlin, whose incomparable body of work is quoted daily; whose thought-provoking perspective inspired generations of subversive artists; and whose contagious love for irreverent language irrevocably poisoned my young mind.

George Carlin
(May 12, 1937 - June 22, 2008)
He was just here a minute ago...

Table of Contents

Foreword 5

Introduction 11

I Quit My Job For This 19

Not So Blue 39

Cats, Pajamas 51

Bored With Buddha 57

Original Recipe 65

Attack of The Show Stoppers 75

Bears Repeating 91

Blood in The Water 103

Vacant Eyes 119

Rare Form 1: Summer 139

The World Has No Eyedea 163

SQUALOR 201

Rare Form 2: Winter 221

Blank Check 241

Fall Children 263

Ravenous 303

PERIL 321

Acknowledgements 343

Artist Credits 344

Foreword

by Carnage The Executioner

Crushkill Recordings SXSW showcase
(Left to right:) Sam, Carnage
Nook Amphitheater (Austin, TX) 2015

I'm Carnage The Executioner. I reside in St. Paul, MN. My brother Sammy Warm Hands calls me Terrell. I've been a full-time, independent artist for twelve years. I book and manage all of my shows and tours, as well as finance all of my musical releases on my Hecatomb Industries record label.

I would classify myself as a *successful* Do-It-Yourself artist. But I'm quick to tell a novice-to-the-game naysayer that maintaining a viable presence and paying my bills has been a tiring struggle. Many on the outside might not see what Sam and myself do as "work," simply because we do what we love as a source of income. But asking us what consequences come as a result of our choices to be our own bosses, could inform you of just about *everything* you need to know about how to persevere as a DIY artist.

I first had the pleasure of meeting Sam in 2011. I was one of two opening acts for Ecid's *Red Beretta* tour, and John Henry's (Eugene, OR) was one of our 13 stops. Before I performed my set, Sam introduced himself as one of the rappers in The ILLusionists - the group scheduled to co-headline our show. I recall him being calm, cool and warm. He was a fan of my past work, citing a connection between us through mutual friend and legend, Eyedea (R.Eye.P.). But equally visible in him was a professional confidence that held my attention, especially after I found out that he was the owner of his own record label, Take 92 Music. After I performed my set and exited the stage, Sam was the first person who spoke to me. His compliments kind of caught me off-guard, due to Hip-Hop shows often featuring rappers on the bill with egos that prevent us from displaying genuine appreciation for art other than our own.

I watched Sam's set when he took the stage. I'll admit that I was borderline taken aback; his untamed energy was twice what I expected it to be! It was a little "much" for me as a first-timer. But I didn't call his abrasive live performance a flop. I realized this was the OTHER side of his approach: professional artist and dedicated live performer were the two labels I gave to Sam that night. This combination would lead to me taking the time out to acknowledge Sam as my peer whenever he reached out to me.

Just over a year after Sam and I met, he was asking me if I'd like to tour with him and The ILLusionists to promote their well put-together *Death Of A Salesman* album. He suggested that I take the headlining position, with his group being billed as the opening act. I was dealing with the craziness of self-releasing my newest album, doing two collaboration projects and five other tours. I can truly say I'd kind of "had it easy" with these other tours, though—they were all booked by someone other than myself. But touring is never as glamorous as it appears to be from afar. My first-hand knowledge of the toil that comes along with touring was partially why it took Sam contacting me a few times before I finally committed to touring with him.

Admittedly, I was fearful of doing a tour that was a *total* DIY effort for the first time. This would be one where I expected to receive more responsibilities than ever before. But Sam didn't let me ignore him or weasel my way out of working harder. He did, though, assure me that he would pick me up from the airport when I flew in to start the tour and do all the driving in his personal van. That was cool and all, but Sam's willingness to spearhead the tour art design, book the entire tour himself, act as tour manager and give me the majority of the money made on the tour - in additional to billing me as the headliner, were the selling points. Out of compassion and respect for Sam's past touring record, his generosity and his dedication to the DIY grind, I decided to give The ILLusionists equal billing on the tour. I also offered to give them a larger cut of the tour money. It was the least I could do as an *attempt* to match Sam's kindness and commitment.

With all the work Sam was willing to do, I felt compelled to ask him if he at all thought I wasn't going to be able to pull my weight. Sam confessed that he deemed it his responsibility as a DIY artist to make these types of arrangements and sacrifices for artists he respected. Sam wasn't afraid to pay the proverbial dues that well-established artists tend to boast about. This reminded me of the dedicated-professional aura I got from him when we first met, not even two years prior. We came up with the title, *(The Attack Of) The Show Stoppers* tour, as somewhat of an ode to my song, "Attack Of The Show Stealer," and our mutual dedication to bringing attendees the rawest, most intense live show possible.

The *Show Stoppers* tour was 8 days long, with most of the shows happening back-to-back, and took place in June of 2013. I consider that year one of notable growth for myself, which came, in part, from our tour. Sam has repeatedly stated that our tour had the same impact on him. On the first night of our tour, I gave Sam and his band mate / our friend Evan (E. Ville) the advice of toning down their live performance intensity a bit. My opinion was that this shift would lead to their strong and relatable messages becoming more easily-digestible to those not familiar with their music. With no resistance at all, Sam explained that he understood where I was coming from. It was then, that a tandem, greatly beneficial artistic exchange happened: Sam became a live performer with a presentation that rivals some of the best performers I've ever witnessed; I headlined my first tour outside of the Midwest and became a more well-rounded independent artist. I met a few artists who I now call my friends on our tour. Quite a few Carnage fans have told me that tour was the first time they had ever seen me live.

During the considerably short time I've known Sam, we have made and lost money together, slept on the same stranger's couches, eaten crappy food with one another and shared, as well as *stolen* spotlights from each other on stages. I've seen Sam do more work than ANYONE who isn't signed to a record label. Most of his accomplishments were achieved while taking time away from his day job and leaving his wife at home alone. Sam's duties have included, but are not limited to: booking agent; tour manager; contract agreement enforcer; graphic designer;

merchandiser; auto-mechanic; conflict mediator; recording engineer; podcast host; label representative / owner and even chauffeur! Sam is the *EXACT* embodiment of what type of strength it takes to survive and solve the DIY pitfall conundrum. I believe Sam has seen it and done it all. He continues to inspire me immensely, especially when viewing myself as needing to measure up to his level of output and match his work ethic. I accept the challenge Sam has initiated. And yes, I've got my work cut out for me. Wish me luck!

Introduction

Tour is a mixed bag. Let's get that straight right now.

On one hand, it's exciting and often romanticized. In reality, it's lonely and decidedly unglamorous. I write this from the waiting room of an auto repair shop, after being stranded all day and night in a Walmart parking lot. You really never know what to expect.

I first stepped onstage at the age of nine. It was the 1995 talent show, and my "band" was performing a lip sync. I could sort of play guitar, if you count nursery rhymes from an instructional book, and my drummer—the immensely talented Leo London—was probably the best of us all, but we had no idea what we were doing, really. So we pretended.

At the time, I had a few random cassettes but no real musical direction. Then my dad bought my first ever CD. (Imagine that —no rewinding!) I've always been reluctant to talk about these years, because that CD was Garth Brooks' *The Chase*, and that musical direction quickly became country. But as my stepdad Steve pointed out, those years seem a lot more important in hindsight.

I dove deep into the Garth Brooks discography, collecting albums, singles, compilations, and even live releases on VHS. I remember watching the second video countless times, becoming obsessed with the live show. The crowd and the energy were captivating. My parents took me to see him in Portland that year.

It was my first concert.*

Even my first fiction book, which is still in my elementary school library, was written about traveling the country to see a Garth Brooks tour. (Yes, I've always been this obsessive.) That line in "The Process"** is true, and quite literal:

I was singing "Thunder Rolls" in the cold and the rain
Years later I wanted to be like Kurt Cobain

I actually walked around outside in my cowboy hat, belting "The Thunder Rolls" in the rain. Alone. You know, for fun.

Needless to say that when my school announced the talent show, I was all in. My friends Rick Lyon and Leo (then known as Mikey Palmer) joined the "band," and The Country Kids were born. We "played" the makeshift instruments (a child-size acoustic guitar, an unplugged keyboard, and some painted popcorn tins, repurposed as drums) and we practiced in my living room. They weren't necessarily fans of the music, but I've always had this weird ability to get people to go along with my crazy ideas.

One of these ideas—and this may have been my mom's, I don't remember—was to make it more theatrical. We recruited my neighbor, Maria Rodriguez, and Leo's sister Tracy to be our dancers. That's right. We had fucking backup dancers.

The talent show was held at a nearby middle school. The bleachers in the gym were enormous, and the "stage" was center court. The audience was literally looking down on us.

---

*In my revisionist history, I skip the country phase (1995) and go straight to my first punk band, EPD (1998). I tell people my first CD was Beck's *Odelay,* and that my first show was Beastie Boys & A Tribe Called Quest. For someone who doesn't have a habit of lying, I've gone to great lengths to hide from my past.

***Bears Repeating,* 2014

Most people would be intimidated, but I loved it. The lights went dark with our backs to the crowd. As the song started, we spun around and jumped into action. The dancers were in perfect sync. Leo's bass drum had our name painted on it. I pulled a Bob Dylan move, miming the harmonica solo at the same time as my fake strumming. Later, I did the Chuck Berry hop across the stage, and people went *nuts*.

It might've just been the sheer amount of preparation and choreography for a bunch of third graders pretending to play a song, but whatever it was, it worked. The crowd loved us. And I loved performing. Probably the strangest part of this story is that our "band" didn't end there.

In fourth grade, the talent show was held at the high school, which meant a giant stage in an auditorium. We played a different Garth Brooks song, and I pulled out the old Chuck Berry move—which, full disclosure, I ripped off from the Garth Brooks VHS—and we were greeted with similar, if not *greater* enthusiasm. But that wasn't enough. I wanted to elevate the show from last year.

When we first entered the empty auditorium, I looked at the stage in awe. It was something impressive; something to be respected. From the ground, I pictured where I would stand. I looked at the lights. I looked at the seats. *All of those seats.* And then I looked up at the stage. It was tall. *It's as tall as I am.* I looked at the ground below, just in front of the seats. The aisles were carpeted, but the front was cement...

Cut to the performance: I do the hop with my guitar, the crowd applauds. This is the show that we've rehearsed. What I didn't tell anyone is what I planned when we got there: I jumped off the stage. I paced the aisles and played right to the people in their seats. They absolutely lost it. My ankles were on fire;

jumping four feet onto concrete—in cowboy boots of all things. But I didn't care. I *found* myself in that performance.

The Country Kids went on to pantomime songs at the Lane County Fair, the grand opening of a Burger King, a Kelly Middle School (*big kids!*) assembly, and—with some arm twisting from my parents—one last talent show in fifth grade.

We had a wrap party with all the band members to celebrate our time together. I was a dick. It was embarrassing to put on the hat and the boots and play that old act again in fifth grade. I had moved on to skateboards and alternative music. But my life was irreversibly changed by The Country Kids.

One year later, my friend Crosby Kneale invited me to play a Green Day song at his sixth grade talent show. With real instruments. By then, I had acquired a full-size acoustic guitar and an electric guitar as well. Crozz played both guitar and bass, so he opted for bass. We had no drummer, but that didn't stop us. Well, maybe a little. Crozz didn't feel comfortable singing in public, so I sang live for the first time. The performance was unremarkable, but by the end of the school year, we formed a real band that would last for nine years.

This Day's End (formerly EPD) is discussed at great length in my last book, but what is most clear about that time (1998-2007) is that I desperately wanted to be a legitimate artist in every way. By high school, I had released multiple CDs in multiple genres, and even began producing sessions for other artists. I designed, printed, assembled, and sold the band's CDs, tapes, shirts, and stickers. I booked our shows. I promoted for other artists. I maintained our website. I fought for us.

We played regional shows on weekends, but half the time we needed rides from our parents. Or borrowed cars. My dream was always clear: move in together, hit the studio, buy a van, and hit the road. We did have a short tour with She (my Arson) in 2004, but me and Crozz drove home every night and went back to work every morning. It was terrible.

TDE came really far, farther than most, and I'm really proud of those accomplishments. By the end, we were packing local venues and having the time of our lives. We had a great record and a great fanbase.
But we fell short of the dream.

In 2008, I had pretty much given up on that dream. All my bands—This Day's End, Outreach, No Laughing Matter, Dead Fucking Serious—were dead and hope was gone. The future wasn't bleak. There *was* no future.

It wasn't until I found rap, specifically The ILLusionists (more specifically my rhyme partner E. Ville AKA Evan Vaught), that I felt it was possible to achieve the dream. By then, we had grown up and I was married, so we didn't need to have a band house. But I had a badass home studio, so making records was easy. The elusive part was the live shows.

I had one solo rap album and one with The ILLusionists, but I didn't see myself as a solo artist. I played acoustic shows once in a while, but that wasn't anything serious. It took a while to get comfortable without a guitar in my hands, but with Evan, I wasn't alone up there. Our chemistry was off the charts.

In 2010, we opened for Eyedea & Abilities* in my hometown, Eugene, OR. Instead of a DJ, The ILLusionists had a

---

*Eyedea & Abilities are an underground (read: not major label) rap group, but they're about as prestigious as it gets in that world. Their skills are unparalleled and I had been listening to them for a decade at that point. So Crozz & I were floored when we convinced the venue to let us open the show. I was even more shocked when they turned out to be amazing human beings.

live band comprised of our beat maker Web The Free Range Human (AKA Web Beats, AKA Gabe Morley)* on drums, and Crozz (AKA Croz K, FKA Odar Beats) on bass, guitar, keys, and samplers.

The support we got from E&A was completely reinvigorating. Before long, Web was remixing their songs and I was mixing and mastering them. I invested in a nicer microphone for recording our third album, *Death Proof*, and we even started tackling more serious material. The goal was to step up our game in case E&A wanted to do more shows together. We printed 1,000 copies of *Death Proof* and played our release show on October 16th, 2010. The next day, we found out that Eyedea had died.

It's hard to describe how it felt, having such an abrupt and tragic end to the most exhilarating time in my life. But as devastating as it was to lose my new friend, it strengthened my resolve. I had my hero's endorsement, and I wanted to honor that. Nothing would get in my way this time.

*Aliases are big in rap. Try to keep up

EPD backstage
(Left to right:) Chase Eichengreen, Ben Arp, me, Crosby Kneale
Portland State University (Portland, OR) 2002

Paying my respects to Micheal Larsen
Cherokee Park (St. Paul, MN) 2017

The ILLusionists 10th anniversary
(Left to right:) E. Ville, Crozz, Gabe, me
Photo by Thomas Hiura
HiFi Music Hall (Eugene, OR) 2018

I Quit My Job For This (2011)

Lineup: The ILLusionists, Sarx

Best show: Eugene, OR

Worst show: San Bernardino, CA

Record store find: Batman *Knightfall* (books)

Evan and I had played as many shows *without* the band as we had *with* them. The more we played, the more we noticed that rappers don't even have DJs anymore. And we were one of the only groups with a band. And the band wasn't really on the albums, so we could easily hit the road as a two-piece.

That eliminated the impossible equation of how six ILLusionists members could all get days off work at the same time. But when I tried booking dates in other cities, every venue wanted to know our history in their town. And our history was in punk and hardcore bands. The ILLusionists didn't have a name outside of Eugene.

Just before *Death Proof* came out, I enlisted a good friend of mine who was a salesman. I drew up a map of cities and asked him to book us a tour. He agreed, but never delivered.

Frustrated, I started to look at the smaller touring acts who came through Eugene. Basically, guys like me now. We had played a few times with Sarx* (Seattle, WA) and he struck me as

*Who, after receiving a cease and desist over rights to the name, now performs as GunsGodsGhosts

a very genuine person.

We first met when he was on tour with Sadistik, and we traded shows after that. I knew that he had been on tour a couple of times, so I tried to convince him to take us with him. It's something that a lot of local guys do when somebody is really active on the road: *hey, if you ever need an opener... well if you ever need a driver...*

But I wanted to make a better pitch. I'm not trying to tag along; I'm trying to *build* something for myself. One night, after a show in Eugene, I asked: "would you be willing to take us on tour? I've tried booking myself, but we don't have the contacts yet. Our best shot is to go with someone who's done this before."

Sarx was hesitant, saying that he didn't have a vehicle (or a driver's license, for that matter). We were standing by my car, a Nissan Xterra, and I placed my hand on its side while making my closing argument: "look, I will sell this fucking car, buy a van, and drive the whole way. But we need your contacts. We need you to book it."

And that was the deal.

I sold my car to a dealer and paid off what I owed. With the remaining $4,500, I searched for a suitable van. The first one was an early 90's Ford with a lot of space. It was a little rusty, cosmetically, but it had really low mileage. Like 25,000 low. Between the low mileage, and the oil change sticker indicating that it hadn't been driven in years, and—this is the most unsettling—the peepholes installed in its windowless back doors, it was enough to make me question its history. My best guess is that it was either a residence or something that was in police impound for a very long time.

Before long, I found a perfect candidate. This one had 107,000 miles, which is still pretty good. It was a 1999 Ford

E150, formerly employed by an electrical company on the Oregon Coast. The graphics had been removed, but it still had a roof ladder and orange flashing light on top. The interior was simple up front, and caged off in the back. The steel behind my seat had enclosed myriad metal shelves and drawers. It was the smallest van of its kind (Econoline models go up to E350), but it had more than enough room for us. It also had a V6 engine, which meant better gas mileage than a V8.

Over the next month, with my stepdad Steve and my brother Travis,* I gutted the back, took off the roof light and ladder, added carpet, two more seats (found at junkyards for $25 a piece), a stereo, AC, cruise control, and exterior decals for both The ILLusionists and my label, Take 92 Music. For the first time in my life, I had a legitimate tour van.

The first step for any tour is to plan your route. Which cities do you want to play? How many days will that take? Which day of the week in each city? And finally, which dates can we all agree on? We did this together, though I think I only booked one or two shows myself. Sarx recommended a longer tour, to acquire more contacts. The trip spanned 19 states in 40 days.

Evan got a leave of absence at his security job, but I was getting a lot of resistance at mine. If you've read *Famous Last Words*, or listened to The ILLusionists' *Death of a Salesman*, you'll know that a lot of that workplace drama influenced the music. But when it became clear that they wouldn't approve my vacation time, I told them I was leaving one way or another. To keep my vacation pay—which I would've forfeited by quitting—I agreed to demote myself and return to a lesser position. There was no way in hell that, after eight years with the company, I was

---

*Who identifies as my sister Emma today

going to start from the bottom when I came back... So we called it *I Quit My Job For This* tour.

I am most content when things go according to plan. Especially if it's my plan. That first tour had so much new territory, and so many unknown factors, that I was definitely out of my comfort zone. By that time, I was 25 and probably had about 200 shows under my belt. But I'm very much a homebody; anti-social and somewhat reclusive. I'm also a control freak. These qualities have only increased with age, but the allure of tour was strong enough to carry me through those mental obstacles.

Ev and I arrived in Seattle ahead of schedule. The van was packed with Costco snacks and sleeping bags. (Fortunately, no band meant no heavy equipment!) We brought portable HD video cameras to document the process.* I made daily edits and put them YouTube for our friends back home. It was an exciting time.

The tour was set to kick off in spectacular fashion: the first show was in Seattle, with Sadistik, Kristoff Krane, and No Bird Sing. Graves 33 was local support, and we were kind of tacked on before him and Sarx. Oh, and nobody came.** Either way, it was one of the best bills I've ever been on. Those guys are some of the early Crushkill Recordings artists, and we were proud to be part of the show.

Earlier that day, I learned the first survival skill of the trip: make friends. Sadistik invited us to a video shoot where we played extras in "Higher Brain." We met another extra named Kelly Nelson, who was visiting from Denver. We told her that

*This was before Instagram and Snapchat

**It was a perfect lesson for Day One—keep in mind that we really looked up to these guys—no matter how good you are, there's still a chance that *nobody gives a fuck!*

we were playing there in a few weeks, and she said "hit me up if you guys need a place to stay." I cashed in on that favor for about eight years.

I was astounded to find how many total strangers would welcome us with open arms. They knew we were far from home and making very little money. People would cook for us, offer their shower—sometimes their own bed or even their entire house! Some of them, like Kelly, have been good friends of mine ever since. It still blows my mind to think about it, and I've tried to be more generous and hospitable when I know other artists will be passing through my town as well.

Many of these friends have, of course, been musicians. In fact, Sarx & I teamed up with Crozz and Carnage The Executioner to form Arcane Amalgam in 2017. Another friend, Ill2lectual, offered us a place to stay in Los Angeles, and we even recorded a song with him that night. We really hit it off with him, collaborating on many future projects, including *Blowing Up The Bandwagon*, *Re-Endtroducing*, and *Rare Form*.

Ev and I actually met so many great artists on that tour that we invited many of them to do a song with us called "Friends & Anemones." Gabe (Web Beats) made the beat, and it featured Sarx, Graves 33, Zac HB (Minneapolis), Irenic (Minneapolis), Masked Avengers (Stockton), and Ill2lectual all together. We ended up doing future tours with both Zac HB and the Masked Avengers, while Graves 33 contributed heavily to my later work like *Rare Form*.

Sarx took us to a place just north of Seattle called The Jet Bar & Grill. They had a good hip hop crowd there, but I mostly just remember the moments in between.

Before the show, and this was documented on our YouTube videos, we started arguing over best (and worst) rappers. First he said something in defense of Lil' Wayne, who was one of the most lowbrow, mainstream artists of the time. In my opinion, he ushered in the "mumble rap" era that exists today. At the time, I was dumbstruck. It was the first time I learned that intelligent underground rappers can also like ignorant Top 40 bullshit.

Then I said something about KRS One, a highly revered hip hop PIONEER, and Sarx responded by saying that "aside from like, Insane Clown Posse, there is no emcee that I despise more than KRS One."

I was so upset that I left the building. Gabe was my closest confidant, and hip hop mentor, so I called him to vent. After a couple minutes, Sarx came to the van. I told Gabe to put him in his place, to which he said "I want my fucking beats back."

We all shared a laugh, and that was probably the first of a hundred more passionate debates that I've had with Sarx. We disagree a lot, and we both love music so deeply that we'll probably never stop fighting about it.

I learned another lesson that week: *always* have a backup. My brand new laptop DIED DURING OUR SET and I ended up rapping a cappella while Graves 33 tried to fix it. But it couldn't be fixed. We took it to an Apple Store the next day, and even though I hadn't bought the warranty, they gave me a brand new computer! That could've been a major setback, financially and logistically, so now I carry a thumb drive containing every instrumental track that I've ever made.

Olympia, WA wasn't much to speak of; just a big empty room and my friend Kellen's parents, who came to support. But I did learn a driving trick that I use to this day.

I tend to pee pretty often, so I loosen my belt when I'm driving. If I really have to go, I might undo the top button on my jeans for a while. The fewer the stops, the better time we'll make on the Interstate.

Medford, OR wasn't much better, but it's a lot more memorable. If you're never stood under stage lights, it's sort of like being under a heat lamp at the deli. I am, for the basis of this metaphor, your chicken nuggets. When I wiped my brow between songs, I uttered something about how if it were any hotter, I'd have to take off my pants. A girl in the crowd called my bluff, shouting *TAKE 'EM OFF!* It was a pretty uneventful night, so I figured *why the fuck not.*

"I hope you know I only have one testicle," I said. The pants came off. I stepped down from the stage, grabbed her hand, and we danced to the next song in our set.

Evan went to a hotel with his wife* Ambur. When we met up that night, she swung her hips in a way that her butt hit me like a wrecking ball. I was still carrying my bags and fell onto them, right into the wall. That was the first night sharing beds with my tourmates, which soon became par for the course.

We played a couple shows in northern California, beginning in Sacramento. The promoter had also scheduled an in-store performance that afternoon, so that we could promote the show. Our understanding was that it was a record store, but the GPS took us to a shopping mall.

Evan was driving the van, and pulled into a parking garage. When we got to the ticket booth, it was clear that we were taller than the clearance. But it was rush hour, and a line formed behind us. Panicked, Ev relinquished the wheel, establishing a rule that he'd help on the long drives, but I'd handle the city stuff.

When we found the record store, they pointed us to a big stage in the middle of the mall. There was a guy with a clipboard

*then-girlfriend

taking names. We weren't scheduled for an in-store. It was a goddamn open mic.

One of the other acts was probably 14, and badly played terrible club rap while his two friends awkwardly stood beside him. Sarx tried to compliment the kid, despite the performance, and got a cocky "yep" in reply.

We waited through seven more acts, only to play one song (each) for indifferent passersby. I was more interested in staring at the fish tank than the "show."

Sarx booked us at a famous punk club in Anaheim. The Doll Hut, he joked, was "made entirely of stickers." It was a tiny little shithole that had endured decades of debauchery. Some of my favorite artists have played there, like Bad Religion, The Offspring, and even Brian Setzer. I spent most of the time in the bathroom,* but we played our most aggressive songs and had a good time.

Every artist has experienced some kind of technical difficulty onstage, but what we didn't expect was the kind of clusterfuck that these DIY bookings can be. Many times, these are venues you've never even heard of before, but you throw everything at the wall and see what sticks. San Bernardino, CA is a good example.

We arrived at a little bar with no stage, and as the other acts arrived with their gear, we realized that we were the only rappers on the bill. The promoter, who I later learned is named Animal—red flag, Sarx!—had evidently not listened to our music when he confirmed us.

So we played a screamo show.

*I'm lactose-intolerant, and my pills were no match for Pizza Hut's chicken alfredo.

Playing with bands can often mean having more sound equipment available, and even a better engineer. In this case, it was just Animal.* I set up the video camera just before we went onstage. There's time lapse footage of me arguing with him because there was only one mic for me and Evan to share. If you've never heard The ILLusionists, we often trade off words very quickly like the Beastie Boys or Run DMC. It was an impossible scenario. We cut a bunch of songs and played a short set that included only our most straightforward arrangements.

A wack bar show is disheartening enough, but the silver lining is that you can always win over a few people if you play your heart out. Without being able to perform the set that we'd prepared, it wasn't our best night. Afterward, Animal told the other bands—right in front of us—to donate anything they could to the tour because the door didn't make any money. So two or three band members opened their wallets and gave us... $9.

San Bernardino left such a bad taste in our mouths that we drove straight to Las Vegas after the show. Sometimes a rough night can make you want to leave that town and never come back.** But because we had to ration our funds for several weeks, we walked around Vegas until the sun came up. That way, we only paid for one night's sleep instead of two.

The Vegas strip is shiny and impressive at a glance, but it's mostly people trying to slip you drugs*** or push you into a limo that's headed to a strip club. But after 10 hours of walking around broke, it's pretty fucking shitty. Our show was on the *old* Vegas strip, so we got the cheapest room we could find over there. Exhausted at 8am, the first thing I see is a dead roach. I'm

---

*He even let the bands set up their gear while Sarx was still performing!
**I still haven't returned to San Bernardino.
***One guy put a baggie IN MY HAND, saying "try before you buy!"

from the suburbs. I had never seen a cockroach in my life. But we were all so tired that we just put a plastic cup over it and went to sleep.

We woke up late in the afternoon and still had time to kill. Fortunately, we stumbled upon some ILL-friendly spots like Insert Coin(s) and the Toy Shack. We played arcade games and I bought a one-sixth scale action figure from *Batman Begins*.*

On the first day of tour, Sarx laid out some ground rules for the trip. He said that everyone should always stay in the same place. We had to keep a schedule from city to city, and that would be difficult if we had to track down people who were sleeping across town, snoozing alarms, etc.

Sarx may have set the rules, but he broke that one in Vegas. He went to an afterparty at another bar and never came back. He swore up and down that we wouldn't have to go find him, and that promise was kept. But Ev and I had to lug his merch tub all the way to the motel on foot... in addition to our own stuff. He stopped texting us back around 3am, so we went to sleep.

I awoke to a violent pounding sound. The room was pitch black behind the hotel curtains. I stumbled to the door and looked through the peephole to find a security guard and a very haggard-looking Sarx. Blinded by sunlight, I opened the door, and plopped back in bed without a word.

The next day, I was editing footage and found that Sarx had filmed his sad, seven mile walk to our room (he couldn't afford a cab). According to his video, Sarx had gone to an afterparty with some people from the bar. When they moved to another bar, the girl who invited him told the bouncer not to let him in. And she

---

*I couldn't help but correct the Toy Shack employee who handed me "the Michael Keaton." I was excited to hear they had one, because I could only see the Christian Bale that I had asked for. Dick move, but still a cherished part of my collection!

was his ride home. He told this story onstage in Gallup, NM and read her phone number to the crowd. She got so many angry texts that just minutes later, she called, and he put her on speakerphone to talk to the audience. It was pretty amazing.

In Phoenix, we played at a really big place that housed a venue *and* a recording studio. We got the impression that they didn't use the venue side very often, but we still had a good time. Everyone hung out for a couple hours after the show and it was a good vibe. The owners even invited us to stay there overnight.

And then they started arguing. Fans trailed out as their voices escalated, and we decided to go to our room. For the next hour, it devolved into a full-fledged fight. They were screaming and threatening to kill each other. Sarx, Ev and I sat motionless in our room with the lights off, wondering if we should sneak out, or if that would potentially make it worse.

That was when I learned to read the room. Sometimes it means knowing which songs to cut, based on audience reactions. Other times it can mean knowing when to turn down a crash pad and find an alternative. I've stayed in every kind of place imaginable: parking lots in the van, RV in the middle of nowhere, Motel 6 (my jam), plush hotels, apartment floors, guest room beds, shared beds with tourmates, shared beds with hosts, basement mattresses, dingy rap pads, family homes, and even mini mansions. Despite my appreciation—and genuine need— for hospitality, I do have a healthy skepticism at times.

I can't stress enough how grateful I am for the generosity of friends and strangers alike. Sometimes it can be the difference between eating dinner or spending all your money on a room. I'm pretty adaptable, but when you park and people say "make sure you set the alarm in this neighborhood," that makes me a little nervous. At times, Evan slept in the van for that very reason.

One night in Texas, we walked into a place and started laying out our sleeping bags. Sarx noticed a pile of dog shit in the kitchen. It was maybe 15 feet from where I was laying on the floor. Our host said that the dog belongs to his roommate, so it's not his job to clean it up.* Ev grabbed his things and went straight for the van. The only sleep I'd had that day was on the ground in a park, so I stayed indoors regardless. Sarx and I slept on the poop deck and hoped for the best.

After Phoenix, we did sleep in the van. At 7am, I awoke to condensation dripping from the ceiling. The GPS had fallen off, along with the rearview mirror, because the sun was so intense that it melted the adhesive. We immediately bought a visor and some Little Trees air fresheners. We didn't have a show that day, so we checked out Zia Records and killed some time. Sarx noticed that one of his favorite rappers was in town that night, so he tweeted him.

A few hours later, we were witnessing Astronautalis perform a legendary freestyle about the life and death of Pizza Baby. It was an incredible show, and that freestyle was only one of the highlights. The crowd was singing along like crazy, and the energy was off the charts. Nobs (of Dez & Nobs) was playing with him on that tour as well.** Astronautalis introduced himself as Andy and we hung out a while after the show. He saw Sarx's tweet—which explained that we were on a DIY tour, with a night off—and was kind enough to put all three of us on the guest list. Hell of a guy.***

---

*Years later, this guy posted spoilers for *Avengers: Endgame* on opening day, so you can get a picture of the kind of fuckface that he is

**We had just discovered Dez & Nobs, picking up their CD in Riverside, CA.

***Update: at the time of this edit, Andy has just been accused of sexual abuse

The more that I travel, the more every city looks the same. One block can look like Olympia, WA and the next block looks like St. Louis, MO. Turn the corner and you could swear you were in Reno, NV. The biggest surprise, however, is that my preconceptions were often pretty ignorant. There's a vast nothingness in the western U.S. that definitely embraces the rural American stereotype. If you stop at a gas station in Wyoming or Oklahoma, it's probably going to be what you expect. But there are some hidden gems, too. If I had thought about it, Eugene and Portland are good examples. Most of Oregon is rural, and we're the exceptions.

Nonetheless, it surprised me when I arrived in Fayetteville, AR and found that it quite closely resembled my hometown. The promoter, Smar-T Jones, invited us to stay at his apartment. We didn't have any shows nearby, so he actually let us stay for three days! It was on the third day that I realized I don't like being thousands of miles away from my wife on my birthday. I had already missed our anniversary while the tour was in Sacramento. Even worse, I didn't celebrate with Steve, whose birthday is the day before mine. It sucked to break a decades-long family tradition like that. To this day, I do my best to be home for the holidays.

In our down time, we went to a bowling alley, cupcake shop, Qdoba, and Dairy Queen. We also went to a sex shop. With the rules established on Day One, chief amongst them was No Jerking Off in Shared Spaces. We decided to take it further, creating a *Seinfeld*-ian pact to see who could wait the longest.

Sarx lasted until Texas, in the bathroom of a Denton bookstore. I don't remember where Evan bowed out, but I won that motherfucker.

There wasn't any money to wager, so we came up with a different prize. One of our popular songs was "Anti-Wack," so it seemed a suitable play on words to dub it the Anti-Wack contest. If we were each delegated to buy gold spray paint, a thrift store trophy, and a dildo, then we'd have all the ingredients for a big golden dick trophy.

I walked in to an Arkansas sex shop and bought a bigass dildo on my birthday. We sadly never finished our arts and crafts project, but I've since used it as a Christmas tree topper and a prop for some hilarious prank photos.*

In Springfield, MO, my wife called to say that our dog Louie was hurt. He's very small and has a history of issues with his legs and eyesight. The injury required an expensive surgery right away or we'd risk having to euthanize him. Birthdays and anniversaries are hard, but family emergencies are terrible. Luckily, my mother-in-law Kathy bailed us out, essentially saving our little boy. (My studio guests will attest that he survived to hump many a leg in the future.)

Our Chicago crash pad was great until it wasn't. Ev and I watched Ghostbusters, which was comfort food at that point. The hosts invited Sarx for drinks and then left him there with no transportation. We were already asleep at their apartment, so he had to find his own way back once again. The hosts woke us up when they brought the party back home at like 4am. They woke

---

*Years later, my wife and I were having dinner with friends. Katie, who was on Tinder at the time, got a message that she thought was a dick pic. Normally people *don't* want dick pics from strangers, but she thought it would be funny in a group setting. She was disappointed that it wasn't a dick, so when we got home, Ang (my wife) gave me Katie's phone number. I put the dildo in the fly of my jeans and clenched it in my hand. I took the picture in the bathroom to make it more believable. When I texted her, she was still out at the bar with our friend Hailey, who was in on the joke. Katie was so confused by the random dick text that she showed it to the bartender and other strangers while they laughed at it. We finally texted her a picture of the [disembodied] dildo from Ang's phone (a number she would recognize) and revealed ourselves. It was one of the funniest nights of my life.

us up again at 10am, loudly drinking *again*. We had planned to go to lunch together, for Chicago deep dish pizza. Given their drunken disposition, we opted to drive separately. We followed as their car swerved, inspiring a made-up excuse (*we got a last minute show tonight!*), so that we could find a parking lot to sleep in the van.

The midwest cold cut through our sleeping bags and winter socks. I genuinely thought I was going to get hypothermia or something because my toes were numb for an eternity. The next day, I vowed, we would get a hotel room. It was the first one of the tour, but we were far from anyone we knew and it was worth it to have a hot tub, a shower, and a clean bed.

Minneapolis was significant because of the people involved. It was one of the best shows, but the true highlight was visiting Eyedea's memorial and meeting his mom at the show. Kathy Averill has done a tremendous amount to keep his name alive, and even continued to run his Crushkill Recordings label. This was just a year after he died, and things were still pretty raw. Kathy came to the show—an event promoted by Crushkill manager Brady O'Rourke—along with Ecid and Kristoff Krane. On the bill, I met Zac HB,* PCP, and Irenic. It was great venue (Cause) and an incredible lineup.

After our success in Minnesota, we were in for some surprises in South Dakota. I remember the tiny highway, passing tiny towns with signs like *Population 9,000*. Soon it became *Population 1,500;* every town smaller than the last. Soon we arrived at the venue, and it was equal parts furniture store, halfass arcade, and music venue. We ate at the Hardy's across the street, which was odd because it's the same branding as Carl's Jr.

*Update: Zac was also accused of abuse on Twitter, the same week as Astronautalis but all the menu items are different.

At the show, a local guy told us that there should be a good turnout because there's nothing to do. Small towns can actually work like that. But he went on to explain that it was approaching winter, where it's so cold that most can't even function, and "almost every year somebody snaps and kills their entire family."

Soooo we put on long johns and got the fuck out of there as soon as the show was over.* Unfortunately, rural South Dakota highways don't have a lot of truck stops. We had to stop and pee in that bitter cold. I can't say for sure—it was dark—but I'm pretty sure my penis had fully inverted and I was left holding the urethra itself.

People warned me about the elevation in Denver. They said to be careful; that it's easy to get short of breath. I have asthma, so that's advice that I wanted to take seriously. Unfortunately, it was Halloween.

I had already found a Green Man costume** at a mall in California. If you haven't seen it, it's just a solid green spandex suit that covers 100% of the human body.

I tried it on at that mall in Sacramento, and walked out of the dressing room, asking if the employees could understand me through the mask. This provoked some questions, so after explaining that I would be performing in costume, they asked me to rap right there in the store. I chose my weirdest rhyme ever—a b-side from the forthcoming "Arms Race" single—just to further exaggerate the moment.

---

*Note to self: remove long johns *before* your performance!

**As seen in *It's Always Sunny in Philadelphia*. I later wore it for the "Vacant Eyes" music video, projecting images on it, much like green screen backdrops are used in film.

I once knew a foreign guy with the foresight
to start a midget porn site for each one of his four wives
He was a sore sight, bright little orange guy
Height right about 4'9
Couldn't quite flip the switch on his porch light
The poor guy dreamed of being up so high
that you could see red around his whole eye
But with his dwarf endorphins, he couldn't feel pain
So he pricked his foreskin to find a good vein
Insane, but he still had good aim
The drugs flooded in through his blood into his little brain
Never anticipating the dissipation of his genitals
Now our little sensation was forgettable
It was regrettable the way his demons had dwarfed him
All four wives packed up and divorced him
So, of course, it forced him to kill himself
This one's for Wilson, the illest elf

Not my most poignant work, but it sure got a rise out of the staff. Back to Denver!

There have been other times when I had to carry my inhaler onstage, but for some reason, the stars aligned. I rapped the entire Denver show in constume. It was slobbery and sweaty inside the mask, and I mostly stood still because couldn't see the edge of the stage! It was a memorable first time in Colorado.

We stayed at Kelly's for a couple days, and decided to head west when the snow came. We had another day to get to Salt Lake City, but we didn't want to get stuck. My Xterra could handle snow easily, but the van is rear-wheel drive and has a tendency to fishtail. The snow continued as we passed Fort Collins, CO. I was starting to get nervous.

By the time we crossed into Wyoming, it was a full on snowstorm. The horizon quickly faded out of view. My windshield looked like the Millenium Falcon at lightspeed. Even the semi trucks were pulling off to the shoulder. I slowed to about 20mph, unsure of what else to do. The windshield wipers struggled to keep up. I could barely see 10 feet in front of me. The van shook like an airplane in turbulance. We fishtailed. I slowed down. We fishtailed more. I panicked.

I can't see!

What the fuck do I do?!

WHAT THE FUCK DO I DO?!

As mentioned earlier, I like being in control. I like to follow the plan. That was not part of the plan. I pulled over. The headlights were caked with snow. It was piling higher all around us. The tires were stuck. It was a full on blizzard.

My anxiety triggered a stomachache, and I worried that I might shit my pants. I straight up *couldn't* go outside, and I told the guys I was going to shit in a bag. Now I'll be the first to tell you that I don't pee in bottles or any of those weird trucker habits. But there I was, screaming at my tourmates that I was going to shit in a bag. I called my dad— my biological dad— because he's a lifelong mechanic. I figured he'd have some advice for what to do besides wait it out. He said to wait it out. We had 20 gallons of gas, which was plenty to keep the heat on and make sure that we weren't going to freeze. I hung up the phone and sat in silence. No words, no sound, no traffic, only snow.* I was frustrated. I was scared. I was powerless.
    *only Zuul

This is why I don't leave the house.

20 minutes passed before we actually saw eastbound headlights. It was a snow plow. I exhaled for what felt like the first time in forever. A few minutes later, the plow pulled up beside us. Apparently, we were the *only* non-commercial vehicle on the road. We followed him to the nearest exit (Laramie, WY) before he turned back to help the semi trucks. We were incredibly relieved. I can't really explain it, except to say that I've never been so happy to sleep in a Denny's parking lot.

Lesson learned: only book the midwest in the summer!

After sharing weeks of daily videos on social media, our Eugene show was incredible. As evidenced on The ILLusionists' live DVD, *A Near Def Experience*, we packed the house. It wasn't quite the last show—we played Portland and Bellingham before dropping off Sarx in Seattle—but for me and Evan, it was the best homecoming we could've hoped for. We had gone to so many new places together and shared countless highs and lows. It strengthened our friendship in immeasurable ways and that was evident in our live show. The band joined us for the Eugene date, and with all the excitement surrounding that first tour, it was one of the greatest sets we ever played.

Blasphemy
Tio's Tacos (Riverside, CA) 2011

Batman Begins 1/6 scale figure
Toy Shack (Las Vegas, NV) 2011

Hanging out
(Left to right:) Sarx, Ecid, Ev, me
Ecid's house (Minneapolis, MN) 2011

Not So Bluish (2012)

Lineup: The ILLusionists, Zac HB

Best show: Los Angeles, CA

Worst show: Albuquerque, NM

Record store find: Beastie Boys – *Paul's Boutique Demos*, *How to Shoot Video that Doesn't Suck* (book)

The *I Quit* tour was a doozy. It was by far the longest tour I've ever done, and we were totally slumming it. That veritable boot camp experience prepared me for everything that came next.

For starters, our resume was now sufficient enough to get booked in other cities. And we made enough good impressions that I could utilize those contacts to be my own booking agent. Mission accomplished.

When we first played Minneapolis, we stayed at Zac's apartment. The show had been really fun—second only to Eugene—and we felt an instant kinship with him. Having kept in touch about the posse cut, he expressed a desire to tour with us.

I was in between jobs, so I started booking right away.* This

---

*By the time I did get hired, this tour was only a month away. Luckily, my new boss was cool with it. He still covers my shifts to this day!

tour would be a more reasonable length, since we weren't so desperate for contacts anymore. Zac had a *friends & family* airfare discount, so he was able to meet us in Oregon.

Because this wasn't our first tour, I thought that we should do something different to advertise. We were already going to release a live DVD/CD set, but *A Near Def Experience* didn't include our new tourmate. Zac suggested that we do an ILLusionists remix of his song called "1% Blue." Gabe made a new beat and arrangement, so Ev & I could add new vocals. The most memorable part though, was the artwork for the single.

Zac flew in a day early for the photo shoot. We searched high and low for non-toxic, washable, blue paint. We covered ourselves in that paint, standing in a kiddie pool, while Ev's wife Ambur blasted us with a hose. It was stupid and fun, which was right up our alley.

The pictures and behind the scenes video got a lot of love online—the local paper even covered our new DVD—but our release show was underwhelming. It was hard not to compare it to the *I Quit* finale, just five months earlier.

My band Judo Pony* had a practice space in the Whiteaker neighborhood called Fusion Bomb Studios. So many venues have been closing down over the years, that it was the only place I could think of to host the show. We crammed a bunch of friends into that tiny room and had a decent time. I was finally booking by myself, but that only meant I had to work harder.

Booking a tour with reliable contacts means emails, texts, and calls for several weeks to iron out the details. But there are *always* those cities in between, or regular contacts who are unavailable. Most of the work is filling those gaps. The only way to have a good tour is to allow yourself to enough *time* to work. My rule is three months, minimum. If I can start the actual

*Possibly a worse band name than The ILLusionists!

booking—not planning the route or reaching out to tourmates or making the artwork, but the actual *booking*—with at least 90 days, then I'm fairly confident that we'll have a solid tour. With four or five months, we can really get ahead of the curve. But even then, we might still be trying to fill a couple days last minute. We might even be adding shows while the tour is in progress.

Back then, I hadn't learned that lesson. We didn't have enough time *or* contacts. So I consider it a success, even though we had more days off than usual. That can mean loitering in parks or coffee shops, trying not to spend money. It can mean overstaying your welcome at somebody's house. It can mean seeing a show, or finding a record store for entertainment. But it mostly means extra long drives.

Driving is a huge part of touring. We spend far more time in the van than we do onstage or even inside of venues.* My goal is to keep the drives short, which keeps the cost down. I still try to make new contacts every time, so that we can add smaller markets in between major cities. I want to play more shows in fewer miles. We traveled 8,500 miles for *I Quit*, but my average tour now is less than 5,000.

Some drives are unavoidable. A-list tours often go from San Francisco to Portland because there's not a lot going on in Southern Oregon or Northern California. For us, that's a nine hour drive to Sacramento or Stockton.

Stockton had a great all ages club called Plea For Peace. We first went there with Sarx, and they had us back many times. It had a punk rock vibe, but their underground rap shows were pretty cool. The ILLusionists had an old school sound, but with a

---

*I spend more time behind the wheel than on the stage or at the cypher
  - "Rough Days," *Figures of Speech* (2018)

punk rock attitude. Sometimes those odd venues were kinder to us than the hip hop crowds.

In San Jose, there is a weekly event called *The Cypher* where all kinds of emcees gather to freestyle and have a good time. They often feature a touring act as well, but it's clear that people are there for *The Cypher*. From what I've heard, it's the longest running weekly on the West Coast.*

Nowadays, *The Cypher* is held every Wednesday at Back Bar. In 2012, it was at Johnny V's. From the moment we walked in, I knew it was my kind of dump. Small room, intimate vibe, punky bartender dressed in ripped fishnets, and a lot of dudes in hoodies who looked like they just crawled out of their basement studios. AudioDru is the DJ, host, booker, and man in charge. I met him through my friend Pariah (of The Architex). The show started off great with their regulars like YDMC, Jeff Turner, Sway D, and LIFE. I can't remember who was there each time I performed, but those guys always stood out as the best. They traded freestyles like true veterans. The whole crew was tight.

When we started our set, people were already leaving the room. I knew we had to catch their attention fast, or everyone would leave until the freestyles resumed. We played our hardest, fastest, most lyrically heavy tracks first. Heads were nodding. The crowd had thinned, but we were winning them over.

Then we played "Real MCs (Just Rhyme)."

"Real MCs" was a single from *Death Proof* and one of our most popular songs. It denounced the fashionable, fame-seeking rap in both the mainstream and underground alike. Lose the holier-than-thou image. Focus on your craft. Elevate the song. Cut the skits. Just rhyme!

---

*Last I heard, *The Cypher* folded in 2018

The song was always a high point in our set. Unfortunately, there's a line in the second verse that turned some heads at *The Cypher*.

I don't freestyle
My words aren't disposable
Fuck what you heard
My verses are quotable

I wrote that because most rap shows have a really lame cypher at the end of the night and I got tired of listening to the same old crap. I take my time and write memorable lines. Spontaneity isn't my strong suit. Obviously there's an artful way to do it, and these guys are some of the best. But they heard that line and instantly turned on us. The people that we *just* fought to keep in the room were leaving. I think our set ended to maybe five people. Some got it. Some took offense. The cypher resumed at the end of the night and everybody came back inside. Zac joined them, and our then-underage friend Tony The Scribe (who let us crash in his dorm) was allowed to perform with them as well.

The more times we played there, the better we did. It was clear that we respected the music, and nobody could deny our work ethic—*wait, where's Zac?!*

Zac was getting pretty friendly with a girl at the bar—he often lost focus at the sight of redheaded women—and when we packed up, he was gone.*

We looked around the venue. We looked outside. We tried his phone. We packed up the gear. We got paid. He and the girl

*Everyone on the first tour was married. Now I keep an eye on the single guys.

walked by in a rush as we called his name, and then they were gone. Nothing. *Fuck.*

A few minutes later, he called me back and said to meet around the corner at this girl's car. Apparently they made out and she gave him a cookie in a ZipLok bag. He waited a week to eat it to savor the moment. Who knows if they ever saw each other again.

LA was cool for a few reasons. First of all, we got to hang with Ill2lectual again. His whole family has been so kind to us. Secondly, we returned to The Doll Hut. The turnout was better than our first time with Sarx—and I didn't get diarrhea from Pizza Hut!—but that's hardly the exciting part.

I should set this up properly: I fucking love record stores. Of course, we all love music. But Sarx will tell you that it's rare to find people like us. I fucking live for it. I wish that other artists still spent their days buying music and reading liner notes and enjoying the ride. Tour allows me to find new music daily. If we have a moment of free time, I'll find a record store—sometimes two or three! So you can imagine my excitement when I discovered that LA has the holy grail of all record stores: Amoeba Records.

There's footage of my reaction to that room. After a few curse words, I immediately said "I want to *live* here!"* I quickly found our friend Ecid's new album, *Werewolf Hologram*, which came out that week. My record store rule is this: if I can find it at home, don't buy it. Spending money comes easily; saving is hard. Another great find was a demo version of the Beastie Boys' groundbreaking album, *Paul's Boutique*. For my favorite band of all time, and my encyclopedic knowledge of their history, I had

*Not in Los Angeles; in the actual store

never heard those early recordings. It was a great day.

My friend Jeff Antons met us at the store. He's a photographer, drummer, and all around good guy. We decided to film a music video for "1% Blue," and he directed it. We filmed a little in the store, then walking Sunset Blvd, sleepily rapping an elevator, and on the rooftop of a parking garage. We climbed on top of the van at sunset and Jeff climbed onto the roof of his car to film us.

The footage was actually pretty cool, but neither of us had time to edit it. Years later, I posted about it on our Facebook page and a fan volunteered to edit it. I never saw a final product, so I guess he didn't have time either. It remains unreleased to this day.

Come to think of it, LA really dominates my memories of that tour. We were off that night, and Sadistik was in town. He invited us to come see him play at an art gallery called CHALK.

CHALK was owned by Chris and DJ Neff, who turned out to be cousins of Sadistik's tourmate, Louis Logic. And although we never met before, Lou offered to let us open the show. Remember when I said that I carry my instrumentals on a thumb drive?

Lou was trying out some new material that would later become *Look on the Blight Side*. We would've fit better with his earlier, more boom-bap material, so me and Evan played first, and Zac—whose music was much more melodic—went second. It was a great crowd, great night, and we ended up playing CHALK on three different tours.

Phoenix didn't come through this time, but not for lack of trying. Instead, we drove straight to Santa Fe, NM and performed at the college out there. The show was unremarkable, but we had a good time. Zac's friend Sarah was the RA of an all-female dorm* and snuck us into her room. She said we could use the upstairs bathroom, which was co-ed. I think we used the wrong one because some girls came in *really* confused, seeing me and Evan brushing our teeth in our boxers.

Albuquerque is a great city if you hit the Wednesday night weekly at Burt's Tiki Lounge. They've had some drama in recent years, but back in the day it was a sure thing. Unfortunately for us, we came on a *Thursday*. There is footage of us playing a daytime show in the park, spitting hardcore battle raps at little kids and their parents. If I've learned anything from tour, it's how to take a loss.

We did have good shows in Colorado and New Mexico, but we had to get back to LA in a hurry. Ill2lectual was paying us for some features** on a side project called *Brothers Ill*, so Zac had booked LAX for his flight home.

Since we didn't have a place to stay in Gallup, NM, it made sense to start driving right after the show. Night drives can be brutal. You've been awake all day and then played a physically demanding show. But it's a lot easier for me to *stay* awake then to get up early in the morning. The other perk is a complete lack of traffic. That way you can cover the same ground a lot more efficiently. The downside of night drives is that my passengers want to sleep. In the early days, I would let Evan take the wheel for a while. But for the most part, I do the driving on tour. All I ask is that someone stays awake with me in the passenger's seat.

*The only two dorms I've seen to this day!
**Features are guest performances, featured on someone else's song

Zac slept in the back after eating a weed cookie in Gallup. When we stopped for gas, he woke up in a state of panic. Not recognizing the rural area, he couldn't figure out how we could ever get out of the gas station parking lot. There was no sleeping after that, so he asked if I'd put on some of Gabe's beats for a freestyle.

I've already expressed my disinterest in improvisation, but it was going to be a long night. I thought *what the hell. We're all friends here.* Before I knew it, me and Zac were trading bars until the sun came up.

We made it to Ill2lectual's house in the morning, and napped in his living room. Zac's flight was in the late afternoon, so the plan was to drop him off at the airport, and record our features that night.

When we got to the airport, there was a police checkpoint before the terminal. They were outside of their cars, lights flashing, directing traffic to the entrance.

Until they saw us.

Maybe it was the white van—usually the decals are less suspicious than an unmarked van—or the two ILLusionists with shaved heads, but for whatever reason, they signaled for us to pull over. From the passenger window, they asked our reason for the visit. All was going well until they asked if there were any weapons on board.

The irony here is that we were touring on my anti-violence anthem, "Arms Race," which thoroughly condemns gun violence. But we had been in some uncomfortable situations on the first tour. Sometimes sleeping in parking lots can be dangerous. When we first rolled into San Jose, it was like that Dave Chappelle bit where he's in the back of a limo going "gun store, liquor store, gun store—*where the fuck are you taking me?!*"

I'm honest to a fault. That's what people say, "to a fault." So when the cops asked if we had any weapons, I looked to Evan and gestured for him to explain. All three of us were pulled out of the van and searched. My phone, wallet, thumb drive, and everything else were haphazardly tossed into traffic behind me. They pressed me against the van and did a full pat down. We were all placed on the curb while they opened the back doors and dug through our bags.

Eventually, they grabbed a backpack that Evan identified as the one containing his gun. One officer dumped its contents on the hood of his police car behind the van. The other two kept searching our merch bins and luggage.

The cops hilariously sorted through Evan's comic books, colored markers, and notebooks until the threat was revealed. Fortunately, it was *unloaded* and stored in a protective case.

We later found out two things:
1. Oregon has different gun laws and you can't take it out of state without specifically registering it there.
2. The fact that it was unloaded meant the difference between getting it confiscated and going to jail.

Once the van was cleared, they believed our story, and Zac was allowed to catch his flight. He snuck a photo of us sitting on the curb next to the cops, which I will gladly include at the end of this chapter.

One cop was a hip hop head and grabbed our hoodies out of the front seats when it started to rain. We were stuck there for about an hour, and Evan had to hire a lawyer to attend his court date and pay a fine. It cost him a pretty penny, but we got to go home. In fact, that's exactly what we did.

There's video of us driving back to Ill2lectual's house, telling the story, and singing along to NWA. It ends with us saying that we need to get the fuck out of California.

We apologized to Ill2lectual and made the 13 hour drive home. It was about 5pm when we got stopped, so it was nearly 7pm when we began our second overnight drive in a row.

Home never felt so good.

(Left to right:) me, Zac, Ev
Photo credit: Beau Owens
Ev's house (Springfield, OR) 2012

(Left to right:) me, Ev, cops
Photo credit: Zac HB
LAX (Los Angeles, CA) 2012

Sunrise in a parking lot
Denny's (Raton, NM) 2012

Cats, Pajamas (2012)

Lineup: The ILLusionists, Masked Avengers

Best show: Seattle, WA

Worst show: San Francisco, CA

Record store find: Nas – *Life is Good*

The ILLusionists were picking up steam. Touring was quickly becoming a way of life. *Not So Blue* was in April; just five months after we got home from *I Quit*. We started booking again immediately, securing a third tour by summer.

"1% Blue" was a really effective photo shoot, but it wasn't the tour flyer. Logistically, it would've been very expensive to have Zac fly out in advance, just to do the paint gag with enough time to distribute the flyers. This time, we were traveling with the Masked Avengers (emcees Braxy and Tendre) from Stockton, CA. We played shows with them on both previous tours, and they were one of our favorite new acts.

I got their permission to do a goofy ILLusionists poster without their involvement. It was their first tour, like Zac's before them, and ours before that. People are pretty open to ideas when you take them on the road.

We're animal lovers. One of the best travel comforts is what we call "tour dogs" or "tour cats." It gets lonely out there, so when someone lets us stay at their house, it's a huge bonus if they have dogs or cats that want to snuggle with us.

We decided to visit the local animal shelter, Greenhill Humane Society, and with their permission, take some photos. My wife Ang and I had just purchased a Canon t2i camera—which was first used for the "Arms Race" music video—and she was getting great shots of our furry boys at home. The three of us went down to Greenhill and she photographed us playing in The Cattery. Ev and I dressed down, with Ninja Turtles and Sesame Street PJs on full display.

The *Cats, Pajamas* tour was easily our most talked about flyer. Every venue recognized us when we walked in, like *hey, you guys are hilarious!!* The image was shared quite a bit online, too. It might be a stupid play on words, but the Internet loves cat pictures and Ang got some great shots.

By then, we had enough experience to know how our tours should go. I was disappointed when the Masked Avengers informed me that they would be driving to the first few shows alone. Some of their friends wanted to tag along with them. It wasn't the biggest offense by any means, but I think we missed some of that initial bonding time in the van.

Nevertheless, our kickoff show was pretty great. Sarx opened the show, which was super cool. It's always comforting to see my former tourmates when I return to their town. He booked an awesome group called Fictitious, and they brought the house down.

We played at the White Rabbit, which was my first time in the Fremont neighborhood. Over the years, I'd go on to play numerous venues on that block, and film the "Vacant Eyes" music video in the alley behind them.

Our merch numbers were improving, as I started to step out of my comfort zone. Sarx had outsold us at nearly every turn, because he was so much more confident asking for sales. I used to do commission sales for a living, and I fucking hated it. It gave me the same feeling on the road.

By *Cats, Pajamas*, I would stand by the door at the end of the show with a stack of CDs in my hand. When people gave me props on the set, I'd thank them and ask if they had our album. If they said no, I'd show them what we had for sale.

Many people will just say "sorry, man—I don't have any cash!" I learned that lesson, too. There's a product called Square, that's a one-inch credit card reader for your cell phone. When I got the "no cash" defense, I'd say "that's cool, we can take cards!"

These are sales tactics, yes, but we're eating one meal a day and it's usually fast food. Selling a few CDs can go a *long* way. These people paid to see us *and* made sure to tell me that they're fans of our work. I had to justify it like that, so I could adapt and survive.

We upgraded in Eugene, returning to our favorite dive, John Henry's.* This was only a short time before that venue was sold and converted into a generic sports bar, so I'm glad we got to play there one last time. The lineup was stacked, including Landon Wordswell and the Cave Dwellers.

After visiting places like *The Cypher,* where the music flows continuously, I was really keen on having a DJ spin between our sets. My friend Josh was making great mix CDs under the name Rock N Roll Damnation, so I asked him to play. His selections

---

*I'm quite fond of shithole venues with an underground vibe. Braxy told me that he walked in on a hobo masturbating in the bathroom! Actually, to quote him, the guy was "violently jerking off." I guess it really was a stimulating performance!

were so perfect that it led to him getting a weekly Saturday night gig at Level Up, which he continues to play to this day.

MA was supporting a new album at the time, and we played their CD release show in Stockton. It wasn't at Plea For Peace, but a place called Blackwater Cafe. The first couple times, people warned us that Stockton could be pretty dangerous. We stayed with a graphic artist called AlterEgoz, who had iron bars over his doors and windows... as did everyone on his block. The second time, we had to sleep in the van. Our friends didn't have room at their place, but they were emphatic that we drive to the next town so we didn't get robbed.*

This time, we were hanging out in front of Blackwater after the show. People were chatting in groups while we loaded the van. I noticed a car driving by *really* slowly. I turned to see if one of our friends recognized it, but everyone had taken cover behind the other cars. Apparently, in Stockton, it's second nature to brace yourself for a drive-by, but me and Ev stood there like dummies because nobody warned us.

The *Cats, Pajamas* tour had noticeably shorter drives, as I was learning how to better plan a tour. We played four California cities within a 120 mile radius. With a less grueling pace, I was inspired to write some lyrics in the down time.

"Finally" became the happy ending on our 2013 album, *Death of a Salesman*. I wrote my verse in one sitting, at Tendre's house in Stockton. It celebrated our newfound momentum as touring artists. It felt like I was finally getting my hands on that elusive dream.

In Sacramento, we played another coffee shop venue called the Midtown Village Cafe. It was a small spot, not far from a

---

*We ended up at a Target parking lot in Tracy, CA.

couple of record stores. The show was ok, but the owner was gave us free food and drinks at the end of the day. We played a couple uneventful shows there that year, and then I heard it closed down. It would've slipped my mind completely if not for the fact that I saw it again in the Johnny Knoxville movie *Bad Grandpa*.

San Francisco is a tough town to get into. There are so many artists that the venues have be more selective, and we just didn't have any history there. My friend Davis recommended a Tuesday night weekly at the Red Devil Lounge. Unfortunately, it was an open mic.* This meant no pay, and two-song sets, but we could at least try to sell some merch.** It was an eclectic mix of styles, but we were the only rappers, aside from MA. The coolest part was just getting to walk through Haight Ashbury and check out —maybe you guessed it—Amoeba San Francisco. It wasn't as big as the flagship store in LA but Nas, Aesop Rock, and The Bouncing Souls had new albums out.

We wrapped it up at Johnny V's (San Jose), and dropped off the Masked Avengers in Stockton that night. It was super late by then, but we drove all the way to Eugene because I had tickets for *The Dark Knight Rises* premiere.** My wife and I went with my cousin, Chris Bradley, who was visiting from Italy. There was no reserved seating in those days, so we had to get there an hour or two in advance. We had so much time that I wrote a rap about it before the previews.

*My booking spreadsheet read:
Venue: Red Devil Lounge
Money: N/A
Notes: We'll just play the fucking open mic
**We did not sell any
**I'm a *huge* Batman fan. It's a problem. See *The Bat Fan Addict Podcast*

It all started with his mother and father Thomas and Martha...

People talk down about that movie, and I'll admit the third act leaves something to be desired, but the scope of that movie is incredible. The first Bane fight scene was one of the best scenes I've ever had the pleasure of viewing. I didn't breathe the entire time. It was all my nightmares and childhood comic fantasies rolled into one. Spectacular.

(Left to right:) Braxy, Tendre, me, E. Ville
Someone's crash pad (Sacramento, CA) 2012

Photo credit: E. Ville
Haight and Ashbury (San Francisco, CA) 2012

Bored with Buddha (2012)

Lineup: Kristoff Krane, The ILLusionists, Zac HB

Best show: Portland, OR

Worst show: Eugene, OR

Record store find: Dark Time Sunhine – *ANX*, Open Mike Eagle – *4NML HSPTL*

This one was pure luck. I was talking to Zac on my lunch break, and he said that Kristoff Krane had invited him on a West Coast tour. Chris (Kristoff) had been offered a private show in Saratoga, CA and wanted to add some dates while he was there.

I congratulated Zac, but he seemed unsure if it would even happen. They would both be flying from Minneapolis, so neither of them had a car. I was a huge fan of Chris' music after Eyedea introduced us in 2010. We had played together once or twice, but a chance to hit the road with him was too good to miss. Me being me, I seized the opportunity and offered to drive.

Soon enough, Chris called and asked about my experience booking tours. I had just done two in a row, and I thought it would be much easier with a bigger headliner like himself. I wasn't even sure I could get the time off—it was less than 30 days after *Cats, Pajamas*—but I told my manager that it was so important, that I would quit for the chance to tour with Kristoff Krane. Luckily, it never came to that.

There wasn't much time to prepare, but I got us a handful of dates from LA to Seattle. To help fund the long drive, I booked The ILLusionists in on the way.

After two full days of travel, we met the guys at Ill2lectual's house (Los Angeles). Chris arrived with his wife Sharri, which was a last minute decision. I've always had a down-to-business philosophy that spouses stay at home. Whether in the studio, or on the road, it's a pretty big distraction when the rest of us are there to work.

To my surprise, Sharri was the most valuable asset to the tour. She is a great person *and* a professional photographer. The problem was that my van had only four seats. With four performers on the bill, it meant having people take turns sitting in the back with the merch. Thank god it was a short enough trip!

That was our first time touring with a headliner, and even though I had opened for some legendary artists at home, it felt different spending so much time together. My behavior was guarded, because I really wanted to make a good impression. To this day, I'm not sure why I was so uncomfortable.

Shortly after we met up, Ill2lectual put on our 2012 remix of "Real MCs." We added live drums, new vocals, and scratches by Ill2 himself. The mix was a *lot* cleaner and more powerful than the original, and I was proud of it. When the beat dropped, Chris excused himself from our conversation and walked straight to the studio monitors. "Who is this??" he asked. "It's awesome."

We had recorded a song with him for our upcoming *Death of a Salesman* (2013), but I was reluctant to unveil what I felt was our masterpiece. It was probably my biggest mistake of that tour. Zac set the stage with his brand of singalongs and good vibes. The ILLusionists played our most aggressive battle raps, breaking only occasionally for introspective interludes, while Chris was speaking heartfelt, often profound messages with clear-eyed serenity.

I always wanted us to stand out, but not like this. The ILL had a *love us or hate us* motto onstage. Either way, our show wasn't easily forgotten. The problem on this tour was that I knew we had better, more relatable material ready to go. I should've adapted to the situation, but I withheld the songs from our set.

My insecurity around Chris made for a much different Sammy Warm Hands. Gone was the crass, creative dictator with iron will. They wanted to get Indian food for dinner—which I've never had, nor could I even identify—so I was trying foods on Day One. Most people who have known me for decades have never seen me try unfamiliar food. It just doesn't happen.

A few days later, Sharri convinced me to eat a cherry that she bought at a fruit stand. I don't think I've ever eaten a cherry in my life, but I genuinely felt pressure to just go along with it and eat the damn fruit for the video camera. It was health food peer pressure!

The tour kicked off at CHALK, which was packed once again. The second day was a private show in Saratoga, just outside of San Jose. Chris had a recent Kickstarter fundraiser for his album *Fanfaronade*. One of the rewards was a private show. Thanks to Brayden Curry's contribution to *Fanfaronade*, we had ourselves a tour.

The house looked massive when we approached the door. Inside, his entire family was eager to please. We had the most comfortable stay, complete with food, showers, and a pool. We set up in the back yard, and soon realized that we were playing for a *young* crowd. I believe Brayden was turning 16, so it was basically a high-end, high school pool party.

The Masked Avengers were also big fans of Chris' music, so I invited them to open the show. The high school kids were super fun, and Chris even coerced a freestyle out of Brayden.

That night, Sharri annihilated us at the pool table, and we played some vintage arcade games in the garage. I talked to Evan, Zac, and Sharri about a song concept that I had called "Crisis of Conscience." I had all these thoughts about the objectification of women in music and media, and wanted to really dissect toxic masculinity.* But I also felt complicit in the culture to some extent. It's easier to write a one-sided argument, but I felt that it would be hypocritical.

We had an honest discussion about how to approach these issues, and I got pretty passionate in the moment. They really helped me process those thoughts, so I took a shower and went to bed.

Later, in Seattle, Chris helped me figure out that I could be both the ally and the scapegoat. Showing both sides, he said, would make for a more thoughtful statement. Good advice.

The shows were great until Eugene, at a hit-or-miss weekly called *Monday Night Mics*. Diablo's (the venue) was a longtime staple of the local scene, and would soon suffer the same fate as John Henry's.

We had an excellent lineup, but Mondays are tough in any city. I remember being so disappointed—and embarrassed, actually—that we brought home our first tour headliner, and nobody came. I switched up the set list a bit, closing with "On The Rise." It was too aggressive for that tour, but I felt so

*We didn't call it that at the time, but you get the point.

defeated that I had to get it off my chest.

We're on the rise 'til we're ostracized
Originals try us on for size
We're packing our crates to the clubs alone
So if you don't like the show, you can go the fuck home

Ev and I were pretty much screaming by the end of it, and I walked offstage steaming. To my surprise, Chris pulled me aside and said "you guys killed it. That was your best set that I've seen." It put my mind at ease, knowing that he wasn't disapponted in me, too.

After the show, Chris complimented my friends The Architex, telling KI Design that their set was really impressive. He went on to ask if they had any songs that weren't about battling, because he really wanted to hear more about who they are, etc. KI took that as disrespect, saying that it felt like the out-of-town artist condescending to the local artist like *you should be more like me.*

I tried to explain that this is the same kind of discussion he had with Eyedea after *E&A*,* which—even by a bigger artist like Eyedea—was received as constructive criticism. His last album *By The Throat* was almost completely without the boastful raps that defined his early career. Frustrated, KI said "well, if you ask me, that's when they got worse." Ironically, KI's solo material was very introspective and probably would've ended the discussion right there. But, much like The ILL, The Architex live show was about high energy bars and murdering the mic.

*As told by Micheal (Eyedea) on the Face Candy DVD, *Waste Age Teen Land*

The best show was in Portland. We stayed in a big house on a huge, scenic property outside of the city. It was a beautiful view, offering a healthy dose of positivity to recover from *Monday Night Mics*.

Sharri staged a photoshoot for us in downtown Portland. It was fun to just roam the streets without having to perform or keep a schedule. We also weren't used to having professional photography on the road. I was grateful that she offered to do it.

At the venue, the turnout was great and we performed as a three-piece. The ILLusionists band was let go after *Near Def*, but we kept Crozz as a second beat maker. Since he lived in Portland, we invited him to DJ. The energy was much lighter, and we were clearly having more fun. It definitely made an impression because I've had numerous people tell me that was their first time seeing me live.

I strive to tour with artists who are good people and good musicians. If we're seeing the same show every night, I don't want to get tired of it. A good performer can continue to inspire, no matter how many times you've seen them. And that's how it felt with Chris. He was always present and giving his all.* Not to mention that I knew all of his songs by heart. It was my first experience like that and I felt lucky to be there.

In Seattle, I saw a much different side of Kristoff Krane. That's not to say that he was serious all the time, but Chris had a very zen-like, spiritual vibe. Between his inverted disposition, and my awkward fanboy feelings, we probably bonded less than my previous tourmates.

All that changed with Sadistik. Here are two of the most straight-faced, artistic rappers on the planet, goofing off together like little kids. We fucked around town that day, had dinner, and

*All? No, ALL!

then Cody (Sadistik) joined us at the White Rabbit. He made a cameo for their song "Higher Brain," which was the video shoot we attended on the first day of *I Quit*.

Personally, the highlight of the *Buddha* tour was paying Chris that night. It was our last show, and he complimented my organization and efficiency throughout the tour. He said that I was a good booker and even better tour manager; that I should consider doing it professionally.*

Back at Cody's house, they upped the ante. It was pretty late, so every TV channel was playing infomercials. Chris and Cody started dialing the 800 numbers and pranking them. It was hilarious to see them playing around like that—granted, Cody has always been super funny offstage**—and the characters they came up with were fucking great. I filmed the first couple calls, but the battery ran out pretty quickly. Then the pranks got more R-rated and we laughed until our faces hurt. It was a great way to end the tour.

---

*Booking is my least favorite part of being an artist, but I strongly considered it for a minute. We probably could've gotten on some bigger tours as a result.

**The first time we met, Cody called me from outside John Henry's and asked if I'd let him in. He said to look for "the most handsome guy in the room."

(Left to right:) no fucking clue. The Masked Avengers are in there, too
Photo credit: Sharri Keller (Satori Photography)
Private show (Saratoga, CA) 2012

(Left to right:) me, Chris, Zac, Ev
Photo credit: Sharri Keller (Satori Photography)
Downtown (Portland, OR) 2012

(Left to right:) Chris, Sharri, Ev, Zac, me
Downtown (Seattle, WA) 2012

Original Recipe (2012)

Lineup: Sarx, The ILLusionists, Man Danno

Best show: Seattle, WA

Worst show: Oceanside, CA

Record store find: Beatsteaks – *Smack Smash*

That fall marked one year since *I Quit My Job For This*. For our fifth tour, we brought it full circle: reuniting with Sarx. He was actually part of a collective with Graves 33, Man Danno, and Name The Uncanny. They were called Fated Empire. Dan (Man Danno) had a new solo release and wanted to join us. He's a great guy, and an absolute *beast* on the mic. It was a no-brainer.

We had just finished our DJ Shadow-inspired EP, *Re-Endtroducing*, complete with music video and a feature in *Northwest Alternative* magazine.* We recruited Ogar Burl and his friends to film some badass skateboarding sessions, cut with our most cinematic performance shots to date.** I don't even remember how the magazine article happened, but they were a glossy, high quality magazine with Suicide Girls-style pinups and music. We just lucked out.

*Ironically, given the lyrics: *the thought of me on a magazine is laughable*
**My performance was shot on a skateboard, holding onto a moving van!

Re-Endtroducing was a turning point, creatively. We had already written most of *Death of a Salesman*, but it wouldn't come out until the following year. With *Re-End*, we saw an increase in fans, and some glowing reviews from people who normally just supported because we were friends. I still cringe at my voice on recordings from that era,* but the writing had definitely surpassed our previous work.

The tour kicked off at The High Dive in Seattle, right down the street from The White Rabbit. I've played The High Dive a few times and, though it's a great venue, the first thing I remember is the green room.

Many bathrooms and backstage areas have artists' stickers everywhere. The Doll Hut (Anaheim, CA) and 924 Gilman (Berkeley, CA) are great examples of that. More often, these places are covered in graffitti. The High Dive's green room is notable for having the biggest collection of dick drawings that I've ever seen. They're on every wall, high and low. It's like the closing credits of *Superbad* exploded into the room.

We had played Seattle quite a bit by that point, so the turnout was solid—even without Kristoff or Sadistik. The energy was so high that first night that Dan accidentally lost his voice after his set. For the next three weeks, he sounded like Clint Eastwood in *Gran Torino*. It was hard to understand him, even in conversation, and he had to push extra hard to perform, which only made it worse.

After a couple Washington shows, we headed back to Eugene. Finding a venue was fruitless, but my friend Ogar Burl had the coolest basement parties where he would DJ.

---

*Beastie Boys are my favorite, but it took a long time to find my own voice.

With all the buzz surrounding *Re-Endtroducing*, I figured we'd have a great turnout. I had a promotional system that worked pretty well: drop a new single, post flyers online, hang the flyers all over town, do local radio, list the event in the local paper, and then text friends directly.

Apparently, we were building our fanbase across the country, but playing a little *too* often in Eugene. Even people who loved the new CD didn't need to see us a seventh time that year (we had a couple other shows between tours—mostly opening slots). Fortunately, it doesn't take a lot of people to have a good basement show!

I remember that one of my long-time Guitar Center coworkers had just been fired, without reason, after working there for more than a decade. In that moment, I was so upset about it that I broke my own rule and performed an a cappella verse from *Death of a Salesman*. It was captured on video, and I heard from my other GC friends that management had seen it and was upset that I aired them out.*

From there, we hit the usual spots like the Midtown Village Cafe, Plea For Peace, and Johnny V's. Dan hooked us up with a new contact in Oakland, where he's originally from. We saw the locals acts do a soundcheck and their DJ, Andy Minty, was incredible.

Andy was a few years younger than us, but he had incredible turntable skills. His style was noisy and chaotic, and he had the showmanship to back it up. Since *Re-Endtroducing* was a DJ-heavy project, we asked if he wanted to freestyle some scratches

---

*That was especially good news to me, since we had a whole album (and documentary) coming out about them.

during our set. It turned out so good that we traded information and featured him heavily on *Death of a Salesman*.

The venue was a two-story building called Nightlight. The bar was on the first floor, and there was street access to the venue stairs. A noise-rap act was headlining, and they brought a second PA... *in addition* to the club's sound system! From the moment they started playing, it was punishingly loud. I immediately left, because I protect my ears very carefully.*

Before long, everyone was outside. The audience, the other acts—even the bartender left the room. The stage faced away from the stairs, and yet we could hear them loud and clear on the sidewalk—even through ear plugs and a closed door! I've had my share of bad shows, where I might've sabotaged the set intentionally. If I perceive the audience is treating me unfairly, I might play my 15-minute NOFX cover or start replacing singalong songs with full-on screaming songs. I've mostly grown out of that, but I've done it. That said, I've *never* seen someone so bent on losing the crowd right out of the gate. I've had my friend Kellen explain noise music to me, but I really don't get it; especially at *double* the volume!

We returned to CHALK one last time.** There's footage of me and Sarx playing his song "Nightingale" together, which was cool. We worked out an acoustic version, where I played guitar and he sang/rapped over that. The response was so good that we played it that way for the rest of the tour.

---

*I've had tinnitus, or loud ringing in my ears, since I was 15 years old

**The Neff brothers were really generous to let us play there so many times. They weren't trying to be a music venue. After all, they were just throwing a party for their cousin (Louis Logic) and I happened to be there. It was one of our favorite spots for a while, but I understood when it came to an end.

Our first time in Oceanside was at a cool dive bar that was blasting metal when we walked in. But only two or three people ever came. That never stops us from putting on a good show, but it is discouraging.

What set this apart from other shitty shows is how the night ended. I pride myself on being able to entertain and engage an audience of any size. It's a direct benefit of playing so many basement shows in high school. But that night was the first time I remember blowing away the employees. If three people attend, then I'm playing for those three people. The bartender and sound man are typically out of my direct line of sight, but once in a while, they'll be so impressed that they come and buy our merch themselves.

Some people have referred to that as making "pity sales." They're clearly not having the conversations that I'm having. These are people who see live music five days a week, probably four acts a night, and not every show is going to turn out. So if they choose to buy *my* album instead of 19 other artists that week, then I'm proud of that. Not to mention that it's their *job* to be there. They're trying to *earn* money, and a dead night is just as much of a burden on their pocket as it is on mine. So that gesture goes a long way.

We stayed at a friend's apartment, and passed a strip club on the way. I yelled *titty bar!* and the guys echoed even louder: *TITTY BARRRR!* It became a recurring gag through the tour.

I don't know how many people have heard of it (I hadn't), but there's a town in western New Mexico called Gallup. I think Sarx found the place by chance, but we played there a lot. The venue was a huge club/hookah lounge called The Juggernaut. It had graffiti murals all over the building, including the classic X-

Men character, Juggernaut. It was run by members of a Native American metal band called Sleep Tastes Pretty.

Last time, Sarx read that girl's phone number onstage. The second time, Sleep Tastes Pretty brought their full metalcore show to us. The stage was under blacklights, and every piece of their equipment was designed to reflect it. Those guys were always super nice offstage, so it was great to see them kill it onstage. Their drummer brought back Sarx at the end for a freestyle, double bass and all.

Tour can disrupt my creative process, so I downloaded some instrumentals from Non-Prophets, Aesop Rock, and others, writing what became the *ILL AT WILL* (2013) mixtape. I remember writing some rhymes on my laptop at *What The Funk Friday* in Phoenix.

By the time we got to Denver, the titty bar joke was getting too real. After weeks away from home, we tend to get pretty lonely. There is a strict No Jerking Off policy in the van, or any shared spaces, so it could affect our state of mind after a while. If we're lucky, we can trade photos with our wives to ease the tension.

We arrived a night early, and went straight to Kelly's apartment. When we caught her up on the latest tour, the titty bar thing came up again. She said, "oh, Janette works at the BEST ONE IN DENVER! We've gotta go!"

Now, my tours are not *sex, drugs, and rock & roll*. They're usually none of those things.* But we were all ready for some female contact. I've been with my wife since 1999, and prior to *I Quit*, if you added up every single day that we were apart, it would be comparable to the first tour. Certainly not *five times* in

*Though, at times, I have to excuse myself when the bongs come out.

a row. I called Ang and asked if she'd be offended, and she was cool. Green light.

It turned out that Janette, who we had also met on the first tour, was a bottle service girl for a liquor company, and that was one of her regular spots. It was one fancy place, so she guest listed us—Kelly, too—and we got a pass on the dress code for looking like bums. The room was enormous, with five different stages and high end sound/lighting equipment. It was like something out of a movie.

We all sat together near the bar, and would break off one or two at a time to check things out. Upon realizing that we were on tour, one stripper told me that she was an aspiring singer and just signed to Christina Aguilera's management company. She probably didn't expect that I would be a big fan of Xtina, but I launched into fanboy mode until she effectively distracted me. You'd think that being all backed up for so long and going to a strip club would make things *worse*, but I actually felt great.

The next day, Dan broke the cardinal rule: Always Stick Together. I don't remember the details, but in his version of the story, I made it clear that we were leaving in the morning—with or without him. (Sounds about right!) Even better, the girl's roommate wasn't happy either. Dan got to be witness to an argument instead of having a good time with her. It wasn't even worth the trouble...

Our SLC date was actually a few miles out of town in Logan, UT. We played a huge college bar, where there was no stage, but an enormous dance floor. The room was in an L shape, and the bar itself was on the other side of the room. Sometimes the architecture itself can ruin a show by spreading the crowd too thin.

Everyone hung out at the bar pretty late, and we stayed with Black Socks, who was one of the openers. When we got to the house, he showed us to the basement where we could sleep. Ev and I set up our sleeping bags on opposing couches, and tried to get some rest after the long drive. Sarx and Dan were hungry, so they went to grab some food.*

Just as I was just dozing off, our host walked downstairs and said that some girls were coming over "if you want to party." Evan told him that we're tired, and married, and thanks for the offer. I'll never forget his reply: "well if you wake up getting your dicks sucked, it's not my fault!"

As soon as he left the room, we started cracking up. It was that special kind of laugh that you get after lights out at a sleepover. The next morning, we packed up our sleeping bags and brushed our teeth. When Black Socks woke up, he said "you guys missed the girls, man! You were both asleep when they showed up!"

As ridiculous as that sounds, it wasn't the first time a host had offered such amenities. On the first tour, we stayed with a guy who was very accommodating. He asked if we needed *anything at all*. I jokingly said "hookers and blow." He instantly pulled out his phone and was like "cool, I'll get some girls over here right now!"

The joke went right over his head, but we intervened before he finished dialing. Unfazed, he continued: "well, do you want the blow?"

We ended at The Shredder in Boise, ID. It's a great, all-ages room with arcade games, a stage, and a halfpipe for

---

*Presumably, Sarx's signature move at Jack In The Box: a cheap taco, placed inside of a cheap burger. Dan said he still eats it that way. Gross.

skateboarding. The shows are hit or miss in Boise, but it's still one of my favorite cities.

Around this time, Sarx told us that he and his wife Ana were expecting their first child and it would be our last tour together. Though it was disappointing to lose our traveling partner, I'm glad that he sacrificed the road life and put his family first.

(Left to right:) Sarx, me
Photo credit: E. Ville
(Oceanside, CA) 2012

Insect cemetery
Rest stop (Unknown) 2014

Ev's happy place
IHOP (Unknown) 2013

Attack of The Show Stoppers (2013)

Lineup: Carnage The Executioner
The ILLusionists

Best show: Albuquerque, NM

Worst show: Denver, CO

Record store find: Christina Aguilera – *Ain't No Other Man* (12in)

Though we had just worked our asses off for the past year, I wanted to go harder. In January, I planned my first Sammy Warm Hands album,* *Assholextraordinaire*, and a solo tour. Ev made a great cartoon drawing of me for the CD, and it was displayed prominently on the flyer. He captured me perfectly with just a few simple lines.

At the time, I was playing bass in a Seattle band called Jori & the PUSH. Since *A-hole* was a rock-oriented album, they were going to be both my tourmates *and* my backing band. I brought Dead Fucking Serious bassist Chris Wilson to play during my set, and that was all it took. Our rehearsals sounded great, and the shows were already booked.

Tragically, my mother-in-law Kathy was fighting off breast cancer at the time, and her prognosis was dire. She had been up

---

*Though I had released an earlier mixtape, it wasn't all original material. Ironically, this SWH album is generally not considered canonical in my body of work.

and down for months, so we held out hope. I waited until the last few days to cancel the tour. Sadly, she died at home on January 17th, 2013.

I believe that Jori & the PUSH played the shows without me, but my mind was elsewhere at the time. I did join them for one cathartic set, on the final night in Eugene.

My album didn't really take off, but it was only meant to be a side project. My real focus was *Death of a Salesman*. The ILLusionists spent three years transforming our tortuous middle-management lives into fully realized concept album, complete with our escape to the open road. It was our pinnacle achievement in songwriting, production, *and* popularity. We needed to do something big.

I had recently seen my friend Carnage The Executioner in Portland. He was on tour with Atmosphere at the time, which he quickly followed up with Kristoff Krane and Toki Wright on the *Short Circuit* tour. I told Terrell (Carnage) about *DOAS* and asked if he wanted to hit the road with us that summer.

His whole strategy at the time was to capitalize on the Atmosphere appearances, hitting those markets again as a headliner. Opening for a bigger artist is an opportunity to make new fans, which is exactly what we were hoping to accomplish with him. In a sense, he paid it forward.

Terrell had a booking agent, but we weren't satisfied with his pace. I decided to take the initiative and put it together myself. In exchange for booking, driving, and supplying the flyer art, we were offered equal billing and a 40/60 cash split.

The name came from a popular Carnage song, "Attack of the Show Stealer." He wanted to include us, so it was modified to *The Attack of The Show Stoppers* tour. Evan illustrated each of our faces, sort of like a hip hop Mount Rushmore. Our go-to graphic artist Char Houweling provided the color, and I did the rest. The *Show Stoppers* tour was official.

Working with Terrell was educational; he is meticulous about his business. I'm a pretty detail-oriented person with OCD tendencies, so I respond well to specific direction. When I confirmed a show, I'd mark it green on the spreadsheet. Once the promoter and I agreed on a guarantee, I'd tell T that it was settled.

With Kristoff, or anyone else, that would be the end of it. There's a certain amount of trust that goes into this business. Terrell, on the other hand, would have me call back the promoter and ask where the money is coming from. An experienced promoter will pay the artist before they step foot onstage. An inexperienced promoter will make a promise to pay, and expect the ticket/door sales to cover the cost. It doesn't always add up. Working with Terrell taught me to ask those questions in advance. We can't prevent every unpleasant surprise, but we don't have to leave it up to chance.

We met at the Boise airport. Ev and I had played The Shredder on the way, just to make some gas money. The first actual *Show Stoppers* gig was about eight hours away in Missoula, MT. It's a beautiful drive,* and it gave us a chance to reconnect as human beings.

Terrell is one of the most genuine friends I've met through music. The kind of person that I feel like I've known my whole life. By that point, we had been in daily contact for months, just to iron out the details. We traded rhymes and stories, and I

*Though Montana birds have a habit of making Kamikaze dives across the Interstate. We hit one on that drive and it dislocated my passenger side mirror. To date, I've hit four altogether! RIP frens.

showed him *Death of a Salesman*. We rapped along to LL Cool J and Beastie Boys albums. We geeked out about the new RA The Rugged Man CD.* In other words, we hit it off.

In Missoula, I was immediately introduced to a local artist named Wormwood. We had *just* entered the room and he came up to tell me how much he liked our new single, "pwnd." The album wasn't even out yet, and it was already resonating with people. Our set had become largely *DOAS* material; working class anthems for starving artists. I knew we were onto something when the crowd sang along on the very first night.

We noticed a difference in comfort right away, too. Since the tour was making $500 a night, we weren't sleeping on couches anymore. There wasn't much sleeping in the van after *I Quit*, but getting a room and a shower every night felt amazing. Motel 6 would be my honorary tourmate for years to come.

In Salt Lake City, our tour collided with Sunspot Jonz (of Living Legends). It was a cool show on the back patio of a bar called The Woodshed. I think Sunspot got there late, straight from the airport, and was a little thrown off by "Attack of the Show Stealer."

Hit the stage after me
You won't even get a cheer
Hit the stage before me
They'll forget you were ever here

That's a good ass line, but it's kind of like his "Real MCs" because it rubs people wrong if they aren't paying attention.

*Little did we know that both me and Terrell would end up playing shows with RA, and Terrell would be featured on his next album, *All My Heroes are Dead*.

Denver was solid, but the venue was too big by a long shot. I think we skipped a size between *Original Recipe* and *Show Stoppers*. It was undersold, for sure. The promoter had agreed to our guarantee, but tried paying me less. I was the tour manager, so it was my responsibility to get the full amount. I calmly explained that a door split wasn't our deal, and that I could pull up the email on my phone if he was unclear about that.

Not only was the door short, but he wanted to pay the openers $100 for promoting the show. I had been talking with those guys all night, so I grabbed one of their emcees and walked outside. "He's saying that we can't get our guarantee because you guys need to get paid. I appreciate you spreading the word, but that's how these things work. The tour gets the money for our travels, and the locals help promote. It's no sleight against you, but we need to get where we're going."

In hindsight, I should've skipped that part. I didn't need to involve them. They were promised payment just like we were. I redirected my attention to the promoter. "Look, we have it in writing that you agreed to this amount. Whatever you worked out with the opener is between you and them."

He didn't have the money. He opened his wallet to prove the point. I wasn't trying to shake him down, but we had a deal. He would do his job and I would do mine. I told him "I don't care if you have to take it from the bar, but we need the guarantee."

He talked to the bar manager, and they gave him the money to pay us. I can only assume it was a loan.

Back in the van, Terrell was ecstatic. We had a celebratory laugh as we drove away. It was super tense at the venue, thinking we were gonna get shorted by quite a lot. T said "you're the fucking *man!* I can't believe you still got it from him! I thought you were gonna whoop his ass!" I would never fight in a physical sense, but I did everything I could to honor my commitment to the tour.

One great thing about Terrell is that he's a good listener. I thought we had our shit down by then, with about 100 ILLusionists shows under our belts. But he was watching closely, and much like the Eyedea/Carnage song "Coaches," he gave us notes every night.

We used to run around all over the place; in the crowd, on the monitors, you name it. There's nothing wrong with an active stage presence, but he pointed out that we are a duo. When one person's climbing the bar and the other person is still onstage, the audience won't know where to look. We needed to act as a unit.

Terrell pointed out that our new songs had "opportunities" for some call and response parts. We used to make fun of call and response, because it was always the same.

When I say "hip," you say "hop!"
Hip! HOP! Hip! HOP!

I wasn't having it. I have a clear vision for my music, and reasons to justify my decisions. In this case, he explained that we don't have to pander to do it. "Your chorus starts with *RELEASE US NOW*, right? And then you have a break before the verse? Well, why not keep that going? When you finish the chorus, just say it again and the crowd will say it back. You don't even have to set it up!"

Sure enough, he was right. It was hard for me to hear that I didn't have my shit dialed in, but we tried his suggestions every night and they worked. Before long, we were killing it better than ever, and he didn't have any notes at all.

Years later, we played a show together in Salem, OR. There were maybe 20 people and it was mostly drunken rednecks. I had three or four people there to see me, and nobody else cared. Illogic and PCP* both struggled to keep the crowd's attention. Most were sitting at the bar, backs to us, never making a sound.

But Terrell knew better. When it was his time, he didn't play a single Carnage song. Instead, he used his beatbox skills to perform unmistakable classics like Zeppelin's "Immigrant Song." In two minutes, people were on the dance floor. In 10 minutes, the barstools were empty and *everyone* was dancing. He invited the rest of us performers to join him and we jammed on Beastie Boys and other popular songs, occasionally mixing in our own verses for fun. It worked because he read the room.

On the *Show Stoppers* tour, we learned that from him. Give them a little aggression and see how they respond. If they're feeling it, then go for the hard stuff. If they recoil, then go with the inspirational stuff.

Carnage is an emcee first and foremost, but he beatboxes all of his own music and scratches. Since we never toured with a DJ, that was our chance to have a live scratch routine for "Re-Endtroducing." Additionally, he would come out for a new song we wrote together, "The Show Stoppers." We had often traded cameos with Sarx and Zac, so it was cool to continue that tradition with Carnage of all people.

In Albuquerque, we played to a packed house at Burt's Tiki Lounge. It was their weekly hip hop night and we were firing on all cylinders. The stage was set up differently at the time, with a small platform in the middle of the room, and a rail around the

*Terrell's tourmates at the time

edge. I remember feeling distant from the audience, so I would stand on it and steady myself with one hand in the rafters. It was a super fun show and Carnage brought it just as hard. Everyone was singing "Star Destroyer" at the top of their lungs.

We were selling merch afterward, when a guy came up to me and asked why we shaved our heads. At the time, both Evan and I shaved our heads in favor of having ugly bald spots.* It wasn't that unusual, whether on YouTube comments or at shows, for people to ask us if we were some kind of skinheads or racists.

My go-to response was (and remains) that I can't grow a mohawk anymore, so I work with what I've got. But that guy was really insistent that I was holding out on him. He kept saying "come on, man. You can tell me. I really liked you guys, and I wanna buy your stuff, but I just wanna know."

Visibly irritated, I said "dude, there's nothing to know. He went bald. Then I went bald. The end."

He whispered in my ear, "but you're Nazis, right?"

I jumped back like "dude, get the fuck outta here! We're RAPPERS. Do you see the man I'm standing with RIGHT NOW, performing with every night, hugging and smiling onstage?!" I didn't want to turn Terrell into my token black friend, but I didn't know what else to say in the heat of the moment.

The guy claimed we were just keeping up appearances and that he knew "the truth." I grabbed our merch and said "get the fuck outta here, man! I don't want your fucking money."

The promoter in El Paso was awesome. Jenna took us out for Mexican food before the show and we had a really good time. I remember one guy was so into our set that he walked up and

---

*I later made peace with my ugly bald spot

asked how much it would cost for everything on the table. He bought one of everything, but in the smallest sizes—he was a big dude—and walked back toward the stage where Terrell was playing.

This place had two very attractive bartenders, and I soon realized the shirts were for them. It was really loud, and we were about 50 feet away when I noticed one girl had laid the shirt face down on a table and went full Edward Scissorhands on it. She held it up so the girl behind the bar could see. I couldn't really hear them while Carnage was playing, but Scissorhands threw it up on the bar and the other girl instantly took off her shirt in front of everyone. Then Scissorhands put on hers, and they were both sporting *Death Proof* skulls with enough cuts to show off plenty of skin.

By that point, people were buying shots like crazy and bringing them up to Terrell. He doesn't usually drink, so it surprised me that he was actually trying to keep up with the Texans. Soon, the girls were strutting onstage to hand-deliver the drinks. Then they started grinding on him. Then he pulled *me* onstage to bail him out! I don't even remember what we played; maybe "New York State of Mind." We got back to the motel later like *what the fuck just happened!?*

It was our third time at the Stray Cat in Tempe, AZ. The promoters Wally and James were really nice guys,* and we usually got to play with our friend Span Phly, who had previously toured with Terrell. We finally had a good turnout in AZ and that was how we left off with the *Show Stoppers*.

---

*Professional, too! I can always count on getting paid before the show.

I booked a longer tour, but Terrell had other obligations, so he could only join us for about half of it. The ILL went back through California—Plea For Peace and Johnny V's—and came across a new spot in Sacramento.

The Midtown Village was closed, but I had recently met a Sacramento artist named Task1ne. He recommended a weekly called *Microphone Mondays*. From what I understood, it was largely an open mic scenario, where anyone can sign up and play a couple songs. That night, there was a battle.

Battles are not designed for performers. People come for punchlines; not to watch your set. In this case, it worked out great: The ILLusionists had no shortage of punchlines.

The battles were fun to watch, and when it was our turn, we fucking killed it. It was our first good Sac show since *I Quit*, and it felt amazing.

I collected some vinyl on that tour, and took a photo of my haul at the motel. Ev and I thought it would be funny—I did mention that us couples will send photos to help with the loneliness—to do a photo shoot. I didn't get naked, but pretty close.* I took a Christina Aguilera record and laid on the bed like George Costanza's famous *Seinfeld* photo shoot. I held the record over my crotch, and bunched up my underwear to look like I was fully nude. Ev took the photos with my cell phone and I sent them home to my wife. Ang was so shocked—mostly that I went to those lengths to stage the shot—that it made the whole thing even funnier.

At Johnny V's, a middle aged biker wandered in during our set. In a room full of twenty-something emcees, he definitely

---

*On a related note, I never take off my socks. Sarx called me a "never nude."

stood out. We talked at the merch table, and he lingered there the rest of the night. If someone set a drink on our table, or leaned against it, he would check them like a bouncer. Eventually, he told me that he's part of the Hell's Angels.*

Apparently, they held events up and down the West Coast, but there was a shortage of young members. He wanted to hire us for one of the events, saying "I don't understand rap music, but you guys clearly have your hearts in the right place... I think they'd really like you." He bought everything on the table, and took my card to stay in touch. We never heard from him again.

We went to Amoeba Records in Berkeley, just to kill some time. I saw that they carried a bunch of our friends' music—Ecid, Ceschi, Kristoff Krane, Onry Ozzborn, and Sadistik—so I asked someone at the counter if they'd be willing to buy some of ours. I was directed toward their hip hop buyer, Evan Litwack.

Evan is a hip hop super-fan whose recommendations were hand written on nearly every one of my friends' CDs. Before I finished explaining who we were, he said "oh, The ILLusionists! Crushkill, right?" I couldn't believe it. "You just did that tour with Kristoff Krane, didn't you?"

It felt good to be recognized, but especially at a famous record store like that. From then on, Evan stocked my new releases whenever I came to town. To date, they've carried *Death of a Salesman*, *Bears Repeating*, *Famous Last Words*, *Vacant Eyes*, and *Rare Form*.

For the grand finale, it was our CD release show for *DOAS*. Our success was largely inspired by working with Eyedea & Abilities, so it was only fitting that DJ Abilities played the show.

---

*I think he had a Hell's Angels back patch or something that looked official, but I can't picture it.

He had just performed in San Francisco, so we picked him up at his friend—and underground MPC legend—Jel's house on our way home. It was another long drive, much like our first day with Terrell, which gave us the chance to just talk and catch up.*

The show was a major success; easily our biggest to date. We packed like 200 people into Luckey's, which was home to The Architex' popular weekly. I couldn't believe the response. Even our longtime friend-fans were passionately singing along. This was our first proper release on Eyedea's Crushkill label and the tour with Carnage was a good look, too. We finally started to see the fruits of our labor.

In hindsight, I should've used that show for another live DVD. It was our biggest headlining show to date, and the crowd was out of control. Many friends drove in from other cities; Jori Teran came from Seattle to sing "Finally," and Andy Minty came all the way from San Francisco to scratch. Crozz played all of our beats on his computer, and Gabe played live drums on a few songs, too. It felt good to put aside our differences and celebrate the album.

Just after *Show Stoppers*, we played another show for Brayden Curry in Saratoga, CA. He was throwing another big party, and wanted us to come back. It felt good being hired a second time, particularly since we had not been the main attraction on the *Buddha* tour.

Brayden had a headliner named milo [sic], who I had never heard before, but these days he's a household name. I listened to one of his songs and it reminded me of Open Mike Eagle.

*His reaction to *DOAS* was priceless. He confessed that lyrics are the least important part of hip hop for him, and yet he genuinely liked what we had done with the concepts. I rewound the interlude where my boss chewed me out for pursuing music over my day job. He facetiously referred to Abilities as DJ Silver Spoon and we laughed our asses off.

Crozz wasn't available to tour for long periods, but he was able to get the weekend off. Sadly, Ev was attending a friend's wedding and couldn't come. Ogar Burl knew the ILLusionists stuff pretty well—particularly *DOAS*—so he subbed for E. Ville. We leaned on the tracks where Ev only had choruses, and mixed in a couple new songs that would later become *Break The Bank*.

It's at least a nine hour drive, so we left a day early. That turned out to be a great decision, because we got a flat tire on the way. We were close to an exit, so I coasted into a Shell station for safety's sake. I learned that the spare tire is kept *underneath* the van. To remove it meant lowering the tire, which was suspended by a thick cable.

First, we had to find a jack. The one that's built into the van was too short (a truly maddening feature), so we went inside and asked the Shell employees for assistance.

The guys behind the counter ignored me, but a nice kid and his grandma overheard and offered to help. Noah Gonzales was just 13 at the time, but he grabbed the jack from his grandma's car and got to work. It, too, was short. We were getting frustrated,* but Noah had another solution.

Noah went home and got a bigger jack from his family's truck. While he was gone, we each struggled to disconnect the spare tire. We followed the instructions in the manual, but it wouldn't release. The tire was on a heavy duty cable, so there was no getting through it with our bare hands.

Doug and I walked to a nearby Walmart and bought some bold cutters. We walked back and found Noah, pulling off the last few nuts.** We cut the cable and Noah got us back on the

---

*I like to describe myself as car-tarded. My dad was a mechanic for most of his life. I learned virtually nothing from him.

**ha

road. We gave him whatever cash we had ($40) and a copy of *Death of a Salesman*.*

I returned the bolt cutters, and we booked a Motel 6 across the street. We were super relieved when it was over, but I later took it to the Ford dealership and they quoted me $500 to replace the whole spare tire assembly. That fucking tire has been floating around the back of my van ever since.

Crozz made a beat called "Flat Tire," and though it didn't make *Break The Bank*, it became the most popular single** from our second album, *Rare Form*. He started it in our room that night and finished it at Chipotle the next day.

When we finally got to Brayden's, the party had moved to a rec room at the neighborhood swimming pool. To my surprise, milo arrived *with* Open Mike Eagle and they both played the show! I've had quite a few shows with Mike, so that was an added bonus. We actually performed a new song where I mentioned his name, so it was cool to do the shout out in person.

The show was fun, but afterward was even better. We all hung out at Brayden's that night, debating music in the hot tub and eating dinner by the fire. It was probably one of the coolest one-off shows of my life.

---

*He wrote us in 2016 to say that he still listens to it!
**"Break the Mold"

(Left to right:) Ev, Terrell, me
Photo credit: Jenna Martin
Downtown (El Paso, TX) 2013

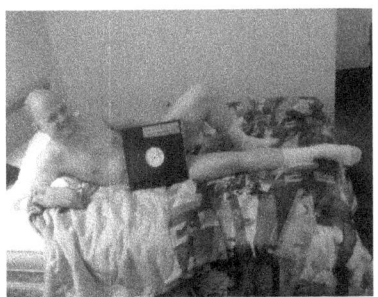

Me and Xtina
Photo credit: E. Ville
Motel 6 (Sacramento, CA) 2013

Bears Repeating (2014)

Lineup: Sammy Warm Hands, Ebb One & KI Design, Ogar Burl

Best show: Portland, OR

Worst show: Sacramento, CA

Record store find: The Used - *Berth*

The ILLusionists went out at our peak. I didn't really think it was over at the time, but *DOAS* took so much out of us—especially me and Gabe—that it just fell apart.

As The ILL got more and more serious, I needed a light-hearted outlet. Ogar Burl was an old friend. He had introduced me to much of my favorite music in high school, so I kept him informed whenever we had something cool in the works.

In 2013, I featured him on my *ILL AT WILL* mixtape and it was his first recording ever. By October—just four months after *DOAS*—we had an album together: *Break The Bank*.

It was a really fun, quick project like when The ILLusionists first started. Doug (Ogar)'s first taste of the mic made him even hungrier, which was inspiring to me. I often work so fast that it's only fun until I have to wait for other band members to do their parts. Story of my life.

With that in mind, I released my first solo rap album* in January. It was a little risky dropping three albums in six months, but if you've read my first book, you'll know it wasn't the first time.

Bears Repeating was entirely fan-funded, through the website Indiegogo, which totally blew away expectations. And *Break The Bank* had sold out so fast that we had to do a second pressing just so that Doug could join the tour.

Doug didn't have much solo material, but he prepared about a 15 minute set and filled it out with our *Break The Bank* "duets." I also featured him in my set, for "Endless Excuses" and "Deluxe Edition." Since the two of us were old friends, and I was sort of hitting the reset button on my career, I wanted to bring more artists from home.

Pretty much all our best shows of that time were a result of The Architex and The ILLusionists working together. The two of us had enough contacts for artists and venues that we made a formidable team. But those guys have so many members that they rarely hit the road. I asked Ebb One and KI Design if they wanted to play some shows as a duo.

The drives were super fun because of Ebb One. The man is always *on*. Doug and I have a sort of big brother vs little brother thing going on, but Ebb and KI just rip on each other constantly. I absolutely loved it.

---

*Apparently, I have a lot of *first* solo rap albums. I don't count *Assholextraordinaire* (2013)—released as Sammy Warm Hands—because it's a weird, rap/metal side project. I don't count *99 Years* (2008)—released as Sam Wartenbee—because it was a joke album, prior to the formation of The ILLusionists. Though admittedly, it was exciting when *99 Years* turned 10 years old. I don't have a lot of accolades, so those milestones are important to me.

Ebb's *Mutiny* EP came out on the same day as *Bears*, so we had a double release show in Eugene. But I was more excited about Portland for many reasons. We were booked at the Hawthorne Theatre, which is where Ang and I have seen tons of our favorite bands like Bouncing Souls, Strike Anywhere, and The Dear Hunter. It's way too big for us, but they offered us the smaller room in the bar.

Portland is never starved for good music, so it can be really hard for small artists to get a show. This was my first collaboration with a booker named Zoe Minderovic, and we did quite a few shows together after that.*

Somehow we wound up in a different part of Seattle, at a place called Dante's. It didn't seem like they did a lot of shows, but they did have our names on the marquee and the manager paid our guarantee. I remember being tied down to really short mic cables, and feeling pressure to play ILLusionists songs, since people were used to hearing them. Sarx and Graves played a group set (as Wings & Wounds), and hooked us up with a cool group called Black Magic Noize.

I remember being overwhelmed by the turnout, and thanking my friends in between songs. As I looked around the room, listing off names, I thought I saw Onry Ozzborn in the crowd. But I was the headliner, so I thought there's no way he would be at *my* little ass show. I must've been mistaken.**

KI shouted "you forgot about Onry!" and I was like "shit, is that really you?" Red faced, I said "I'm sorry man, I didn't even realize it!"

*Later that year, we played at the Hawthorne with Prem Rock and DJ Halo, and Onry Ozzborn just showed up and jumped on the bill!

**We had just opened for his group, Grayskul, in October. Maybe he was there for Graves 33? Come to think of it, it wasn't the last time he came to one of my shows. Maybe he's just cool like that.

At the merch table, I talked to a regular ILL fan named Jen. She said that it was always fun to see me—even if I had just played there—because I always brought a new set, with super talented artists on every tour. I had become a conduit for new music. It especially meant a lot because the *Bears Repeating* tour was my hometown crew. For the first time, I was taking our typical Luckey's bill—which was slowly becoming stale in Eugene—and blowing people's minds in other markets.

Ebb and KI had some songs together and some solo, but they shared the middle slot together. Some of the songs ended up on their first duo album, *Coffee Table Clutter* (2016). The highlight was often their freestyle song. KI does a classic hip hop routine, asking the audience to hold up any object during his freestyle. It's a good way to prove that it's not written, and it's fun for the crowd to see if they can stump him. Then he and Ebb would pass the mic back and forth, playing off what each other had just said.

One memorable freestyle was at a dance hall in Arcata, CA. It was an EDM night, and the vibe was a *lot* different than we're used to. People were there to party, not to listen to lyrics. So when a girl was shaking her ass during his freesyle, KI rapped about her yoga pants. She seemed flattered, and exacerbated the booty shaking, but he finished by saying he'd like to "jam it in [her] uterus" and the crowd went crazy. Her face had probably the most embarrassed expression I've ever seen at a show.

Earlier that day, we had a long drive into town and ate at the only restaurant that was still open. I was so broke that I had to borrow Doug's money to afford that place! The promoter arrived well before soundcheck, and we met at a bar around the corner. He looked gaunt, and possibly strung out. As soon as I could leave the room, I told the guys that he looked like Rickety

Cricket from *It's Always Sunny in Philadelphia*. They unanimously agreed. We knew there were a lot of drugs in the area, so it was suspicious from the start.

Then we met his lady, who introduced herself as Baby Devil. I am not exaggerating or changing a word. For the rest of the night, she was flirtatious and kept insisting that we stay with them because she wanted to make us pancakes in the morning. Don't get me wrong, I fucking love pancakes, but it seemed like she wanted more than breakfast.

The venue was really cool, and it was easily the biggest crowd of the tour, but we didn't sell much given the rave or whatever the fuck it was.

We were dodging Cricket and Baby Devil, so we left in quite a hurry.* About two hours later, I'm driving and everyone's asleep. KI wakes up in the passenger seat, screaming. *FUCK...* He punches the dash. *FUCK, FUCK, FUUUCK!* It turns out that we left a little *too* hastily: he forgot his insulin. From what I understand, it can be life threatening for a diabetic person to go without, so I offered to turn around without hesitation.

"No," he said with a pause. "We're too far away. I'll figure something out." The other guys woke up, but remained silent.

"Let's just go back," I said. "It's not a big deal." But KI was firm. We stayed the course to a janky Motel 6, in a small town called Willow. The guys walked to the get some coffee in the morning and Ebb said that people looked at them like aliens.

*If I leave pissed, I'll flee to the next state
Find a Motel 6 / After some time to rest, late
checkouts are the best / If we left too early,
we walk around bullshitting and spend the little we're earning
Then it's back to square one / Negative funds
Gotta borrow each other's money to make it through lunch
and it sucks, but you can make it up another night
No matter how rough it gets, never give up the fight
-"Before Doors Open," *Famous Last Words* (2015)

In Sacramento, we met up with Task1ne for a video shoot. He and I had recorded a song on *Bears Repeating* and I wanted it to be a single. We improvised the whole video at a record store called Dimple. It's on a famous block where Tower Records was founded, and you could see the old Tower sign in the background of our performance.

The show was *Microphone Mondays* at Sol Collective, where The ILL had last played on battle night.

Unfortunately, there were some noise complaints and the venue was shut down. But they didn't tell us it was cancelled. We got there and called the promoter to see where everyone was. He told me that the show was *moved*... to a Mexican restaurant.

Skeptical, we plugged in the location on the GPS and got some burritos. The food was good, but it was well past show time and nobody else was there. On top of that, the restaurant was a walk up window with outdoor seating. It was overlooked by an apartment complex, literally a stone's throw away.

I told Task what happened and we laughed at the ridiculousness of the situation. Eventually, people started pulling up, but they didn't get out of their cars. Then some more people wandered up on foot. I saw the host and asked him what was going on. He said we'd get started soon, but I didn't see a PA or anything. I asked again and he brushed me off like *just wait*.

Then somebody stood up on a bench and started loudly reciting poetry. For like two minutes. People were rolling down their windows, leaning on hoods, and one guy was even sitting on top of his car, through the sunroof.

They applauded.

A man on foot raps a verse. More applause. I look at Task like *what the fuck is this shit*. Sunroof guy freestyles about God for an eternity. More applause. All I'm thinking is *I can't do my set here. I'm not gonna sell anything tonight. This is a fucking waste of time.* I whispered to the host that we're "not really into slam poetry" and we bounced.

Task said the guy dissed us on Facebook for leaving. Said we didn't have the balls to perform in their city without the safety net of a beat. Not sure why he couldn't wrap his head around it, but we didn't drive 500 miles from home just to do a lame parking lot cypher.

The next day, we drove to Oakland. I have a strict rule about not using my phone behind the wheel. For that reason, I had some missed calls. When we stopped at a gas station, I listed to my voicemail. It said that Ang was in the hospital.

I couldn't talk to her because they were running tests. I spoke to her aunt and uncle, who picked her up after she complained of crippling pain that left her immobile. Her sister had appendicitis before, so they guessed it was something similar.

In the meantime, I was unsure what to do. *My wife is in the hospital. She's the most important thing in my life. Do I call off the tour and go home? Do I just wait and see what they find?* I put on some sad songs and continued south. I tried not to show the tears behind my sunglasses, but I was falling apart.

We stopped again and I got an answer. After a series of inconclusive tests, they did a scan and found a mass inside. Upon closer examination, it was identified as an ovarian cyst. To my relief, and hers, they put her on some medication and sent her home after six hours.

It hurt being so unable to comfort her that day, but she was home safe and the show must go on...

DJ Halo hosted us at his Tuesday night weekly in Oakland. The Legionnaire is a small-ish bar with an upstairs venue. We played downstairs on flat ground, where he regularly performs.

Another show was happening upstairs, and we were right in front of the staircase. Halo knocked it out of the park, but it was hard to ignore all the people walking *right past us* from the bar to the stairs with their drinks.

In San Jose, *The Cypher* had moved to a new venue. While Johnny V's was a bit of a shady dive bar, Back Bar was all new and shiny. It looked a bit *too* nice for an indie rap show, but they've been holding it there ever since.

On that particular night, our tour collided with my friend P Chill from Sacramento. We all shortened our sets, because five acts is long enough as it is. Five acts *and* a cypher is a *lot*.

P Chill went up after his opener, and was immediately plagued by technical difficulties. His DJ was struggling to get the computer to work. P Chill said "man, I told you to go to Best Buy today and figure that out!" To keep the show moving, he said "I'm just gonna do this one a cappella."

After performing no less than two entire songs a cappella, he turned back to the DJ. The tension was high, and almost everyone in the crowd had left. Doug and I were looking in disbelief. We felt terrible for him.

While that was happening, the DJ bent over to check the connections. He accidentally bumped the table, and his laptop fell right on the ground! We were literally speechless. *How could it get any worse?*

Thinking quickly, P Chill asked his tourmate to bring something from their merch table. He had a 12-inch single for sale, and there was an instrumental version on Side B. He handed that to the DJ and used AudioDru's turntable to play one last song before he had to go.

While all this is happening, Pariah from The Architex walked in. Watching the shitshow unfold, he yelled in full battle rap voice, "this is HORRIBLE," and walked out. I felt so bad for P Chill, and he even apologized for ruining the show. I refused to accept his apology, insisting that he made the best of a really bad situation. He decided to leave for the next city on his tour, and I didn't blame him for skipping town.

We stayed with KI's brother in San Jose, and had to get up early the next day to drive home. Doug and I had been added to a Sapient show in Eugene, and couldn't pass it up.

I have a hard enough time waking up before noon, but there was a complication that meant waking up *extra* early. KI had been in contact with the venue in Arcata, and they found his insulin bag... he wanted to pick it up "on the way."

Arcata isn't exactly on the way home. We added four extra hours to the trip by cutting over to Highway 101 and getting the bag. I wished we had just turned around that first night.

I was a fucking empty shell of a zombie, but I made the *14 hour drive* by myself. At Doug's house, I got out and fell in the yard. I couldn't stand on my own, so Doug helped me up. When we got to the venue, I was *fucked*; so disoriented that I couldn't form a coherent sentence.

Doug carried everything inside and performed soundcheck duties for the both of us. He sat me down at a table and I dozed off on my forearms.

A few minutes later, he poked my shoulder and set down a slice of pizza. I still didn't have words, but the food started to make me feel a little better. The sound guy was an old friend, but when I tried talking to me, I could barely muster the word "tired." *So tired.*

When it was our turn to play, Doug looked at me like I wasn't going to pull it off. To tell the truth, I didn't really know what was about to happen. I wasn't sick; I was burned the fuck out. Clinically exhausted.

We were sharing a time slot that night, mostly doing *Break The Bank* material. The set had Doug rapping first. I stood lifelessly still and did all his backup vocals. The chorus got a little more blood flowing, and by the second verse—my verse—I was giving an adequate performance. I didn't say much between songs, but we *did* play the songs well.

During "Blood in the Water," my speed-rap solo track, I planted my feet still and closed my eyes. My mind was blank, but I didn't miss a fucking word. Our friend Bryan filmed the whole show, and it was hilarious to watch later.

We had one last date with Ebb and KI, at small bar called The Triangle (Salem, OR). Our friend ThatKidCry frequently hosted shows there, and it was our first time. Normally, we'd finish at home, but I was thinking about the future: I needed the contacts.

The turnout was average, but we had a great time. With years of collaborations and now a whole tour behind us, we were in rare form. Even Ev drove up to play a song with me. KI often stayed onstage for all three acts, acting as our DJ. We all had guest appearances rapping in each other's sets, too. The *Bears Repeating* tour was really a cohesive show, and I continue to use that model to this day.

First day of tour
(Left to right:) me, Doug, KI, Ebb
Doug's house (Eugene, OR) 2014

(Left to right:) me, Doug
Downtown (Salt Lake City, UT) 2014

(Left to right:) me, Task
Dimple Records (Sacramento, CA) 2014

Rasputin's Records (Berkeley, CA) 2014

Blood in the Water (2014)

Lineup: Sammy Warm Hands, Task1ne, Ogar Burl

Best show: Phoenix, AZ

Worst show: San Jose, CA

Record store find: Metallica – *Live Shit: Binge & Purge*

After *Bears Repeating*, I had a vasectomy. It was probably the worst day of my life, but totally worth it. I had started planning a spring tour, and then Doug got a hernia. With back to back crotch surgeries, we decided to push it back a few months.

That summer, I had the "Blood in the Water" video ready to go, and Task1ne had agreed to join me on tour. Task had a lot of buzz and we all thought he was going to do big things. Putting out our joint single worked well to promote the tour, and Doug returned to open again.

Blueprint (Soul Position, Rhymesayers) reached out to me about booking Eugene. I was booking the *Blood in the Water* tour, and coincidentally, I already had the dates he wanted in Eugene and Portland. We agreed to combine shows, and I worked out the rest of the details with his booking agent, Tony Caferro.

Normally I'm focused on getting my *own* guarantees on tour, but I couldn't pass up a chance to kick off my tour with Print!* I talked to KI and we split the Blueprint guarantee between me and The Architex.

On the day of the show, we trimmed and combined sets to accommodate both tours. With Print and his tourmate Count Bass D, plus The Architex, there wasn't even time for me and Doug to do our own sets.** Task worried that he wasn't going to have an audience at 10pm and refused to go on. I said that if he pitched in on the guarantee that he could play whenever he wanted.

A few minutes later, Landon Wordswell calls me on the phone. Landon was the one who introduced us, so I guess he felt compelled to mediate. Irritated, I explained the whole thing again. I wasn't budging.

The show was fucking awesome. Luckey's was packed to capacity; just like the *DOAS* release show with DJ Abilities. Print played songs from his entire catalog, no matter how obscure. The highlight was when he performed "Alchemy"—a collaboration between Print and Aesop Rock—and the whole crowd sang along.

The second show was at The Hawthorne Theatre, and they wanted Portland-based openers. They offered me a solo slot, and I had the other guys come up for a few cameos. Our 90 minute show was condensed to a 30 minute support slot. The room was packed, and a lot of my old friends had come to support.

We returned to Dante's in Seattle, and Man Danno opened the show. We had such a good time that it led to a collaboration on *Famous Last Words* (2015) called "Dan Sammo."

*And *two* days at that!
**We played a duo set, comprised of mostly *Break The Bank* songs

There was a stripper pole near the stage, and I had played with it a little at the *Bears Repeating* show. This time, Task—who is a very large man—had his turn. There was a point in his show, toward the end, where he took off his shirt and started rapping extra hard. That night, he took off his shirt and spun around the stripper pole. It was fucking awesome and the crowd loved it.

Doug and I played air hockey by the merch table. I beat him, because I don't lose at air hockey.* He gets a kick out of seeing my competitive side. Sarx had dubbed me the "Anti-Fun" on the first tour, and with good reason. Anything other than music and movies is pointless to me. Air hockey is a rare exception.

At the end of the night, there was a miscommunication and the venue didn't have our guarantee. I pulled up the email on my phone and sorted it out, but it was my last show at Dante's.

The Missoula show started another practice that I use to this day. We couldn't get our full guarantee, which usually means settling for a percentage of the door. In this case, we accepted a lower guarantee with back end (the possibility to earn more if the door did well). If someone is hell-bent on a door deal, I'll fight for a small guarantee. Even $100 shows some kind of investment from the venue.

This is how you avoid showing up to find that nobody even put up a flyer. Just prove that you actually *want* me to play there. Sometimes it works better for the promoter, and sometimes it

---

*We played once on Doug's birthday, and after I won, his friend called "next game." I beat him, and his friend after that. By then, a crowd had formed around us. Doug had left after the first round, and by the fourth, I was battling strangers. I beat the stranger and moved on to a fifth competitor. He seemed genuinely upset that I was doing so well, and absolutely crushed me. It was the fastest game I've ever played. Evidently, the last two guys were semi-professional and asked me to join their Sunday night air hockey league. I was flattered, but did not join the team.

works better for us. But at least we're all committed to do our part.

That night was much different than the *Show Stoppers* tour. The CoDependents* booked both shows, but all we could get was a VFW. I've played a lot of granges and legion halls in my early days, but that one wasn't exactly thriving. By the time I went on, all but one of the openers had gone home and I played for three or four people. It was one of those nights where the sound guy bought my album and said "I've seen a *lot* of shows, and never seen anyone put on a show like that in an empty room!" At least it softened the blow.

Boise sucked, even though we had both Arthur Maddox and Oso Negro on the bill. It was so embarassingly empty that we only used the closeup photos for social media. The venue (The Crux) closed shortly after that.

We still went to one of my top five favorite shops, The Record Exchange. And we had fun trading verses in friendly competition. I remember piling our stuff into the van and Task just kept going and going like the fucking Energizer bunny. He out-rapped both of us after a while...

Salt Lake City was interesting. We showed up early and they had us on the marquee. That's usually a good sign. We walked around to kill some time, and got some goodass street tacos on the corner. The locals—Dine Krew and Dusk—were great, but there wasn't much of a crowd that night. It was starting to feel like my worst tour in a long time. I had hit these territories repeatedly–both opening and headlining–but it wasn't affecting the turnout at all.

*The CoDep's would go on to become my Crushkill labelmates in 2016.

We still got some love before the show. I remember one of the openers saying it was "an honor" to share the stage with me. Producer Melvin Junko and his wife came to the show. We talked about music and her work with Suicide Girls. They bought some merch and were really supportive. If you have any interest in boom bap beats, I'd highly recommend looking him up.

Task introduced me to his friend Gage Luce. He was cool to me right off the bat, but before long he was coming up to me and telling me what to do; set times, etc. I said something to the effect of "I've got it under control, man."

Gage came up to me again and tried to say that Ogar Burl could only play for 15 minutes. He only had 20 to begin with, but it didn't matter because Gage wasn't running the show. I pointed to the bartender and said that I booked the show with her, and cleared our set times in advance.

Then it got *really* weird. Gage walked onstage—WHILE DOUG WAS PERFORMING—and just stood there. He lingered for multiple songs, even grabbing Doug's beer, thinking that it was his own. Doug was ready to snap.

I walked onstage for our duo songs, and Gage was in his ear saying "you've got one left." I took the second mic and said to the crowd "alright, we've got three left—let's do this shit!" I think Gage must've had too many drinks, but he left us alone for the rest of the set.

Task usually went on immediately after Doug. But Gage grabbed the mic and provided an introduction. That would've been fine, but again, he never left the stage. Through the whole set, Gage drunkenly hyped Task like they were in a group together. He kept putting his arm around him and doing the backup vocals like it was a singalong song when it wasn't. I could tell that Task was irritated, even telling him verbally to "chill," but he played it off like a pro.

My set was normal, except for a couple girls who danced to my feminist anthem, "Crisis of Conscience." Ironically, the booty shaking only happens during that song. I had jumped off the stage to be closer to the tiny crowd. When I climbed back up, the girls came along for the last song. Our numbers were small that night, but we made the most of it.

Gage needed a ride home, and we obliged. But when he got out, he said that Task owed him a burrito. Task got out like *seriously? I'll be right back...* and bought this motherfucker a burrito. It was a strange way to meet, but Gage and I would eventually work together again.

In Denver, we played a newer venue called Lost Lake. Finally, a room that was the perfect size. Crushkill's label manager, Brady O'Rourke, was living there at the time and took us out for Thai food. I astonished my friends by ordering beef and broccoli,* and we had a good time.

At the show, I was excited to show off my new set. Brady had only seen me live with The ILLusionists, but he was incredibly helpful when it came to releasing *Bears Repeating*. His only objection had been my use of the word "retarded."

> *They say home is where the heart is*
> *That shit's retarded*
> *My heart is in the music*
> *It's why I'm an artist*

I'm pretty careful about the words that I choose, but I

*vegetables!

haven't stopped saying that one. My bad. I actually raised the stakes, turning it into a call and response. Doug hated it as much as Brady did, but I thought it was fucking funny.*

Burt's Tiki Lounge was remodeled after the *Show Stoppers* tour. They had a new stage with better sound. We walked around the block to Jimmy John's, next door to a strip club. I was feeling pretty lost in my head that day, so I asked Ang if I could go after soundcheck.

When I walked into the room, the door guy yelled super loud about me looking like "the guy from The Prodigy."** For some reason, he had a wireless mic in his hand, and I couldn't politely get around him. I was already off my game, so I didn't know what to do. He said "yo, say 'smack my bitch up!'" and put the mic in my face.

I didn't want to say that,*** but I remembered a different Prodigy song and said "I am the firestarter! Twwwisted firestarter!" It was embarrassing in a specific way, like the time I bought condoms and it set off the alarm when I walked out. The cashier took them out of my bag and waved them in front of the alarm sensor, which set it off again. She then tried to deactivate the sensor, waving it again for what felt like an eternity. It was the longest 30 seconds of my life.****

I returned to the merch table feeling better. One guy walked in before the show and bought our stuff without ever hearing it. He said that Quentin Tarantino's *Death Proof* was is favorite movie, and he had seen my van parked out front. I told him that I

---

*At the time of this edit, I've now taken tests that imply I'm moderately autistic
**See also: Beetlejuice, Super Saiyan 4, Tekken, Rick & Morty, Troll doll, etc.
***See, I have *some* limits
****That's what she said

saw it three times in the theater and sampled the theme song in addition to the logo. He was so stoked that he asked if I'd take his picture by the van with his new CD and shirt.

We had a great show that night, but it was double-booked by mistake. Some venues don't offer door deals *or* guarantees; they prefer to have free shows and pay the artist a percentage of bar sales. It's almost always a good deal because more people tend to come.

In this case, we had a deal with the bar. I was waiting to settle up with the promoter when I noticed the host of the show taking money from the bar... and giving it to another act. I ran to the promoter and asked if we could get paid, now that the host had settled up with the bar.

The host said that our tour was added to an existing show and he didn't even know who we were. That was a blatant lie because I had a history of texts, and the promoter corroborated our story. I pointed to the *Blood in the Water* flyer on the door. My face was on it. I grabbed a newspaper ad from *The Alibi* that was stuffed in my laptop bag. It was an ad, paid by Burt's Tiki Lounge, which listed all the shows that week. The only names on it were Sammy Warm Hands & Ogar Burl.

The dude opened his wallet and gave me $20. He said it was all he had. The promoter opened his wallet and did the same. I wasn't trying to be an asshole, but we can't afford to play for free when we're 1,400 miles from home.

In Phoenix, there was a long-standing weekly called *Blunt Club*. People had talked it up since the first ILL tour. We finally got a foot in the door, and it was worth the wait.

We shortened our sets to make room for another tour—Jabee and The Jivin' Scientists—who let us open for them. We still got our guarantee, and the crowd was amazing. We got along so well that Phen (Jivin' Scienists) would later appear on my *Vacant Eyes* album.

It's worth mentioning that I stopped shaving my head that year. *Blood* was the first tour where I had the aging punk rocker look that I have now. It made for some pretty hilarious looks when we walked into rest areas and truck stops. We had a scrawny bald man with blue hair, a tall skateboarder with glasses, and a large black man with colorful comic book shirts.

That night, Jabee was the headliner. He looked at me like those strangers did at rest stops. Everyone had mingled before the show, but he never acknowledged me.

When I got offstage, I made my usual trek to the merch table. Within seconds, Jabee tapped my shoulder and said "wow, dude. That was awesome."

After the show, everyone was in good spirits. Most of the gear was already packed, but the artists all hung out for a while longer. We were laughing and having fun when Jabee noticed me. "*This* motherfucker!!" he yelled. "You *surprised* me, man. That was incredible."

We accepted an offer in San Jose, opening for an act that I had never heard of: Wildcard. (AudioDru said he was big on YouTube; that he would have a built-in crowd.) It was a 12 hour drive from Phoenix, but I sure hate having days off... I figured a Friday night show with a headliner would be bigger than our typical crowd at *The Cypher*.

It was not.

Another line from "Before Doors Open" could sum this up quite well:

Trust when I say the saddest part of the day
isn't only being homesick / Putting away
seven CDs and three different shirts from the merch booth
without having sold a single thing is the worst, dude

I finally let Doug take the wheel in San Francisco. Unfortunately, it was late and we hit some overnight construction. The lane was narrowed to that of a compact car, and the van was hauling ass around these turns. It takes a minute to realize that you can't drive the van like a regular car, so Task and I were both yelling "slow down, man!"

Task hooked us up with a Sunday night weekly at the Boom Boom Room called *Return of the Cypher*. The format was super cool: tons of emcees, singers, and a live band. The band played all night along, both originals and popular beats, while other artists freestyled over the top.

Task did his damn thing that night. People went fucking nuts. He was really on the cusp of making a name for himself.

We combined sets again, and when Doug and I started, it was totally packed. But everyone was starting at me like an alien again.

Our first song was "Surprise," which meant that Doug rapped first. There's a musical break after that, where I stepped to the front of the stage, put one foot on the monitor, and looked out at dumbfounded faces. I jokingly acknowledged their skepticism, saying "yeah, I know, right?"

"Surprise" is a monster of a song. On top of that, I had been collecting 12-inches since the *Show Stoppers* tour, so that I could mix in some famous beats with our live show.* This song had an *awesome* break from El-P, with a really old-school vibe. It was time to show and prove.

*I got this idea from watching Mixmaster Mike play with the Beastie Boys.

Insubordinate, exorbitant
Flip words like contortionists
You've been blessed by the presence
of two extraordinary vocalists

People started going nuts. They had set the bar so low, that I annihilated their expectations. It turned out that I could look however I wanted and it would only help me in the end. The band resumed and we each had little cameos in the cypher. Task was especially on fire that night.

Pete Feliciano was one of the people in the front row during our set, and we quickly became mutual fans. He had a phenomenal voice; unlike anyone I'd ever met. He blew my mind *again* when we shared the stage in 2016. We always talked about working together, and I finally got him on a Star Wars-themed track called "Hearts of Kyber" in 2018.*

After the tour, we parted on good terms. I say that because I haven't spoken to Corey (Task) in years.

About 10 months after *Blood in the Water*, my friend Gradient messaged me late at night: "Have you heard what they're saying about Task?!"

Someone made a YouTube video, comparing a new Task1ne verse with an old song by a rapper named ChrisCo. Line after line, the two songs were identical. Comments were already piling up, calling him more than just a thief, but attacking him personally, as well. I assumed that he had heard about it, but I texted him to anyway, to give him a heads up. There had to be some explanation.

---

*Shortly afterward, we had a falling out over the use of racist humor on his podcast

By morning, it was all over social media. Corey had admitted to using a ghostwriter* to keep up with the workload from his newfound popularity. He blamed this unnamed person and feigned ignorance about the plagiarism.

Before long, there was outcry from artists across the country. I still couldn't get ahold of him, but I made a statement saying that whatever artistic crime had been committed by Task1ne did not equate to the personal attacks that Corey was receiving.

I consider the van to be a sacred place. It's where friendships are formed and solidified; where lonely nights reveal secrets and personal truths; and it's where we can be completely honest without the scrutiny of being onstage. I felt like I really knew Corey. Even though he was a newcomer, I could tell that he had a genuine love for the music.

It was a bitter pill for me to swallow, but in a matter of days, more and more of his verses were exposed as fraudulent. He was accused of biting** a long list of underground rappers: Apathy, Diabolic, Jon Conner, Demigodz, Nino Bless, and even Wu Tang Clan's Inspectah Deck. Most of the accusations came with side by side comparisons, so there wasn't much he could do to deny it.

By then, rappers who featured Task were starting to Google their own song lyrics. There wasn't a lot of good news. Corey was taking people's money under the guise of selling a Task1ne verse, but usually it was a hodgepodge of other people's lyrics. Gradient was able to get a refund from him, since he was among the first to ask. (It's common that indie rappers get paid for features, just like they would on a major label.)

*A ghostwriter is someone who writes on an author's behalf and doesn't receive credit. Corey's claim was never corroborated by anyone else.
**"Biting" is a rap term for stealing lyrics or styles from other artists

Gradient asked if I had Googled lines from "Blood in the Water." I thought it couldn't happen to me. Task had lines like *me and Sammy rap from Dusk 'Til Dawn and Transform like motherfucking Destructicons*. I knew that it was written for me. He didn't even charge me.

Well, Gradient did the research. Turns out that the first 12 lines were original lyrics, like I thought. But the last four bars belonged to Diabolic.

"Dangerous" by Diabolic:

...Do the math equation
The world revolves around me like the sun's gravitation
Now shots of Jack are making everybody aggravatin'
I'm a snap and slam you on your back
    so hard you crack the pavement

"Blood in the Water" by Task1ne:

...Now I'm aggravated
I'm a slam you so hard I'm a crack the pavement
You're just mad that the world revolves around me
just like the motherfuckin' sun gravitation

In one case, my friend Araless (from Black Magic Noize) had released a Task feature that was 100% stolen. Every line belonged to Sha Stimuli. In an interview with *Complex*, Sha claimed to have found "well over 20 [Task1ne] verses ... with my verses mixed [in]... word for word verbatim." That last part is revealing because one of the YouTube videos showed Task performing an ENTIRE SONG from Sha Stimuli with a different beat and no mention of its original author.

At the end of a brutal week, Corey released a video called "Response." He described the backlash, saying that he even received death threats from strangers. I felt for him in that regard. Nothing in the music business should be *life or death* like that. But my sympathy was damn near erased when I reached the end of the video.

In five minutes, he never once used the words "plagiarism," "steal," or "bite." He did not name the artists or apologize to them. He didn't really admit wrongdoing of any kind. The closest thing to a confession was "I am guilty of overworking myself and cutting corners." He even turned it back on the hip hop community, saying that his actions "brought out the worst in all of you."

Are you fucking kidding?!

Apathy, Diabolic, and Sha Stimuli were the biggest victims of his plagiarism. They all expressed disappointment after seeing the "Response" video.

I repeatedly called and texted Corey. The most I ever got was secondhand, from Gradient. When they worked out the refund, he said something to the effect of "tell Sammy I'm sorry, and I appreciate everything he's done for me."

Cool.

After a couple months of radio silence (deleting his social media pages), Task1ne appeared as a guest on the *Blind Box* podcast. I wasted no time downloading the episode. The hosts were on his side the whole time, and basically accepted any answer he gave. Even Corey dismissed their indifference when it was referred to as a mistake. "It wasn't a mistake. A mistake is when you do it once and then you realize it was wrong. Once you do it more than that, it's a choice." Right!

But after that, they finally asked a great question: "what percentage of your catalog is original Task1ne material?"

Corey estimated that, of his *entire* catalog, he only wrote "about 25 to 30 percent." That's *70%* stolen!

SEVENTY.

PERCENT.

STOLEN.

Did the host have a follow up question? Did he take a moment to digest the significance of that statement? You be the judge. He said "that's real. That's real. Again, I respect your honesty, man."

The last Task1ne appearance was just a month later. Carnage held a contest for "Attack of the Show Saver,"* awarding one contestant a featured verse on the 7-inch, and a part in the music video. Ironically, that meant playing a character in the song, performing Terrell's lyrics. Even better, Gradient beat Task and won the contest. We never heard from him again.

---

*Sequel to "Attack of the Show Stealer"

Sunrise on a night drive
Chevron (Unknown) 2014

Marquees are cool
Bar Deluxe (Salt Lake City, UT) 2014

(Left to right:) me, Blueprint
Level Up (Eugene, OR) 2018

Vacant Eyes (2015)

Lineup: Sammy Warm Hands, dubldragon., Ogar Burl

Best show: Santa Cruz, CA

Worst show: Salt Lake City, UT

Record store find: Czarface – *Every Hero Needs a Villain*

In late 2014, I was in a weird place. No tours were planned; no release dates on the horizon. I had released the *Freewrites* mixtape, and nearly finished my upcoming *Famous Last Words* (2015), but I was waiting for some more beats from KI.

When *Famous* dropped, it coincided with the 10 year anniversary of my label, Take 92 Music. To commemorate, I wrote about my musical history, and many of the albums that informed my path as an artist. *Famous Last Words* was both an album (CD, tape, digital), and my first paperback book.

The free time was productive. In addition to the *Famous* book and album, I recorded several *Stolen Songs Sessions** albums as well. I had a lot on my plate, and the thought of a booking agent was on my mind again.

I booked another pair of shows with Blueprint that summer,

---

*The *Stolen Songs Sessions* are video albums of cover songs from the bands that have inspired me. As opposed to *Stolen Songs*, which are various artists, *Sessions* would dedicate the entire runtime to one artist at a time.

which put me in touch with his agent again. Tony Caferro is the owner of DTR45, or Deep Thinka Records. It's a national booking agency from Buffalo, NY and Print is one of its many clients.

I pitched myself to Tony, and he agreed to consider it. In the meantime, I played a few spot dates in the Northwest and Midwest to promote *Famous Last Words*.

Coincidentally, I was contacted by dubldragon. [sic] to join them on the road. We had the stage once before, and they hoped to go out with a more experienced headliner. I was flattered to be the person they asked. Additionally, Skeptik (their emcee) offered to book it. He said that he was a professional booking agent for—wait for it—DTR.

It was dumb luck, and I couldn't have been happier. I told him that I was trying to convince Tony to sign me, and they talked it over. We would use it as a trial run. I was told that if it went well, then it was basically a done deal.

The dragons wanted to tour that fall, which was rapidly approaching. I had already started working on remixes for *Famous*, so I debated whether to tour on the album I just released or rush to finish the remixes. To readers of my first book, it will come as no surprise that I gave in to temptation. *Vacant Eyes* premiered a mere five months after its predecessor.

The Vacant Eyes tour kicked off in late September, which is one of my most favored times to travel. It circumvents the summer heat, and the winter snow. Perfect timing.

The dragons are from the bay area, so we started the tour near them, meeting in Reno. I actually lost my voice on that first drive, since Doug and I were talking for nine hours straight.

When we walked into PB&J's on the first night, someone immediately made a reference to me looking like [then-alive] Keith Flint from The Prodigy. I was already tired of it.*

A few minutes later, we noticed there was a Prodigy photo on the bathroom door. The venue actually had a ton of great rock memorabilia. The only downside is that it was way too big for us, so even our good-sized crowd looked underwhelming.

In the morning, we had breakfast and got to know our new friends a little better. Danny G was the dragon who made—and performed—all the beats, while Skeptik supplied most of the vocals. Danny brought his leftover Denny's from the night before, and carried it in the other restaurant.

Weirdo.

He casually asked the waiter for some silverware and ate his cold pancakes while we ordered from the menu. We all gave him shit, but Danny is the thriftiest motherfucker I've ever toured with.

Neither dragon lives in the same city, so their "hometown" show was in Fremont, CA. Doug and I were instantly suspicious of the bar. It was full of rednecks and the jukebox was playing country and lame classic rock. After setting up, the two of us took a walk** to Taco Bell.***

The energy quickly changed at 10pm. The barflies shuffled out, replaced by our friends and fans. I've actually played a few venues like that, and consider it a lesson learned. I had my reservations at first, but anything can happen.

*I referenced that on a song called "Hands Down."
Let me start with an apology
I'm not the motherfucker from The Prodigy
**It's rare that *I* would suggest unnecessary physical activity.
***I have a famously sensitive stomach. It's rare, too, that I would suggest Taco Bell, but it was the only thing nearby.

We stayed at Danny's work that night, Whiskey Dick Studio. He's a skinny guy, and the alcohol had gotten the best of him that night. It was dark, and he couldn't get the key in the door. We watched from the van as he deteriorated into a puddle on the ground. Skeptik used a flashlight and tried to open the door. Danny puked into a grate in the ground. It happened to be right in front of my headlights, so we had a great view. Doug and I looked at each other like *what did we get ourselves into?*

Chad (Skeptik) had a lot more California contacts. We played a nice room in San Francisco called Amnesia. It was a good show, but all I can remember is the opener leaving right after his set, and taking most of the crowd with him.

I was also looking forward to Petaluma, where my cousins lived, but it wasn't what I had hoped. Everyone was really nice, but not everybody's music is my cup of tea. There are plenty of artists who I love as people, but can't get into their music. Maybe I'm that guy for you. Who knows.

But this one set was loaded with so much stereotypical rap bullshit that it embodied every local opener I've ever hated. Still bitter from the night before, I walked to the van and wrote an eight-bar verse called "Amateur Hour" (*Rare Form*, 2016).

> *Shifting gears, 50 cities a year*
> *and every night a lazy writer's rhyming titties and beer*
> *Not to mention all the locals rapping over their vocals*
> *Another hopeful acting like he's stacking racks*
>   *with the moguls*
> *Want to go to the other artists and show their respect*
> *But they flee the scene the second that they finish their set*
> *Diminishing the position of every attentive listener*
> *Devaluing potential paying people into visitors*

In Pomona (near LA), we played with a great emcee named Adder. The bar was named Characters and boy, did it live up to the name. There were quite a few middle aged regulars who had a lot to say about the performers. Some guys would linger at the merch table and drunkenly tell stories about their glory days. Others would interrupt the show by shouting over the top of us. One guy was really bent on telling me what we should be doing differently. I kept trying to end the conversation, and eventually he latched onto Chad.

The guy had rapped at me a little, and it was all just LA gang shit. But when he rapped to Chad, he was overtly racist and sexist.

My girl tried to dump me, so I beat her
Stupid bitch, caught her cheating with a beaner

Wow. On that note, we were done being nice. I've never consumed alcohol before, so I have a hard time understanding how to deal with drunk people. (Doug usually intervenes on my behalf.) In that case, we all gave him the cold shoulder after that.

Since it was outside, the audience was smoking, which triggered my asthma. I was uninsured at the time,* so I didn't have an inhaler. Between songs, I explained my condition and asked if people would be willing to put out the cigarettes. I started the next song and noticed that *now everyone's cigarettes are out.* Before I started the next verse, a guy walked up to the stage and handed me his own personal asthma inhaler.

It was like an episode of *Popeye*. I felt supercharged and finished the show no problem. After the set, I thanked him and offered to return it. He said that it's 100% covered by his

*Still am!

insurance and that I should take it with me. I was touched by his generosity, and that gift saved me many times in the future.

Adder was not only great onstage, but he let us stay at his house. I always like waking up with cats and dogs, but Chad was particularly enamored with Adder's ferret. The apartment was near Sunset Blvd, so we started the day at Amoeba and made plans to meet with Ill2lectual.

Chris (Ill2lectual) worked at an aquarium at the time, and offered to get tickets for us. It was a great way to spend our day off. I've grown up near the Oregon Coast Aquarium, which is pretty damn impressive, but this one was awesome. We got to pet sharks and even tour behind the scenes where they access the tops of the big tanks.

Chris joined us for lunch—for which Doug treated him—at PF Chang's. I'm a picky eater: no condiments, no fruit, and almost never veggies. Chad is just as bad in his own way,* so we've grown to trust each other with food. Chad looked at the menu for something resembling a hamburger or chicken strips, and decided to abstain. I told him to have what I'm having—the crispy honey chicken—and that he would not be disappointed. Such advice is meaningless to a picky person, because one "wrong" thing could ruin the whole meal. And on tour, we only get one good meal a day! But Chad and I understood each other. It was a safe bet.

The tour was strategically planned with seven California shows: Fremont, San Francisco, Petaluma, Santa Cruz, San Jose, Pomona, and Los Angeles. We had short drives every day, which considerably increased profitability.

---

*He calls it a Ninja Turtle diet.

LA was the eighth show, and the birth of a long-running inside joke...

See, there are promoters who seem great *on paper*. Maybe you've never done business with them before. Maybe there's not even a flyer at the venue. Maybe they don't even charge at the door, and then we don't get paid. Maybe we get to the venue and it's not even a venue at all.

But on extremely rare occasions, it's all of the above. These promoters just want to look cool for their friends. When this happens, we call it a Birthday Party.

"How was Oakland?"

Alright. Felt like Joey's birthday or something.

"Fuck."

Yeah.

So, it was a Birthday Party. They even tried to charge us for the hot dogs they were serving. It was the only night of the whole tour where we didn't get paid.

Phoenix was unremarkable. *Blunt Club* had ended its long run, and *What The Funk* was over, too. We played a mixed-genre bill with all kinds of bands. Highlights include: napping on the sidewalk (before the venue let us in) and dogs peeing on my sleeping bag at the crash pad. One of the bands was straight out of a 2001 nu metal flashback. It was so incredibly loud that I had to stand outside until they finished.

The title track on *Famous* has a call and response that is distinctly Sammy Warm Hands style. I'd make an announcement and the audience would shoot me down:

I just dropped a new track
NOBODY GIVES A FUCK

I've got a video, too
NOBODY GIVES A FUCK
We got CDs and shirts in the back
NOBODY GIVES A FUCK
Yeah, well fuck you, too

That song can save even the weakest shows. There's something satisfying about feeling let down and then poking fun at yourself a little bit. But on slow nights, my tour mates carry the bulk of that call and response. Other times, it's impossible.

By the time I went onstage in Tuscon, everyone had left, including the openers.* Doug and the dragons were my lifeline for that chorus, but there was only one other person there. I decided that, if there's not at least a *handful* of people in the room, I'll just cut the song. It isn't fair to my friends.

We stayed with the Jivin' Scientists, who are native to Tuscon. They met us for lunch and were kind enough to let us crash at their place. After the show, it was late and totally dark. I didn't see a broken bottle in front of their curb and we got a flat. That's when I realized that I never replaced the ill-fitting jack in the van.**

By now, you know that I panic when things don't go according to plan. Runt—the emcee for Jivin'—said not to worry about it. He drove to Walmart to buy a better jack. They told us to go inside and relax. "You've had a long day."

After a couple episodes of *Always Sunny*, I realized that Runt hadn't come back. I went outside to look for him and was shocked to find that he changed our tire! *What a fucking guy!*

It was so dead that—unless they all lied to me—the bartender flashed her tits to all the guys while I was in the bathroom.
**Come to think of it, I still haven't*

We went to a tire shop in the morning, to ensure that we had a good spare. The mechanics were playing some garbage rap that was popular at the moment. The artist's name is escaping me, but it had a Lil or a Yung in it. Wait—possibly Slim Jesus? Is that a real thing? I'm not even going to fact check it.

The shop owner commented on my van right away. "What kind of music do you play?" I told him it was rap, but looking at us, he didn't quite believe me. He asked "can you spit?"

"Better than the shit you're playing here!"

Then he wanted proof. They fixed us up and I gave them a copy of *Vacant Eyes*. All the employees gathered around his car —windows down, doors open—and he cranked it up. "Nobody Gives a Fuck" started and they were giving me a surprised *alright, alright* of approval. Then I suggested another track.

"Redefine the Flow" is Gabe's remix of my rap contest entry for RA The Rugged Man. It's the most bar-heavy collection of punchlines that I've ever written; a staple of my live show at the time. Then the guys were cheering and giving me props. It was a nice pick-me-up after a shitty show and a flat tire.

We had a good thing with dubldragon..* For the first time, we split the work load between us: I was the driver—no surprise there. Doug was the biggest, so he carried the merch bins. Danny is a great engineer, so he performed soundcheck for all three acts. It only took a couple days for him to get a feel for my preferences, and I never, ever had an issue onstage.

Chad—and Skep hates when I call him Chad in public, but that's his goddamn name—Chad was the booking agent, but he was also the tour manager. It was super helpful to have someone else running the show. All I had to do was drive, sell merch, and perform.

*Fuck you for this, Chad. Two periods? Two?!

Most days, I could ask Chad "what time is load-in tomorrow?" He'd tell me 8:00, and without missing a beat, "it's about six hours away, so we should be out of here by 1 to be safe." He was so good that we'd actually give him shit if he had to check his phone. Sometimes he even memorized the *addresses!* I'd fire up the GPS and he didn't even to look at his notes. The man was on top of his game.

That did not, however, prevent every unwanted surprise. Our third Arizona show was new territory for all of us. That means seeking recommendations from existing contacts, or if that doesn't do it, using resources like *Indie on the Move*. In this case, we booked a coffee shop gig. A small show is better than no show: it's a chance to make some merch money at the very least.

We showed up early, ordered drinks, and plugged in our laptops at the bar. Chad went to find the booker, and he wasn't there. There were no flyers in the venue. The employees didn't even know we were coming.

Plenty of people were there, and the staff offered to let us perform... but there wasn't a PA system. I used to carry one on the ILL tours, but that was years ago. No one could reach the booker, so we just called it a night. We had Five Guys for dinner and headed for the nearest Motel 6. After 10 consecutive shows, we weren't too disappointed with a night off.

Later, I had *just* dozed off* when Doug scared the shit out of me. I shot up in bed to see him dancing in a Chewbacca costume, making wookie sounds. Apparently, he had gone to Target and happened upon a Halloween sale. We all had a good laugh and called it a night.**

*Doug snores a lot, so I go to bed extra early when we share a bed. At Whiskey Dick Studio, he slept in a vocal booth because it was soundproof.

**There's another reason that it's hard to sleep when Doug and I share a bed. If we go to sleep at the same time, it's nothing but farts, back and forth, for the first 20 minutes. We probably laugh harder at that than any other time on tour.

I heard The Juggernaut had closed, but Chad found that they reopened as a guitar shop, with a venue in the back. Ernie, the owner, always took good care of us, so I looked forward to seeing it.

When we got there, it was full of kids on skateboards. There was one small box in the middle of the room, and 10 or 15 kids taking turns doing tricks. Doug and Chad grabbed their boards and had a great time. The Juggernaut was alive and well.

Personally, I was having a rough day. My wife had called the night before and we had warnings that our cable and utilities would be shut off. Since I started touring, we had devised a split of the bills that worked in my favor. We really didn't think I'd be struggling for this long, and it was clear that our short-term plan had to change. I hated myself for putting her in that position, but I didn't know what to do. I tried to reach my married friends at home and got ahold of Kellen Holte (Dead Fucking Serious).

I was completely lost. Was I supposed to stop touring? Abandon the plan after all this time? Kellen was also married with a job and a band that required him to travel. We had a good talk about long-distance relationships and shared responsibilities. I took on two more monthly bills and picked up some extra shifts when I got home. It would be my last tour for a while.

We killed some time at a Dave & Busters in Albuquerque and someone suggested that we go to Walter White's house. The real address was used on countless *Breaking Bad* episodes:

308 Negra Arroyo Ln.

We pulled up across the street and the dragons walked up to take a picture. Someone was in the driveway and tried to kick them out (we weren't on the property). They snuck a quick photo as an RV turned onto the street. Apparently, there are *Breaking Bad* RV tours, and we were seeing the main attraction!

We hit Burt's Tiki Lounge, and a new spot in Cortez, CO. The promoter also worked at a radio station, so the four of us performed on the air to promote the show. It was fun, though it didn't help the turnout that night.

The show was at a trophy hunting bar in the middle of nowhere. The crowd was deceiving, in that it *seemed* like they were ignoring us. Most were at the bar, about 100 feet from the stage. We were so alone up there that when Doug referred to a front row fan, he pointed at an electric fan next to the monitors.

Very few people stopped by the merch table, but if one of us walked across the room, the barflies would speak up. Doug sold some *Break The Bank* CDs at the bar. Guess they were willing to support, but less willing to leave their stools.

From the second day of *Vacant Eyes*, we would often play the same city as Sadistik's, on the very same night. It prevented us from booking Denver *at all*, so we decided to see the show.

Cody guest listed me, and we all pitched in for the other tickets. With him was Ceschi (Fake Four, Inc.), Sapient (Sandpeople), Early Adopted, and Graves 33. I first heard about it when me and Graves were filming the "Vacant Eyes" music video in Seattle. Our overlapping schedules meant that I wouldn't get to see them, so it was a nice surprise that we could hang out.

The venue was amazing and their show was really, *really* good. Graves had a big flat screen on his DJ booth (he was the DJ for his tour) with graphics and music videos for each artist.

Ceschi played his posse cut, "Kurzweil," but he only had one verse. In the middle of the song, he pulled me up onstage. I grabbed a mic. Unsure of my freestyle skills, I frantically searched my memory for a verse that would fit the tempo. The *Vacant Eyes* set was so ingrained in my head that I couldn't think of any other songs. Before I knew it, the chorus was over and I was up. I freestyled about half of the verse and ran out of steam.

It felt good being included, but I wanted to leave a good impression. There was no doubt in my mind that it was the biggest crowd I would to see on that tour. A couple people had even recognized me in the audience earlier. They cheered my name when I walked onstage, and I hated the thought of letting them down.

I filled the empty verse by addressing the crowd and we did the last chorus together. Ceschi later told me that his friends used to mess with him like that all the time. Might not have been my best work, but it was nice of him.

We still had eight shows left, but it was a long drive to Salt Lake City... and it ended up being for nothing. The venue wasn't prepared and hadn't promoted. To appease the opener—and amuse ourselves—we each played a couple songs without an audience. By then, we all knew the words to each other's songs, so we passed the mic, doing each other's verses. It wasn't a show, but it was a good way to blow off some steam.

Since my first time in Boise, people told to play at Grainey's. There was a Sunday night weekly that everyone talked about, so we planned our route around it. Lo and behold, we booked the weekly... and it ended right before we got there.

It moved to an enormous dance club called Fatty's. There was no stage, just an impressively long DJ booth and a little catwalk. It was their first time at the new location, and word through the grapevine was that Grainey's did not tell people about the new location. So we played another wack show.

But even the shittiest shows can have silver linings. That time, it was one of the locals. He wore a strange bodysuit and a mask, punctuating every song with a rant, explaining that the audience didn't understand how good he was. It's always important to be respectful when you're coming to someone else's town, but we were cracking up.

Afterward, the masked guy tripped and knocked down Danny's laptop. We were stunned. It was higher fall than P Chill's DJ in San Jose! Luckily, all that broke was my 1/8" cable.

I got a bad impression when we walked into The Sickhouse in Idaho Falls. There was a small room with a disco ball and tiny little speakers. It looked like a DIY middle school event. As I mentally prepared myself for disappointment, I noticed that I was alone in the room.

I found the guys upstairs, in a much nicer, much bigger room! There was a good-sized stage, and a really nice JBL soundsystem. *Thank the fuck Christ.*

Our tour collided with another DTR artist, Prem Rock. He had a jam-packed roster with him (Billy Woods, Mo Niklz, and Henry Canyons), so we all played a little short again. Honestly, it was the best roster of the whole tour.

My performances were really dialed in by *Vacant Eyes*. Going solo is *much* different than playing in a group, where you don't even have lines half the time. The first two solo tours had really informed my new direction as a performer. Gone was the screaming, jumping guy from The ILLusionists. A Sammy Warm Hands show is much more of a quiet intensity. I move less, make more eye contact, and *sell* the song. Every word of every line is clear; its emphasis deliberate; every show consistent.

My strong suit is not just flashy wordplay, but my point of view. I try to build an arc to my set. It should be memorable and entertaining, but it should also make you *feel* something. It generally starts high energy, and the middle songs are more heartfelt. That was the first time I had three solo albums to draw from, so there was a lot more material to work with.

There were some punk rockers hanging out at The Sickhouse when we arrived. One girl even made a Tim Burton-style drawing of me. It might've been my first fan art!

I was still closing with "Blood in the Water"—sans Task—because it's really high energy, and the tempo makes for an impressive climax. When I finished, there was one more local on the bill. I handed him the mic as the host talked to the crowd. I remember a lot of *goddaaamn*s and *hoooolyyyy shit*s. The other guy took the mic and looked perplexed. He look at me and said "how am I supposed to *follow* that?"

It felt like all that hard work was paying off.

In Missoula, we went straight to the record store. As we pulled up to the storefront, Danny pointed at a guy on the street.

"That guy just said 'hey, it's Sammy Warm Hands!'"

I looked in the rearview mirror and saw Keenan from the CoDependents! Apparently there's a skate shop next door, and he was shredding some gnar, or whatever the kids say.

The van was parked around the corner from a pizza place that smelled amazing. I'm lactose intolerant, so any amount of dairy can give me diarrhea for hours. To be safe, I refuse pizza and ice cream on the road.* People commend the willpower it takes to follow my dreams, but I'm *addicted* to making music. True willpower is avoiding comfort food after weeks on the road.

*Easily my favorite foods!

I knew we had a comfortable place to crash, so I doubled up on my pills and took a chance. That place hit the fucking spot. They even had another one of my favorites, Virgil's root beer. I couldn't have been happier to have a little taste of home.

That night, we upgraded from the VFW. Stage 112 has main room and a basement-level room. We played downstairs with the CoDependents. The sound guy volunteered for the shift, because he remembered seeing me play at the VFW for three people. He was the one who bought my CD. He even hooked us up with a 1/8" cable, since that guy tripped on mine in Boise.

At the merch table, I received some very nice photos from home. It was 20th day on the road, and my reptilian brain had taken over. Apparently I had a big, dumb smile on my face, because the dragons took one look at me and knew why I was happy. We always rooted for each other in that department.

The CoDeps killed it, and we all hung out at Keenan's after the show. I was already in my sleeping bag when they turned on a movie, and it wasn't long before the weed came out. When it happened earlier, I pretended to make a phone call and just sat in the van for a while. But I really didn't want to go outside in my pajamas. Chad read the situation and suggested that they smoke on the porch, so I could sleep in peace.

When booking a tour, people will often tell you "don't worry, I've got you covered." That's usually the person who isn't going to book your show. It's wise to cover your bases with multiple promoters and venues. Seattle was taking a long time to confirm, so we accepted an offer in Olympia.

But Smart-T Jones* came through with a Seattle show after all. We already accepted Olympia, but he was insistant. It was a

*Formerly of Fayetteville, AR

6pm show, only an hour from Olympia... so we took a risk and confirmed both appearances.

It sucked not being able to watch the locals, but it was definitely memorable; having to rush offstage, sell our shit as quickly as possible, pack up the van, drive to another city, unload the van, and rush onstage again. Smar-T even sent us the money via PayPal, so we didn't have to stay and settle up.

When we got to Olympia, Doug started playing right away. During my set, I actually asked for a show of hands as to who had opened the show. I felt bad that we hadn't been there to see them, so I wanted to acknowledge them at the very least.

Kellen's parents—John and Candy Holte—came to the show, took us to dinner, and let us stay at their house in nearby Chehalis, WA. We had a great time, but Chad got some terrible news in the morning. His brother was in a car accident, and his condition was unknown. We told Chad that he could leave the tour, no questions asked, but he talked it over with his family and stayed for the last two shows.

Chad did a great job, finding new contacts in smaller markets. Portland wasn't looking good, so he booked us just east of there in Hood River, OR. It was a weird layout, playing on flat ground, right by the front door. Anyone who walked in or out had to do so RIGHT IN FRONT OF US.

During the dragons' set, Chad held the door as people left. He didn't realize it, but they were performing a chorus that said *the world doesn't care about you* over and over. It seemed like he was ushering them out the door with some attitude.

Joel Weichbrodt is a long-time supporter of mine, penning reviews for a website called *Sound Convictions*. He first discovered my cover of "The Decline" by NOFX, and dove into my catalog. I've been privileged for him to take an interest in me. Joel is a true music lover, covering my work with more depth and nuance than anyone before. He's even reviewed my friends.

When we finally met, Joel was carrying a box of t-shirts. He had asked, before the tour, if there were *Vacant Eyes* t-shirts. I said "no," that my money was tied up in the CDs. As an early birthday present, Joel had printed not just one, but an entire batch of *Vacant Eyes* shirts! I was completely at a loss. Over the years, I've sold those shirts all across the country. Ogar, Gradient, and even C-Rayz Walz* have worn them on countless stages. It was a gesture of friendship that I'll never forget.

Earlier that year (2015), I started *The Take 92 Podcast* and aired hour-long interviews every other week. For the ninth episode, my tourmates joined me in the studio.

Normally, we'd discuss the guest's history with music and end with their latest release. Since everyone was there, we discussed the highs and lows of our tour.

The tour ended at Luckey's. It was billed as my birthday show—two days before my actual birthday—and it was even more special because Grayskul (Onry Ozzborn & JFK) was headlining. Everything was in place for this show to be huge, but we didn't get half the crowd that I anticipated.

Danny had figured out the bass line to "Famous Last Words," and I suggested that we play a "live band" version for Eugene. Durazzo was on the bill, so he played the drums on his MPC. That song is always the most fun for me, but it was even better with my friends backing me up.

*Update: C-Rayz Walz was charged with rape and sodomy in early 2020. I'm sorry these editor's notes are so depressing! A lot has changed in a couple years...

We parted ways that night at Doug's parents' house. I counted the remains of our gas fund. We didn't just break even; there was more than $400 left. I felt that everyone had done their part, so we split the money evenly. The other guys were grateful to have walked away with a bonus, and Chad said it was his most successful tour to date.

"Oh my god, Kirk Hammett!"
(Left to right:) me, Chad
Amoeba Records (Los Angeles, CA) 2016

(Left to right:) Chad, me, Doug, Danny
Photo credit: Daniel Gensel
Somewhere outside a radio station (Cortez, CO) 2016

Birthday show
Photo credit: Karly Dewees
Luckey's (Eugene, OR) 2015

(Left to right:) Joel, me
The Take 92 Podcast (Eugene, OR) 2016

(Left to right:) Chad, Danny
dubldragon.
Uprok (Salt Lake City, UT) 2015

Rare Form 1: Summer (2016)

Lineup: Sammy Warm Hands & Ogar Burl, dubldragon., Gradient

Best show: Hood River, OR

Worst show: Billings, MT

Record store find: Johnny Cash – *Ride This Train*

After *Vacant Eyes,* I made good on my promise. For the next ten months, I stayed off the road. I worked four days a week (instead of three), which boosted my income without ruining my creative output.

Doug and I had been slowly chipping away at a sequel to *Break The Bank*. Neither of us expected to be touring on that album and wanted to ensure that its successor was much better.

Chad is connected with 924 Gilman St, a legendary punk club in the bay area. I first heard of it in high school, watching Green Day's *Behind The Music*. Gilman was home to many of my favorite bands like AFI, Rancid, and NOFX. I was honored that they asked me to headline the third anniversary of Gilman's *Conscious Hip Hop Night*.*

*Later headliners include Ceschi, Blueprint, Sage Francis, and more!

The show was in January, and our second album—*Rare Form*—was close to completion. Playing live is one of my favorite ways to get good performances in the studio. There's an intangible stiffness that occurs when artists record "on paper." When you've performed a song live, you've rehearsed it enough to memorize it. Onstage, you learn better timing for breath control, and which words to emphasize (or remove altogether). These nuances can transform a good song into a great one, and that's why I test all new material live.

The show was booked as Sammy Warm Hands, but I secretly invited Doug for a Sammy & Ogar set. I showed him the new DFS demos on the drive. We also had one of many conversations that acknowledged our unlikely bond. I grew up playing with his younger brother, Chris. Doug influenced us through music and skateboarding, but it's not like we hung out one on one.

"If you told me in high school," he said, "that the little green-haired motherfucker in Chris' band was going to take me across the country on a bunch of rap tours... I'd probably laugh in your face."

The weight of the Gilman legacy was on my mind. It didn't feel right to play a regular set without acknowledging the history. I borrowed a guitar from Pete Feliciano, who was performing as well. I stepped down from the stage, off mic, and belted out "The War's End" by Rancid.* I was full on screaming that chorus, and some laughed, in shock, as they cheered me on.

Doug and I came hard with the new stuff. We each had one solo track on the album, I debuted mine that night. I told Chad to pay attention because I knew he'd like it. "God Paparazzi" is a 64-bar diatribe on organized religion. I almost cut it from the

*You can hear my version on *Stolen Songs 3* (2014)

album, but Doug said it was the best thing I'd ever written. He might be right.

We didn't have the best turnout,* but we really *did* have the best night. Danny filmed our set, which became the video for "Slubberdegullion," and returned home feeling inspired.

Doug had moved to Portland, so we stopped in Eugene, recording all remaining vocal tracks for *Rare Form*. Ill2lectual recorded the scratches in LA, and I sent the mix to my friend and mentor, Eric Munch.

That summer, we had already dropped videos for "Slubber," "God Paparazzi," and "Break The Mold." The album cover was an original painting by Pat Jensen, which I revised for the tour flyer. We were ready to work.

Normally, we have a three act bill. dubldragon. was on board but Doug and I were headlining as a group. Two acts. I invited my friend Gradient to join us. I had produced his first album, *Ambition* (2014), and I liked the idea of being his first tour as well.

Chad's family owns an RV, and the dragons really wanted to use it. The RV accommodates refrigerated groceries, beds, and a toilet. The gas mileage wasn't much worse than the van, and it's was basically free lodging, so they had a pretty good argument.

I do not welcome change in nearly any capacity. I make a plan, find a routine, and that creates my comfort zone. I didn't like the idea of being a passenger. I especially didn't like the idea of being a passenger when one of the drivers smokes weed. I

---

*There were a lot of acts, starting at 6pm, and one act not only played too long, but took his entire crowd with him and *left* right after his set. It shouldn't surprise you to learn that it's the same guy who did that to us at Amnesia (San Francisco) on *Vacant Eyes*.

didn't like the idea of not running our daily schedule, the CD player, the AC, or any other aspect considered. I didn't like losing control.

My fate was decided when Gradient joined the tour. If you're keeping count, that's too many bodies for my van. And it was a lot longer than the Kristoff tour, so we couldn't stick someone in the back for three weeks. The RV won.

On the first day, I felt unbearably sick. I was sitting on the [side-facing] couch, just behind the passenger seat. It was August, I was sweating profusely—I hate the heat—and the whole cabin was shaking like a turbulent plane. I was nauseous, dizzy, and pretty fucking mad. *Why did I do this to myself?* Dramamine kept me from puking, but it didn't make the trip any easier.

Our first show scheduled at the Panic Room in Portland (formerly The Tonic Lounge). Doug and I had recently played there with Blueprint. But the Panic Room *closed* right before our tour, and we were left without a replacement. After crossing off virtually *every* venue in Portland, Doug asked his neighborhood bar if they would let us have a show there. They were sympathetic, and generously opened their doors to us.

The venue was a *Big Lebowski*-themed bar called The Big Legrowlski. All their drinks and decorations were an homage to the film. Probably my favorite moment of the night was when I introduced "God Paparazzi," quoting John Turturro's famous line, "nobody fucks with The Jesus." I'm still proud of that laugh.

Our friend Lisa Vazquez had also moved to Portland, and we asked her to open the show. Gradient went next, and I was somewhat nervous about his first performance. Doug and I had insisted that he got some more stage experience before we left.

It's important that my tourmates put on a great show, and I was serious about that agreement.

It didn't happen. Thomas (Gradient) started the tour with only *three* shows under his belt. Ever. The first night, I remember enjoying his songs from *Ambition*, but noticing the rough edges. I felt responsible for that. Then he said "Sam's probably going to kill me for this..." and performed a karaoke version of the popular 80's song "Take on Me."

I had just got up to refill my water and it looked like I walked out on him. Though, I'm sure that's what he expected when he introduced the song. I listened from the bar and shook my head. *This is going to be a long tour.*

The dragons did their thing, and it was good to see them again. I had given them notes on the *Vacant Eyes* tour—mostly about the order of their set list—and it was great to see those changes being implemented. Their set was much tighter, and it felt good to pass that on, like Terrell had done for me.

Doug and I were excited to premiere the new album. It was my best rap album to date* and we were getting great reviews. *Know More Music* called it "a massive step up in every facet" and *Sound Convictions* said it was "so far past *Break The Bank* that I'm left to wonder where [were] the two or three albums in between." We put everything into that album, and after only three years writing and performing, Doug earned that co-headlining spot. He's an absolute beast. Seriously, stop reading this and listen to Ogar Burl. I'll be here when you're done.

Welcome back. Our closer was the posse cut from *Rare Form*. You may recognize the name from the last chapter: "Amateur Hour." We had The Architex on the album version, but on the road, we invited our tourmates instead. I usually had

---

*More than a dozen preceded it, so that's saying something.

Doug or someone come back up at the end, but this was all five of us, which made for an explosive finale.

We stayed with Doug and his girlfriend, Kelly Rae. From the moment we opened the door, everyone asked for the WiFi password and pulled out their devices. That became the routine. These guys had backup battery packs and laptops and all kinds of electronics to keep them occupied. I got my own room there, and received an exciting message before bed.

Durazzo is a talented beat maker who has twice retired. He contributed a song to both *Vacant Eyes* and *Rare Form*, but he didn't put out a ton of material on his own. He texted me that night, complimenting the show and offering to give me a free beat for my next project. I hit him up the next morning with my choice. It would be quite a while before my next solo album, so I put it away for a rainy day.

It was a short drive to Eugene, so we went to Ang's salon. I had gotten used to some pretty long spikes, but my hair was becoming unmanageable. Having failed the first attempt, I didn't even put my hair up in Portland. It was fucking long. Ang not only cut my hair, but Thomas and Chad's as well. Chad isn't quick to trust people with his flowing locks, but she fixed his unwanted curls and he walked away quite pleased.

Luckey's had me on an emotional rollercoaster. The *Vacant Eyes* show was a letdown, so I took action: I turned down *every single show* for ten months straight. With that break, and lots of buzz for *Rare Form*, I hoped that we could pack the house again.

Cerebral Coretext (of The Architex) hosted the show, debuting some new material that we had worked on at my studio.* Thomas played a better set, performing for more

---

*That album, *Polarities*, was entirely scored by Durazzo.

familiar faces this time. But despite a few friends in the room, I was nervous about the turnout. During dubldragon.'s* set, I was getting upset. By their last song, I was fucking pissed.

After years and years of trying to build a fanbase, it's easy to feel entitled to support. I think the success of my first band had tainted my expectations. The success of The ILLusionists had affected me, too. *Death of a Salesman* is a great album, and I'd put it in my top five releases for sure. But my writing has improved dramatically since then. My delivery is night and day different as well. It's hard to accept that I'm doing my best work, but fewer people are hearing it.

My parents still come to the shows, ever since The Country Kids. If I'm playing nearby, they're almost always going to attend. That night, my folks walked in and it was *dead*. I told my mom that I was "fucking done with this town" and vowed to only play on the road.

Cerebral introduced us, and I reluctantly took my place on stage. When I turned to face the empty room, it was full. Our people came through. We celebrated *Rare Form*, selling so many copies that the vow was entirely forgotten.

We returned to Hood River and Shea Wooten. Doug and I had been invited back earlier that year. Shea traded that tiny bar with the door by the stage for a big, basement level music-school-meets-concert-hall called the Underground Music Station. He had hired us as support for Open Mike Eagle. It was an awesome show, and we couldn't wait to come back.

On *Rare Form,* our tour collided with Nocando, who is also part of the Hellfyre Club with Mike Eagle. It was another great night and UMS had cemented itself as one of my favorite venues in the country.

*Goddamn it, Chad!

One day, early in our 5,800 mile adventure, Thomas was riding shotgun. I was in the cabin on the opposite side. You know how, on a plane, you can see what somebody's watching in the opposite row? Well, it didn't take a closer look to know what was doing.

Wait, what?—yep, that's porn! I was so surprised that my motion sickness was all but forgotten.

"Yo, what the fuck are you watching?!"

Sometimes the long drives can lead to sexual conversations, but I had *never* seen that before. We caught him—I guess—but he wasn't exactly trying to hide it.

Thomas tilted the screen to show off the... display. When I saw the whole screen, my surprise turned to curiosity. I might have said "oh shit, is that Staci Jaxx?" I might've also moved a couple feet closer.

Doug came down from the loft like *what is wrong with you idiots?* and I realized that I had been sucked into it, too. Then it turned into a game. I sat back at the table in back again. Thomas started to make comments about the guy in the video, as if to remind everyone that he goes both ways. We were already laughing at the ridiculousness of his commentary, and the overall insanity of the moment.*

And then he made the most hilarious statement of the whole tour:

"What? I like dick!"

---

*Fun fact: Thomas named his porn folder *Stroke of Genius* after one of my lyrics:

I'll be stuck in your ear
My CD's a corn holder
Another stroke of genius
Ivy league porn folder

We decided to book Boise on a Monday, since the turnouts were so frequently disappointing anyway. We went to The Record Exchange, and headed back to The Shredder to see Art Maddox and meet the openers, Illumneye and Psycho Flores. I told my tour mates that it's a great venue, but the crowds are often not.

That time, I was wrong. The Shredder had a great crowd and everybody killed that night. It was probably my favorite Boise show to date. We were on a roll.

Twin Falls was a new city for us.* Chad was still adding more connective tissue every time we hit the road. Again, short drives make for a more sustainable tour.

We climbed out of the RV into a strip mall parking lot. An enormous historic building was on the corner of the lot. It towered over the rest of the block. Half of us were still wiping the sleep from our eyes (RV naps were common), but we heard a commotion near another car. It sounded like a fight, so we went straight inside.

The building was just as impressive indoors. The entrance planted us in the middle of a massive hallway. On the right was our venue, The Rogue. It was clearly a high end club, with brick, stone, and hardwood *everything*. Velvet roped VIP tables lined the walls. We piled our stuff near the stage, but no one else had arrived.

On the other end of the hall was a restaurant, The Brickhouse. It didn't appear to be open, but the bartender seated us just as our host arrived. Eddy was warm and generous.

It's worth noting that I always confuse Twin Falls, ID and Idaho Falls, ID. When you're in a different city every day, that's just too similar to remember.

He said to order anything we wanted *on the house*, and when we saw the prices, we understood why: there was no way we could've afforded it otherwise.

The food was great (Chad ordered an off-menu hamburger to be safe), but the conversation started to get a little weird. It turned out that the commotion we heard in the parking lot *was* a fight, and it was Eddy who had the guy beaten. He was really nice to us, but we got the impression—especially as he laughed off the attack—that it would be best to stay on his good side.

As the meal came to an end, Eddy said that the club only runs on Fridays and Saturdays. We all looked at each other in uncomfortable silence. It was Tuesday.

"It's a small town," he said, "and nobody's gonna come out tonight." He didn't even try to promote. We were duped. But he fed us and paid us the full guarantee.

Then he asked if we wanted to freestyle.

Ohhh... birthday party show.

Eddy continued to surprise us in every way. Danny picked up his Maschine sampler and started drumming on the pads. Doug led the freestyle, as usual. When Eddy took the mic, he had the distinct sound of New York City in the 1980s. The birthplace of rap. It was incredible. He made a joke about his age, and kept on rhyming. Thomas joined the cypher and even I came in with some written verses. Before long, we were all trading verses and it morphed into us playing short, 10-15 minute sets while Eddy sat on a lone chair at the center of the empty dance floor. Every one of us would've rather played a regular show, but there's no denying that we had a good time.

We weren't getting a lot of hotels with dubldragon.. They were much more accustomed to sleeping in the RV and saving their money. It's smart, but it's also a downgrade from the hot shower and clean bed that I was used to. Most nights were spent in Walmart parking lots. Many stores allow RV parking along the outer rim, but that means walking 100 yards to pee in the middle of the night. If you're me, that happens twice a night. After a 200 yard round trip, my heart rate is elevated and now I can't sleep. So I wasn't loving it.

Since there were no showers, I started buying jumbo packs of baby wipes. Evan swore by them on the ILL tours, but we had enough shower opportunities that I never converted. Now, I'm waking up hot and sticky, after playing a show and sleeping in those same clothes, in a barely-ventilated RV with four other people in the summer heat. I would pull the privacy partition and have what I called a "hooker bath" every day. Baby wipes head to toe. It wasn't my favorite routine, but I sure felt better afterward.

The RV didn't have a stereo, so the guys made one with a power inverter, Doug's computer speakers, and an iPod. There were usually two phones running out of this thing simultaneously, which I worried would drain the battery. I mentioned it often, and would remove it from the cigarette lighter whenever we stopped for gas, but no one else seemed worried.

We hadn't booked SLC, so we planned to use the day to drive to Denver. We were almost there, but they said we needed gas. It was late, probably 10pm, and we had easily been on the road for 10 hours. We probably weren't more than an hour from town. I texted Kelly and told her to expect us between 11 and 12.

Chad went to fire up the RV, but it wouldn't start. They checked under the hood and tried a couple things, but no luck. Danny called AAA and we waited for a tow.

I have a bit of an anger problem,* and being stranded gives me a big dose of anxiety. I had finally gotten control of my motion sickness in that giant thing, but I was still uncomfortable being relegated to the back of it. I was not in control. I had repeatedly stressed that the RV should be checked out before we left. I had repeatedly expressed concerns about that power inverter. I was grasping for something to blame and decided to go cool off.

I was an outwardly angry person in my early twenties. I was more blunt, crass, and unapologetic. Through the years—partially through Guitar Center management trying to tame me—the anger started to go inward. It's nicer for people around me, but I'll hold a lot in to avoid conflict. That lack of release causes me to explode now and again.

I grabbed my iPod and took a walk through the enormous parking lot. It was after hours and we were the only ones there. It was also cold, which is my favorite, so me and my headphones retreated into my hoodie and hat. It had been a week since I'd actually chose what *I* wanted to listen to, so I took my angry moment to listen to Death By Stereo.

I walked the perimeter of the lot and eventually found a nice spot on the concrete to lay down. Flat on my back, eyes closed, I let the aggression of the music run through me. Toward the end of the album, the guys walked over to tell me our tow had arrived.

I acknowledged the news with a nod, and closed my eyes until the last song was over. The driver had given us a jump. My friends were visibly cheering with excitement. I slid into the back and we took off.

*No shit!

By the time we got to Denver, it was late. I always stay with Kelly, but she had to work in the morning and I had no idea how long it would take for us to get back on the road. I had told her we'd figure something out, and she went to sleep.

We rolled into a Walmart parking lot and before long, the security car was circling back toward us. We wanted nothing more than to sleep. It had been a long day, and we were all dressed down in our sleeping bags. Lights out. Shades drawn.

TAP TAP TAP

The RV door doesn't make much of a knock, but a metal *ping*. Chad answered the door and we all heard what was said. That location doesn't allow overnight parking. We had to leave.

Fuck.

Chad opened up the cab and turned the key, but nothing happened. Dead again. We were stuck. We flagged down the security guard and explained the situation. It seemed like the battery was shot, so we would have to buy a new one when the store opened the next morning.

Normally, I'm the one leading the pack; finding solutions. But it wasn't even my vehicle. Apparently, no one thought it was their responsibility... I woke up late the next morning, and it was surprisingly quiet. Everyone was still in bed. Doug and I took it upon ourselves to get started.

We knew it was the battery, from the tow truck driver who helped us. Doug popped out the old battery and we went inside to trade it in for a new one. We found three different compatible batteries, and came back to relay that information to Chad. The RV belonged to his parents, so he called home and made the decision. Doug installed the new battery, but it still didn't work.

Fuck!

Danny called AAA, and we learned that most tow trucks can't handle an RV. They couldn't even find a shop who would *service* an RV. It was going to be tough.

Chad called every shop in town and got turned down every time. We waited about four hours for the tow. It was the middle of August and we were *cooking* in there. Then, out of nowhere, it started pouring. I thought of Eyedea, who famously said *I will be reincarnated as rain*. It reminded me that, even though we were facing an obstacle, I was out there doing what I loved. It was going to be ok. We were going to be on the road for two more weeks, and I had a lot to look forward to.

The tow truck arrived as the rain rinsed away my resentment. He recommended a place that repaired semi trucks. It was so big that it looked like an airplane hangar. There were semis as far as the eye could see. They agreed to check out the RV, but we weren't going to make it to the show.

Since we don't have much equipment (as opposed to a band), we got a Lyft driver to pick us up. Chad stayed behind and dealt with the vehicle.

I had never heard of Quixote's in Denver, nor did I have any clue how to pronounce it.* As the GPS led us toward our destination, the scenery became more and more familiar. She dropped us off in our usual parking lot, right across the street from Kelly's apartment. The venue was right there! We had walked by this place every damn time and never gone in.

There were two rooms, and I think we got the cooler one. Opening was Les One, who was a fan of mine that became a friend. It was one of those nights where we played for a dozen or

*Kee-ho-tay's, apparently

so people, but every one of them stood up front and participated and bought merch when it was over. Sometimes a small show can be better than a big show, if people are genuinely there to see you. Sometimes a big crowd means they're just tolerating you before a bigger headliner, or maybe it was free admission and they came just to drink with their friends. In our case, people paid for a $10 ticket and got the show they wanted to see. The audience engagement can be much like booking a venue; a little investment can make all the difference.

Chad had also taken a Lyft to the show. The repair wasn't going to be finished until morning. We had survived the day and had a good show to boost morale. In the morning, we ate downstairs at my favorite teriyaki spot, Tokyo Joe's. All was good again.

Since *Rare Form* was such an accomplishment, we wanted to promote it a lot. The plan was to do two separate tours: Midwest in the summer; Southwest in the winter. I hadn't been to Minneapolis almost a year. Being the home base of my label, it's important to keep a presence there.

I hadn't actually *toured* the midwest since *I Quit My Job For This*. The consequence of that was working with unfamiliar contacts. In the midst of our RV fiasco, Chad got a call from the promoter in Nebraska.

Last we heard, he had not secured a venue and it was going to be a house show. We had no problem with that, and he assured us that we'd get our guarantee "no matter what." Even if there was no show, he said, we would get paid.

But that call informed us that there was no show. We were on our way to pick up the RV, and it looked like we'd be on a long road to nowhere. The show was canceled and we never got that guarantee.

Remember what I said earlier? The promoter to worry about is the one who says "don't worry, man. I've got you."

We settled down in another parking lot, which was getting pretty old to me. It was summer, but the Midwest still gets cold at night. I wore my long johns and wrapped a sweatshirt around my feet for warmth. After about a half hour, I had to pee.
Goddamn it.
I tried to go inside, but the entrance was closed. An employee was cleaning the parking lot and gestured to go around the building. It was a longass building, but I had to go. Unfortunately, it's hard to sleep after doing a mile walk that gets your heart rate up again.

The next two shows were in Iowa. Doug did a lot of the driving on those Midwest dates. We probably went four days straight where the only thing we saw was cornfields. It got so mind-numbingly repetitive that Doug started faking us out, like "oh shit—GUYS! Look! CORN!!!"
The corn gag repeated, in a variety of different wordings—sometimes just tapping my shoulder and pointing out the window—until it wasn't funny anymore. And it continued for so long that eventually, it was funny again!

I had never been to Des Moines before. The venue was really cool. They were finishing up with an early show when we arrived. I set my stuff in the green room as the other performers exited. What I saw in that room was even more glorious than the dick drawings at The High Dive.
The green room at Vaudeville Mews had a handwritten list of films on its wall. What made it great was a simple twist: each title had one word replaced with "cock."

A Cockwork Orange
City of Cock
A Beautiful Cock

Chad and I spent a long time adding our own items to the list, and had the time of our lives. Highlights include:

Suicide Cock
Dude, Where's My Cock?
The Sixth Cock
There Will Be Cock
Twelve Angry Cocks
A Fistful of Cocks
For a Few Cocks More

It went on endlessly, as we giggled like third graders who just discovered their first dirty word. Sadly, that was the highlight of the night. The opener was good, but left for a hip hop festival that was apparently happening at the same time. That explained the lack of people in the room.

The next day, I couldn't find my new Smashing Pumpkins hoodie. I paid way too much money for it, because it commemorates my favorite album of all time, *Mellon Collie and the Infinite Sadness*. I was sure that I left it in the green room at Vaudeville, but no one there could find it.

I posted about it, asking anyone we stayed with could take a look. It never turned up, but when I returned home, there was a package from the Smashing Pumpkins online store. Chrissy Meyers, my brother's girlfriend's sister, had seen my post and replaced it for me! I couldn't believe it; astounded, once again, by the kindness of [almost] strangers.

The venue in Iowa City was rad. I took a picture of the GABE'S marquee and sent it to Gabe. On the walls, there were framed pictures of Sage Francis, MCA (of Beastie Boys), and Eyedea & Abilities. It was my kind of place.

A rock band opened the show. There were no rappers present. During our sets, most people smoked on the patio, adjacent to the stage. We basically played for ourselves. The sound girls were into it, but we left with $25 and low spirits.

That night, I was startled awake. It was pitch black in a Walmart parking lot, and the RV was *moving*. Fast. I rushed out of bed to find Chad behind the wheel. We raced out of the parking lot, hitting every bump along the way.

"Sorry, guys. I have to do this."

I've already explained how lonely the road can be for us married folk. I don't try to rob my single friends of their own tour experience, but I don't want to have to track everyone down when it's time to go. In that case, we all slept in Chad's vehicle, so he didn't technically break a rule by taking us—however unwillingly and *unknowingly*—on his Tinder date.

We pulled off the main road, onto a dark side street. It was 4am. Chad found the address and parked. "Well... wish me luck!"

By then, almost everyone was up. I was at the driver's side window of the cabin, peaking through the blinds. Danny was on the couch across from me. We looked around in the darkness and saw nothing but some sketchy mobile homes. No main road, no street signs, no landmarks of any kind. We were delirious and confused as to where we were. Danny fished around in a cabinet and pulled out a hammer. He handed it to me. "Ogar's asleep," he said. "You'll have to defend us now."

Doug let out a groan and asked what the fuck was going on. He slept in the loft above the cab, so looking down on us—peeking through the blinds with a hammer in hand—was probably pretty funny. We filled him in, and he took a quick look around. I think he was more amused than the rest of us.

About 45 minutes later,* Chad reemerged with a spring in his step. We were actually a little jealous, demanding details on the drive home; a sexual lullaby, if you will.

Madison, WI was a new stop for us. The bar was kinda like that first night with the dragons in Fremont. It was a dive bar with a decidedly white, crusty clientele. I expected the worst, but by 9pm, the tide turned.

There wasn't a stage, but the PA was pretty nice. We played with a Milwaukee artist named Taiyamo Denku, who was part of the Carnage-founded collective, Hecatomb. Gradient was part of the crew as well, though they had never met in person.

Denku is hop hop as fuck; an emcee's emcee. His friend Rambunxious opened the show, but forgot to bring his beats. He started spitting a cappellas. Doug and I wondered if this would be a repeat of the P Chill incident.

After a couple full songs, Denku grabbed the other mic and started beatboxing. The energy shot through the roof. It was awesome. They finished with a collaboration between the two of them. Denku had the beat on his own computer, so they at least got one real song out of it. Denku—like Carnage himself—saved the show.

We stayed with Danny's aunt in Minnesota. I hung out with the cat, and they made us *three meals* from scratch. We had a

---

*None of us thought it would take that long, so we had accepted his early demise.

good talk about how weird it was that the shows were so white, no matter where we were. It was the same year that Carnage released *MN Mean*, examining whether the "Minnesota Nice" mentality was unhealthier than it seemed.

> *Can't love a place where you're often*
> *subtly reminded you're from the "other" race*
> *I'm proud of eloquence; articulate and sound intelligent*
> *But how white Minnesotans point it out?*
> *Grounds for questioning*
> *Rockin'* My State's Better Than Yours *lanyards*
> *Snobs with liberal, best-place-to-be-born standards*
> *Greatest of places for raising your babies in*
> *Maybe then more amazing when*
> *you're Caucasian or Scandinavian*

I also shared a song from *Murs 3:16* where he (Murs) talks about selling less than his white contemporaries.

> *What's the reason that my album doesn't sell like his?*
> *And don't front like you don't why the hell that is*
> *It's because he's white, you can relate to his face*
> *Through the years you've been taught that Black is unsafe*
> *Plus it's only natural for your own to be embraced*
> *Conscious or subconscious, you can't say that ain't the case*
> *Only reason it took so long to take place*
> *Was up until now your only choice was 3rd Bass*
> *Or others like Ice, wasn't really that tight*
> *Now you got some white dudes who can truly rock the mic*
> *You relate to their stories, 'cause you share that past*
> *Question is, why would you listen to Murs' Black ass?*

After several different shows, and working the Soundset festival for a couple years, I finally got back into a good Minneapolis venue: Honey. CMJ (Christopher Michael Jensen) set up the show, and we had a great bill. A few friends came out like Brady O'Rourke, Ecid, and Brandon Crowson.

Brandon had just finished *The World Has No Eyedea* documentary, in which I appeared. He was looking for ways to promote the film, so we recorded a podcast interview in the RV.

The next day was a blur of driving through the Dakotas and sleeping at Walmarts. Every time we'd pull up to one, Doug would pop his head out of the loft and ask "I live here now?"

Yes, Doug. You live here now.

Thomas had been playing a lot—a LOT—of the recently debuted *Pokemon GO*.* I actually got video of him sleeping while the game was still *on* in his hand. The nature of this game is to physically go do stuff around town. He was able to utilize our travels to benefit his gameplay, but sometimes he'd just disappear.

It was hard traveling with so many people. Two people would wander off, and somebody else would get a phone call and take off in the other direction. It was hard to keep track of who was where, and who they were with.

We found a barcade in Billings, MT. It was good to play some mindless games and feel like a kid again. The four of us played *Turtles in Time* while Thomas scoured the parking lot for Pokemon characters. Doug pointed out an air hockey table, and I proceeded to beat everyone in the crew.

---

*He even wrote a line about it in "Amateur Hour."

We also went to the movies. After two drive days, we needed a break. I'm a huge fan of Batman, and had been talking a lot about *Suicide Squad*, so we all went to see it.

The movie trailers were different than when I saw the film at home. Usually they're relevant to the genre. These ads were straight up horror flicks.

When the lights went out, I noticed that the MPAA rating was wrong.

This movie isn't rated R.

When the film started, the opening frame was different, too. It was a long, aerial shot that slowly panned down to the street where—*wait, what?*—a man was dragging a dead body down the street.

Okay—wrong movie!

I walked out after 30 seconds and informed an employee in the hallway. He got on the phone and paged someone to fix it. Looking at the signs, there was a horror movie playing right across from us. Simple mistake, but the guy made it seem like a big deal.

We hadn't got there in time to buy popcorn, so I took the opportunity to get some. The family in front of me took fucking FOREVER, so I texted the guys to tell them I'd solved the problem. Danny said that they already started playing the movie, so I'd better come back! I was fucking furious that I missed Harley Quinn's first scene, but I had a good time after I calmed down. At least the popcorn was good.

We stayed with my friend Jessica Pelatt and her family. They made us spaghetti and waffles (not at the same time), and we had the whole downstairs to ourselves. The venue was really cool, but there was a music festival just a block away, so we basically just played for Jessica.

That night, I appreciated Thomas' set in particular. With a dozen more shows under his belt, Gradient was coming into his own.

We returned to Stage 112 in Missoula. That time we got the main room upstairs. It was too big for our crowd, but the sound was great.

Thomas and I walked there to get some food. It was just getting dark and the streets were thick with people. There were food trucks and musicians as far as the eye could see. There was *another* street fair. *Fucking summer tours!* I scored some decent hot dogs and a delightful lemonade.

Wormwood opened the show. We met on the *Show Stoppers* tour, and he had written a glowing review of *Rare Form* for *Know More Music*. All in all, it was one of the more enjoyable shows of the tour.

The tour wrapped up at the Columbia City Theatre in Seattle. I remember seeing flyers all over the door, but not ours. We actually spotted one with the *same date*.

When Araless (of Black Magic Noize) arrived, we realized they had an early show and a late show. The late show was in the back room, and we were in the front. Our room was jammed full of tables and chairs, but I always insist on an open dance floor. It took some coercion to get the bartenders on our side, but it opened up the room a little.

My artist friend AlterEgoz had just moved up there from Stockton, so he and his wife came out to see us. My friends Eric and Jori (from Jori & the PUSH) came out, too. Eric taught me everything I know about recording—and they accidentally helped me and Doug form our group—so we've all been friends for a *long* time.

Outside by the RV, I remember confiding some of my frustration. It had been a tough tour. We had a great record on our hands, but the shows weren't turning out. Jori looked right into my eyes and gave me a moving pep talk. *You've done amazing things. Think about how far you've come. Keep pushing.* She was right.

(Left to right:) me, Pat, Doug
Unknown gas station (Minnesota) 2016

R. EYE. P.
(Left to right:) me, Chad, Danny, Thomas, Doug
Cherokee Park (St. Paul, MN) 2016

(Left to right:) Chad, Thomas, me, Danny, Doug
Jessica's house (Billings, MT) 2016

The World Has No Eyedea (2016)

Lineup: DJ Abilities, Carnage The Executioner, Sammy Warm Hands

Best show: Oakland, CA

Worst show: Fresno, CA

Record store find: The Dear Hunter – *Act V: Hymns with the Devil...*

In 2015, Brandon Crowson flew to SXSW (Austin, TX). His goal was to interview all of the Crushkill Recordings artists for his documentary about Eyedea.

He and I hit it off almost immediately, bonding over conversations like *how people don't understand how to sacrifice for their craft,* and *how small talk is like setting my own brain on fire.* The interview itself was great, even if most of it didn't make the cut. Micheal (Eyedea) may have played a big role in my life, but I played a very small one in his.

Unfortunately, the project caused a rift between me and Gabe. Things had been rocky since he left The ILLusionists, and we had quietly continued writing in his absence. Gabe and I did our best to find common ground and focus on the positive things we shared, but he resented my career after we parted.

Kathy (Micheal's mom) broke it down in the simplest terms: if I hadn't been performing at SXSW, then I wouldn't have been in the film. In fact, I almost wasn't on the show at all.

The first annual Crushkill Recordings SXSW showcase was booked through our man on the ground, Joey Alpha (of Slop Musket). His group was based in Austin, so he could Kathy set up an event in Micheal's honor.

Joey and I hadn't met, and I guess he hadn't seen my Crushkill releases either. I was off his radar. The show was announced, with a completed flyer and everything, and I found out on social media. I contacted Brady, who sent me to Kathy, who sent me to Joey. There was enough time that I could play a short set and get my name on the flyer, but it was too late for me to be featured on the stage banner or other merch. Kathy had already budgeted the trip, based on the other acts (she assumed that I had declined an invitation), so I had to fly on my own dime.

The Foo Fighters had just aired their HBO documentary series *Sonic Highways*. I watched the episode about Austin's music history and left Eugene with a lot of excitement.

Kathy put us up in one big house, owned by her long time friends. I shared a room with Brady, and got to hang out with Terrell, Ecid, Seez Mics, Slop Musket, and I even got to know some of Kathy's friends like Brandon, Michelle, and Syd.

Since the E&A story involved Gabe's *By The Throat* remixes, I made sure to tell that story in great detail, ensuring him proper credit.* I even showed Brandon my *Death of a Salesman* documentary, *Mental ILLness,* where Gabe tells the story himself. We talked about maybe having me film an interview with him when I got home.

---

*The remix project was entirely his. I only assisted with some mixing, and later brought it to Brady's attention so it would finally get released.

I called Gabe to tell him the good news, but he wasn't as thrilled as I'd hoped. He liked the idea of telling his own story. As far as I was concerned, I had told The ILLusionists' story and represented our shared experience fairly. No one has even seen the footage of that story, but in the next few months, Gabe accused me of stealing his story, building my career "on a dead man's name," and attacked Brandon publicly for not following through on the interview. Before long, we weren't speaking at all. I was dead to him.

It was bittersweet when the trailers started coming. I was excited to be part of the project, having listened to Eyedea & Abilities since high school. More than that, I was just excited to *see* the fucking thing. There aren't a lot of movies about underground artists like that.

But as the trailers came, Gabe would comment on them. It was more than a year after my interview—I had even done the 2016 SXSW in the meantime—and he still wouldn't let me off the hook. I went from elated to devastated, over and over again.

That summer, Gage Luce reached out to me. He was booking *The World Has No Eyedea* tour, where they'd show the film and have performances by DJ Abilities and Carnage. He knew I had a van, and a history with everyone involved, so Gage recommended me to open the tour (in exchange for providing transportation.)

At one point, on the *Rare Form* tour, I heard that Brandon and Gage weren't getting along. *TWHNE* tour was about to be cancelled. From a Walmart parking lot, I rubbed the sleep from my eyes and called Brandon.

Brandon had taken over the booking, but he said there wasn't enough money to pay the film after the artists were compensated. He wanted to renegotiate the contracts with the promoters. I knew that we were making good money for an indie rap tour, and we shouldn't push our luck. I told him that there's got to be a compromise to make sure that everyone is covered.

Though they were no longer working together, both he and Gage were making inflammatory posts about each other on Facebook. Brandon told me he was going to pull the film and we could do a regular tour by ourselves. I knew that these guys were ready to kill each other, but I also knew that there *was* no tour without the movie. That was the whole point. Anticipation was high, and promoters might back out if we changed the deal last minute. Most dates were already being advertised.

I talked him down, and immediately called Brady. He informed Kathy and she stepped in as the tour manager. She got Brandon and Gage to stop attacking each other online, and gathered all the information that we'd need to salvage the tour.

Gage was out of the picture, so Kathy gave us each a hard copy book with addresses, drive times, load-in times, compensation, and promoter contact information. It was a life saver.

Brady and I worked out a deal where he would ship the Eyedea merch to me, and I would sell it at my table for a cut of the sales. He trusted me to do the job well, and I trusted him to pay me. Good deal.

I was home for one week after *Rare Form*. I was as nervous as I was excited. I might've been the opener, but I had more responsibility than anyone. I was the de facto tour manager, driver, and merch guy for the whole label. That means I would wake up, get my tour mates out the door on time, fill up on gas, drive all day, find our hotel, get the guys out the door on time, find the venue, unload and set up *four times* as much merch as usual,* perform soundcheck, sell merch at the moment doors open, perform after the film, sell merch during the other sets, settle up with the promoter, tear down and load everything into the van again, drive back to our hotel, and spend the next hour counting/recording the money while everyone else slept. If I was lucky, I'd have time to grab a burrito after sound check. And I wasn't always lucky.

The money was more complicated than usual. Normally, the tour makes X amount every night and it goes into the gas fund. Sometimes, like *Show Stoppers*, we'd just split the money up front and pay for gas out of pocket. Easy. That time, the guarantee broke down into three individual guarantees; one for each artist. (Brandon came along with his own merch table, which allowed him to earn some money after all.) Then I had to count all the Crushkill/Eyedea merch money, which I kept separately from my own.

From there, I had to go through all the credit card sales on my Square app. I had built a menu, so that I could tell which purchases belonged to Take 92, and which were for Crushkill.

My menu items were already separated:
CD - $10
Shirt - $15
Bundle - $20

I added items that would help me tell it all apart:
Eyedea CD
Eyedea shirt

Coming right off the Rare Form *tour was even harder because I hadn't been driving or carrying merch at all!*

At the end of the night, I'd count the cash and the Square sales, add it all up, and report back to Brady. He never asked me to do that, but I used to be an Operations Manager and was more comfortable documenting it daily.

I mentally prepared, to the best of my ability, and tried to enjoy my last night at home with Ang. We were getting ready for bed when I saw something scary on Facebook. It wasn't about the tour...

My aunt Sue shared a poem about losing a grandchild. No other information was provided. Comments were piling up, as people wondered what had happened. I texted my cousin Jason, who told me that his son, Hayden Thompson, was dead.

"Suicide," he said.

It was a slap in the face. Then a punch in the gut. Ang hardly believed the words I was speaking. It was after 1am, and I had just packed my bags. I called my parents and woke them up.

"I'm coming over."

I called my brother, but he lived a little farther away. I broke the news to my parents while we waited. Hayden was always a mischievous kid, but it appeared to us that he had becoming kinder and gentler with age. He came over, just two months earlier, for my mom's birthday party. In the past, Hayden might chase the cats or get into trouble, but this time he was serene. He was sweet to the cats, took family pictures, and came up to nearly everyone with unexpected hugs. It seemed like he was in a good place.

When my brother got there, my mom called Jason on the phone. No answer. I texted him to say that we were coming over. You never know what to do in that situation. We just had to do *something*.

He texted me back, saying that he and the other kids were at my cousin Jen's house. We spent the next few hours with them, sharing stories and trying to digest what had happened. Jen told us that Hayden's life was harder than we understood. His struggles hadn't gotten easier in time; we just didn't see them often enough to know what he was going through.

It sucked that we weren't close enough to help in some way. I'm not good with kids in general, but he was getting to the age where we could find common ground. We liked some of the same music, and he had even appeared with me and Doug on the front cover of *Break The Bank*. I was so out of touch, apparently, that I recently looked at that CD and his name was misspelled "Heyden," like a hybrid of his and a luthier I know whose last name is Heydon. I misspelled it on *two* different pressings and had no idea.

By 4am, we were talking about what to do next. Hayden had used a gun, which is why the family left the house. I offered to help clean the house before they came back, and everyone looked at me like *that's nice, but aren't you leaving?*

The tour was the last thing on my mind. I figured I'd call everyone in the morning and let them know that it was cancelled. Without me, there was no transportation and no E&A merch, so it would've been tough to make it profitable any other way.

My family had different opinions. There was nothing I could do to undo that night. There were people counting on me to honor the memory of my friend and rap idol, and it was important to a lot more people across the country. It was also an opportunity to *finally* tour with some bigger audiences. They expressed these concerns and convinced me to leave on schedule. It was probably the most conflicted I've ever felt.

The first show was in Phoenix, so I broke up the drive into three days. I stayed with Chad in northern California. It was late when I arrived, but we had a good talk and a decent night's sleep.

I stayed with Ill2lectual in southern California. I had dinner with his family, and they made me feel right at home. It was actually my first time at his new house. Those were some long, lonely drives, and I felt lucky to be in the comfort of old friends.

The next day was the first show. As I drove through the vast emptiness of southeastern California and western Arizona, I passed a sign that read Other Desert Cities. Wind turbines lined the periphery. There was nothing to do but think.

I drive by wind mills and wonder why it feels
like life is an anvil and time's at a standstill
Traveling over pavement and gravel in amazement
Wonder when I get back where have all the days went?
Thoughts of loved ones lost, but what you didn't know
is future family reunions are at the funeral home
Whether elders, or youngsters, no longer amongst us
it feels so surreal every time that it punctures
the fabric of our family
Everything's unraveling
It's in the back of your mind, even when living happily
Forgive me if I'm rambling or stumbling some
It's a struggle when it comes to saying goodbye to my cousin
I won't hide from it, no matter how much I hate it
I just want to say his name again
This one's for Hayden

I wrote the verse in my head. I named it after the exit sign. It was impossible to write at 70mph, so I'd construct a line and repeat it until it was memorized. I have a strict No Phones While

Driving rule, but I broke it that day. My voice recorder allowed me to capture four lines at a time, which was about as much as I could memorize. I did the whole thing that way, in short increments.

By the time I got to Phoenix, there was just enough time to stop at Zia Records before the show. I wanted to get the new Dear Hunter album, who has been one of my favorite bands since Sarx played them for me on *I Quit*. I have no recollection of picking up the guys at the airport. I remember unloading our bags in the hotel parking lot. Maxx (Abilities) and Terrell were really considerate, offering hugs and condolences.

As we closed the van doors, we were greeted by a loud, friendly dude with big, gold chains around his neck. I didn't recognize him, but Terrell knew him as C-Rayz Walz (of Def Jux Recordings). He was shouting *"this* motherfucker right *here!"* he said, extending his hand to me. "Bring it in! I watched some of your shit on YouTube," he turned to Terrell and finished his thought. "And this motherfucker is CRAZY!" C-Rayz definitely raised my spirits right there on the spot.

That night was not only our kickoff show, but it collided with C-Rayz' own tour, featuring Luck & Lana (with Luckyiam of Living Legends). It was an all-star lineup.

Maxx liked to rest and get cleaned up before the show, so most nights he'd stay at the hotel until his set. I hoped he would've wanted to see me and Terrell, but I wasn't too offended because it seemed like his normal routine. On top of that, we were celebrating the life of his best friend and partner. It was going to be harder on him to see that film than the rest of us. For that reason, Brandon usually picked him up during the show.

The promoter showed us around the venue, and we completed soundcheck on time, but it when doors opened, there were no seats for the film. I wondered how it was going to work, showing a film onstage at a bar.

I asked the promoter about seats, and he said that it wasn't in our rider. He wasn't prepared to meet that demand. Worried, I called Brandon. He was unaware, but the tour had been passed off from Gage to Brandon and then to Kathy. Some things were bound to slip through the cracks. It wasn't a minor detail, but there wasn't much we could do in the 11th hour.

Unfortunately, that set the standard for the rest of the tour. In many cities, there was no seating. That created a typical bar atmosphere, where people are talking *over the top of the movie* while it was playing. I knew Kathy wouldn't be pleased, but there was no use worrying her from a distance. *The show must go on.*

The film ends on a sad note, as you might expect, but Luck & Lana brought the energy to a celebratory crescendo. It was palpable.

Prior to the tour, I had carefully crafted a new solo set. Eyedea was known as a razor-sharp battle rapper in his early years. I knew people would expect high-caliber bars. But he also pushed the envelope as a songwriter, creating some of the most beautiful, empathetic pieces of music I've ever heard. People have his lyrics tattooed on them. People say he saves lives. And above all, we missed him. We mourned the loss; fans and friends alike.

I knew that I had a good set up my sleeve, but my emotions were all over the place. The harder edged tracks were getting a great response. That crowd was *all* in. As I went a little more personal, I could see people's eyes looking into mine. I had their full attention. Terrell was watching from the side of the stage.

I played an acoustic version of "Hay Fever" by E&A. It was the same version I played on the very first tour, as a thank you for Micheal's support. That night it was even more raw. It wasn't just an ordinary show. We had watched his life unfold onscreen before our eyes. Old wounds were reopened.

Having lulled the room to a more quiet intensity, I took the opportunity to talk about Hayden. I couldn't believe I was 1,200 miles from home that night. I couldn't believe what had happened. It was all such a blur.

"On Tuesday, this week," I said, "my 13 year old cousin killed himself." People cried out. Most were gasps. I heard one *I'm sorry!* "I wasn't sure if I should come, but my family encouraged me to do so."

I introduced the song "Other Desert Cities." I told the audience that I wrote it on the way there, and asked for permission to recite it, using the my phone for notes. It was raw. It was vulnerable. It was angry. It was sad.

The love in that room was overwhelming. I segued into my suicide-themed "Vacant Eyes," and poured myself into it.

Some days I want to live
Other days I want to die
Well, maybe most days I want to die
But no matter how it eats me,
it never defeats me
Keep moving
Never stop to wonder why

The sound of that crowd was deafening, and it was healing. Through the applause, I said "if anybody is dealing with that shit, just know that we are here for you.* You are not alone in

*"Here For You" is a popular Eyedea song from 2002.

your pain. Goodnight."

Terrell gave me a big hug and said "that was amazing" in my ear. He looked at me and said "I have to follow *that?* How the fuck am I supposed to follow that?!" He picked up the mic and said it again. When The Show Stealer (AKA Show Saver) says that, it's the highest praise. He threw out his entire set list and tried to build on the vibe that I had established with the room.

My friend James Morales greeted me with a hug as I walked through the crowd. Everyone gave me love as I went to the back to man the merch table. (Brandon had two merch people, Sara and Justin, so I would get one of them to cover for me while I performed.)

C-Rayz gave me props and asked if we could do a merch trade. Normally, a smaller artist would ask the headliner for something like that. I was beyond flattered. He grabbed a *Vacant Eyes* shirt and wore it on his tour. When I saw Luckyiam, *he asked me for a CD trade, too!* Holy shit. I couldn't believe it. Maybe doing the tour was a good idea after all.

A few minutes later, a young lady came to the table and told me about her own experience with suicide. Throughout the night, people would tell me of parents, siblings and friends who had taken their own lives. These weren't 30 second "good set" conversations, either. By sharing my story onstage, people were emboldened to tell me some of their darkest secrets.

Having already performed "Vacant Eyes" on the road, I knew that it affected people, but that was on another level. I think that sharing about Hayden was cathartic on its own, but pairing it with a song about my own suicidal thoughts made it much more impactful. To my surprise, I wasn't sitting at that table alone every night. I had plenty of people to talk to, and plenty of healing was had.

After speaking to the first woman for a while, she asked "this is weird, but... can I give you a hug?" We shared a sincere embrace; the first of many more to come.

I hardly remember the rest of the show. It sounds crazy, being two of my favorite artists, but I've seen them both countless times and was truly caught up in some heartbreaking conversations.

What I do remember is that C-Rayz offered to go last. Almost everyone left after Abilities, but he put on a great show nonetheless. At the end, he spit an absolutely stunning freestyle about Eyedea. It was one of the best shows I've ever played.

Maxx and Terrell are both used to being the headliner. They're veterans with very clear expectations, and a lot of experience to back it up. Maxx got the lion's share of the money, so when we had to make compromises, it was important to him that we shared the loss evenly. I was probably making about 12% of what he made, but it was fair if we all lost the same amount, respectively. Terrell didn't see it that way, and seemed annoyed that Maxx even brought it up. For as long as they'd known each other, I had to let my big brothers work it out on their own.

The Vegas trip was only five hours, so we actually had some downtime at the hotel. It was a giant, fancy casino hotel and we were living large! Terrell and I always shared a room, and Maxx got one to himself. (Headliner perks!)

The venue seemed kinda small, and was already packed when we arrived. The promoter led us out back, to a much bigger area, with a huge stage.

That was our first time touring with any sort of video component to the show. We quickly learned that, not only was seating important, but so were the projector and BluRay player. The promoter had a DVD player, but the film was on BluRay. Eventually, he went home and got his Playstation. By the time it was fixed, the doors had been open for a while.

The promoter was really nice, offering "anything you need," but all I ever asked for was a chair that never came. We all had to sell merch on our feet that night, which made it drag on forver.

The turnout was strong, though not as packed as Phoenix. I played a solid set and Terrell's videographer, Andy Stemig, filmed it. We used "Other Desert Cities" from the first two nights and released a video for my family to see.

Carnage fucking destroyed that night. We used to recap in the van, saying who "won" that night. Maxx had skipped sound check, so there were some unforeseen issues when he arrived at the DJ booth. The crowd had thinned a little after the film, and as the night progressed, but there were some E&A diehards (like myself) who loved seeing a new Abilities routine. I was lucky enough to have played with him at SXSW that year, and a few months earlier at a huge Eyedea celebration in Minneapolis. He still never fails to amaze me. He does things that are simply inhuman. If you're not familiar with his work, or turntablism as an artform, look him up. No, seriously. I'll wait.

L.A.—much like the whole fucking tour—almost didn't happen. The drive was short, so we didn't need to wake up early. Maxx is a morning person, and I am definitely fucking not. I need to sleep as late as possible if I'm going to drive and then perform later.

Terrell gave me a purple, Pat Jensen-designed *MN Mean* shirt before we hit the road. About an hour into our trip, I noticed the battery light was on. Within seconds, the A/C was blowing hot air. We shut off the A/C and took the next exit. I frantically unplugged the GPS, the CD deck, and anything else I could find. The power went right back on, and the battery light turned off.

Under the hood, the battery connections were corroded. We drove to the next truck stop and asked for help. The gas station attendant suggested a steel wool cleaning tool and some Coca-Cola. It was unbearably hot, and that Coke sounded pretty fucking good at the time.

Everyone was calm under pressure. Between me, Terrell, and the gas station guy, we disconnected everything and cleaned the fuck out of it. The soda worked like a charm (and it hit the spot).

Cleaned up and fully charged, we continued driving. Maxx played us four or five songs from his long-awaited solo album* and Terrell brainstormed some new ideas on how to improve his live show.

Given the nature of the tour, and the shared history between us, the conversation inevitably turned to the film and our first impressions of it.** Then it shifted toward Micheal himself. I learned a few things about the E&A hiatus that occurred before *By The Throat*, which Terrell had mentioned to me in Vegas. I listened as the guys shared their still-raw emotions over Micheal's drug use, and how they tried to deal with it at the time.

As their friendly chat veered toward some truly personal moments that I will leave unsaid, the van started losing power again. Google Maps had recommended a smaller highway for less traffic, so we were in the middle of fucking nowhere. That winding road didn't have any stops for another mile or two, so

*It's fucking awesome, but I'm not allowed to tell you about it.

**I'm proud to be part of this project, whether the interview, the closing credits song, or the tour itself. It's really exciting to watch, as a fan of E&A, and a friend of Micheal; not to mention the other artists involved. I am a fan of it. But I'd be lying if I didn't admit that some technical issues—primarily sound and lighting—left something to be desired.

we unplugged everything again and endured the heat.

When we came to the end of the road, I hesitated to continue in that condition. We each had different opinions, but ultimately it was my decision to get it checked out or not.

We stopped at a rural gas station and popped the hood. It still looked good after the Coke bath, so we let it rest a minute before resuming our course. That might've been a mistake, because it never started again.

The front of the gas station had a wooden porch where several truckers drank beers in broad daylight. Faced with our collective incompetence,* we asked the drunken townfolk for help. They looked at me like the idiot that I am, offered no help, and said "good luck finding anything open on a Sunday night." One by one, they finished their drinks and drove away in their pickup trucks.** Apparently they don't give DUIs in small towns.

Suddenly I felt sympathy for Chad. I always get the oil changes and checkups for my van before tour, but they said everything was in good shape. *Hell, it got me this far...* I called State Farm and requested a tow. It took a long time to figure it out. Like the man said, it was a Sunday night in Bumfuck Egypt.

I decided to take one for the team. *The show must go on.* I called Terrell's videographer, Andy. Brandon's crew was riding with him. They were in L.A. already, so he had an empty vehicle for Maxx and Terrell. Andy's was so enthusiastic that the call lasted less than a minute. He jumped right in the car and bailed us out.

*In my experience, musicians are generally inept when it comes to adult/man stuff like vehicle repair.
**One guy actually drove off in a tractor!

Andy arrived right after the tow truck. The guys took their essentials out of the van, so it could be loaded onto the truck. The driver popped the hood and attempted to give me a jump. He quickly diagnosed the problem: I needed an alternator.

He was sympathetic to our situation, too. I pointed to my friends as they packed up and drove away. They were going to our show, and I was not. It had never happened to me before. I was alone without a solution or even a *destination* at that point. He offered to help.

As the sun set, I rode with this man for a few miles, to a nondescript auto shop on private property. I nervously texted my location to the guys.

The driver introduced me to his brother, who owned the shop. His son had just finished school, and was trying to get into the family business. It was after hours, but he was willing to do the work.

The kid was probably 18, but he knew his way around an engine. The van is built in such a way that you have to dissect it completely to access certain areas. Within a half hour or so, he had torn into it and found the bad alternator. He drove me to the nearest AutoZone, where we tested it and purchased a replacement. It was not cheap, but the first two shows had made me enough money to cover it.

By time we got the part, the guys were already at the venue. The film hadn't ended, and there were two local openers. *I might actually be able to pull this off....*

About an hour later, the kid had me up and running. I borrowed a couple hundred from Crushkill to pay for the labor, but I was incredibly grateful for the help. I gave him a *Rare Form* CD and hit the road as fast as I could.*

*I've been giving merch to repair guys since a rock chipped my window on *I Quit*

I haven't been a speeder since I was 19. My first ticket was $430. I was caught racing to Eugene after a late night recording session in Seattle. Ever since then, I drive "like a grandpa."* The only ticket I ever got on tour was from Evan driving too fast through a speed trap. They mailed me a photo with the ticket, but it was a picture of him!

This time, there's too much at stake. I was pushing 90 the whole way. I finally popped in that new Dear Hunter and hauled ass. When I arrived at the venue, there were all kinds of texts on my phone. One was from Chris (Ill2lectual). He met me in the parking lot and helped me carry everything inside.

I had just enough time to pile everything by the merch table** and get my equipment onstage. I missed soundcheck, so I had to actually plug in my stuff while Vel The Wonder was performing. That's really disrespectful, but I had no choice if I was still going to play. Maxx said he would've let me headline, but I'm glad it didn't come to that.

After all that stress, and already tumultuous week, I finally got onstage. It was a sold out show with a line around the block. I had gone from survival mode to being thrust back into work mode. *Let's do this.*

The crowd was showing love from the first song. It felt so good to have made it there! The room was great, the crowd was packed, and the sound was loud and clear. But by the second song, another sound was cutting through the mix.

I looked around and spotted a very drunk woman, maybe four "rows" back. She was waving her arms and yelling the same curses over and over again. She booed, shouted "speak from the

---

*My wife's words, not mine...

**Sara and Justin were kind enough to set up while I was onstage. It might have triggered my OCD, but it saved me a lot of time and money.

heart," and cried "Eyedeeeeaaaaaaa!" repeatedly. She'd say each one probably 10 times before moving on to the next phrase. I made the most of it, pointing at her when I said the most aggressive punchlines, but she wasn't slowing down.

I was performing "Morning;" a song about my wife's struggles through school and her path toward starting a business. *PLAY FROM THE HEART!!! PLAY FROM THE HEART!!!*

"Really? I'm not rapping about my dick right now. I am literally telling you a story about my family."

People were starting to get just as annoyed as I was. Some turned around and told her to shut up. Several people in the front row plugged one ear and leaned away from her, with the other ear in my stage monitors. They just wanted to watch the show.

As I began to set up the next track, I was cut off with *BOOO!!!! YOU SUCK!!!! EYEDEEEEAAAAAAAA!!!!!* After all that I had gone through to get there—my stressful day, my horrendous week, and my long and fruitless career—I snapped.

"Look bitch, Eyedea told me I was dope TO MY FACE!" People cheered. "Does anybody actually work here? Where's the promoter? Where's the security?"

I only had a 30 minute set, and I wasn't about to let some asshole talk over me the whole time. It was worth it to lose a few minutes and just get her out of there.

The promoter stepped onstage and asked what was wrong. We met a few minutes earlier, but I was in such a rush to get there that I already forgot his name.

"This lady is wasted," I said into the mic. "You can't hear her screaming the whole time? These people in the front row can't even hear what I'm saying."

By then, everyone was turned and facing her. The promoter nodded to security and they threw her outside. I heard she was out there talking shit about me for a while, but I was lucky enough to never see her again. Back to the show...

Do you guys have love for me?

(YEAH!)

Do you guys have love for The World Has No Eyedea tour?

(YEAH!)

We've got the director in the house, give it up for Brandon Crowson!

(Cheers)

Now help me out with this next one. Everyone wants to get out of the—

(RAIN!)

Everyone wants to get out of the—

(RAIN!)

The rest of the set was fucking perfect. "Redefine the Flow," a song full of fast-paced battle bars, turned around the show immediately. I always play the first verse with music, and the second verse a cappella. Sometimes it's fun to ditch the beat, and play with the timing of the rhymes. It helps people understand the lyrics as well. When I said *I got more Technics than DJ Abilities*,* the crowd was howling. It was probably one of the best rooms I've ever played in my life.

I had cut two songs to make up for the interruption, but there was no shortage of good vibes. It's supposed to flow seamlessly from "Other Desert Cities" into "Vacant Eyes." It was the third night, so I had my transitions down to a science. As I spoke about Hayden, my usual segue, I noticed the house DJ at the turntables, and the host reaching for the mic. *Goddamn it.* I hit

---

*Technics is a turntable brand, pronounced like the word "techniques." It can sound like a diss at first, but hip hop fans already know the terminology.

play on the track and finished my set. I was still on time, but for some reason my a cappella had indicated to them that I was finished. I wasn't going to walk off without playing my closer, and I still clocked in at 25 minutes.

I fought tooth and nail for that fucking show, and the crowd respected it. They gave me a huge ovation before Carnage took the stage. It was a crowd of true E&A fans, and I was just the warm up. Carnage and Abilities' sets were flawless. We shouted out each other's names every night, asking the crowd to give it up, and they fucking gave it up in L.A.

The merch table was always busy, but that night was *insane*. These fans were insatiable. I shook hands and signed CDs and sold more E&A stuff than any show in my life. There was no time to go to the bathroom, and no time to catch up with friends, but I was sure smiling a lot.

A few minutes after the music ended, the venue was kicking people out. Maxx had *just* got to the table for autographs and photos. I probably had 20 people lined up, and we were making good money from each sale. I wasn't about to turn people away. Sara and Justin came to help fulfill the last orders, but the lights went out! They fucking turned off the breaker and kicked us out. Not just the fans—us, too!

They were putting the keys into the lock and all my stuff was still offstage. Chris grabbed my hand truck for the merch, while I gathered my laptop and guitar.

When we got to the van, I realized I wasn't the only one upset. As Terrell and I loaded the van, Maxx came in hot. I was so busy selling merch that I didn't even hear that his set got *cut off!* Who the fuck would cut off DJ Abilities?

Regardless of who made the call, we were booted too quickly to make sense of it. Maxx had no time to process the shock, so he set his sights on us. "If the night's running long, *I* don't get cut off. *You do!* Those people are here for me!"

"Those people are here for the *movie*," Terrell shot back. "This isn't even about us!"

These two are headstrong artists; masters of their respective craft. They kept trying to assert dominance back and forth, but that remark was actually deeper than we realized. With everything else that happened on tour, our emotions were heightened because we were there for Micheal. The two of them traded jabs until it was full on screaming.

While that was going on, Chris was politely standing in the background. He not only helped me in and out of the venue, but I told him that I'd get Maxx to sign his E&A records. Micheal had signed them years ago, when he stayed with Chris on tour. It was his best chance to complete them.

As things went south, I suggested that we try another time. I put Chris' records in the van and told the guys we should go. The drive remained tense, and it didn't get better at the hotel.

I called Kathy the next morning, just to keep her in the loop (lack of seating, breaking down, feuding, etc.). She thanked me for guiding the ship and assured me that their brotherly rivalry would pass. After talking for 10 or 15 minutes, I had an incoming call. It was Maxx.

He said that it would be best to take advantage of our day off and stay with a friend. It goes against my tour rules, but I trusted that he wouldn't be hard to track down. Unfortunately, Maxx's ride arrived as Terrell was walking outside and they got into it all over again. I nodded to Maxx's ride and we took a walk while they talked it out.

Thankfully, Kathy was right (she always is) and both parties apologized. Maxx took off and we waited for Brandon's crew to wake up.

L.A. is the best place to have a day off. It was where we toured the aquarium just one year earlier. But that time, my Crushkill friends Michelle and Sydney—mother and daughter—had a treat for us.

When we met (SXSW 2015), Syd was going to school at the Conservatory of Recording Arts & Sciences. I had recorded there once before, so we connected on that. Now, she lives in L.A. working at the historic EastWest Studios.

EastWest—formerly Frank Sinatra's Western Recorders—boasted sessions from absolutely *legendary* albums like the Beach Boys' *Pet Sounds*, Michael Jackson's *Dangerous*, Red Hot Chili Peppers' *Californication* (and *By The Way*, by the way); even famous film scores like *The Godfather*, *Gone Girl*, and *La La Land* were recorded there.

Michelle took all of us down there—right on Sunset Blvd—and Syd gave us a full tour of the facility. It was cool to see behind the scenes where rock stars made their dinners, but when we walked into Studio One, it was breathtaking. Frank Sinatra's podium was front and center, before an array of mics and orchestra seating. It was the same room where he tracked "My Way" and "New York, New York." I thought of my Grandma T, who had died in January that year. We both loved Sinatra. She would've loved that I was there.

Studios Two and Three—the *Pet Sounds* rooms—were occupied. I had just read *I Am Brian Wilson*, as well as the 33 1/3rd volume about *Pet Sounds*, and was obsessed with the *Love & Mercy* film that portrayed those famous sessions. It was disappointing, but I was honored just to be in the building.

We saw Studio Five and talked with Syd about some of the acts who were currently working there.* I was especially pleased to hear John Mayer was back with Steve Jordan and Pino Palladino; he wouldn't announce *The Search for Everything* until early 2017.

After the studio, we walked around Hollywood and just enjoyed ourselves. We saw the Walk of Fame, where I wrote EYEDEA on a blank star. I remember being bummed that we were so close to Amoeba, but my van was like 10 blocks in the other direction. Terrell and I had a dinner date with Chris' family, so we started to walk back to EastWest.

Everyone was spread, and I was walking with Syd. We passed a guy who was hustling CD-Rs on the street. He was going on and on about how I had a beautiful lady and how lucky I was. I said "yes, she is—but she's not my lady!" Syd and I kept walking, so he locked onto Michelle. Flattered for her daughter, she got suckered into buying a CD.

When we got to the van, Andy realized that his car wasn't there. He walked another block, just to be sure. The Jeep was towed, and he had to retrieve it from impound. Couldn't have happened to a nicer guy.

Terrell and I had a great night with Chris's family. I edited the footage of "Other Desert Cities" and shared it on Facebook. I also took the opportunity to call my cousin Jason and see how he was doing. They were managing ok. He said that Hayden loved my music and would be glad I was playing a song for him. I made Jason promise not to have a funeral until I returned.

---

*She didn't tell us at the time, but Syd assisted on the forthcoming Foo Fighters album, *Concrete & Gold*.

We picked up Maxx the next morning and started a new routine. I generally save money by bringing snacks and eating *one* meal a day. To avoid fast food, Maxx likes to visit Whole Foods and get fresh supplies every morning. I had never shopped there, and loved their hot food counters. I found a good bowl of teriyaki chicken with rice, and I even ate my vegetables.

He credited the idea to his former tour mates, Grouch and Eligh. I soon found a new breakfast routine that included a Naked juice smoothie and a protein bar.* It wasn't exactly a meal, but sure better than Pop Tarts.

Fresno was the first show that actually had seating for the film.** Unfortunately, there weren't a lot of butts in those seats. To make matters worse, nobody *left* those seats when the show started. We played for a couple dozen people, but they were all sitting there like we were the post-credits scene. The applause was unenthusiastic, and every call and response fell flat. Even Carnage The Executioner—The Show Saver—couldn't get these people on their feet.

The show was a dud, but Maxx was undeterred. He tailored his set to fit the intimate vibe, and interacted with the crowd a lot more. By the end, most people were on their feet; moving and making noise. I chalked up another victory for DJ Abilities.

It was a short drive to Oakland, and Maxx wanted a legitimate breakfast. He was adamant about The Cheesecake Factory, for some reason. It was out of my price range, but it was also the best breakfast I'd had in a while. More importantly, it gave us a chance to hang out and just be friends again. The gang was back to normal.

*Maxx insists that I only drink it for the name.
**Terrell informed me that there were seats in L.A. as well.

When we got to Oakland, I had to pee like a motherfucker. I thought I could hold it, but I really should've stopped sooner. The hotel had our reservation, which Kathy made in advance, but they wanted to verify her card *in person*. We obviously didn't have the card, so Maxx got her on the phone. She offered to pay us back, at which point I offered to pay in cash.

They had a no cash policy, and there wasn't anything they could do over the phone. Maxx offered to use his card, but the reservation was in her name and there wasn't any vacancy. I was a little distracted by the feeling that my dick might fall off at any given moment. I excused myself and let Maxx take the lead.

I searched up and down the street, in alleys, behind dumpsters, and nothing could provide cover in broad daylight. I got back in the van. Not only was my belt loosened to keep the pressure off, but my shorts were fully unzipped. Nothing could stop what was coming.

I could see the guys weren't making much progress in the lobby, so I did the only thing left to do: climbed in the back of the van and peed in a water bottle. I'm not proud of this. I was really worried about spilling. That shit went off like a fire hose and it filled the bottle in seconds. With only an inch to spare, I painfully pulled the emergency brake on my peehole. Using extreme caution, I switched bottles without spilling a drop. The second bottle was damn near full by the time I was done. I tossed them into a dumpster and washed my hands.*

Feeling human again, I walked toward the lobby. They still hadn't come to an agreement, so we searched Google Maps for the nearest hotel. It was a really nice place, with a fancyass separate shower and jacuzzi tub. I took a half hour nap before Terrell and I left for soundcheck.

*I keep a hand sanitizer pump in my cupholder. (This is before Covid-19.)

The GPS took us on a route that was under construction. I followed the detour signs and ended up back at the hotel. I tried following Garmin, and it took me to a closed road.

When you combine a control freak with an anger problem, a small thing like getting lost can be catastrophic. I must've gone four different ways and kept getting lost or stuck. I was seething with rage; unleashing the most foul curses with every breath. Terrell tried his best to calm me down by offering words of encouragement.*

Chad booked the Oakland show with his crew, the Lobetrotters Collective. I had talked up my former tourmates and promised a great show.**

The venue was enormous. The lobby was big enough to be an entire venue by itself. Danny was already onstage setting up. DJ Halo was on the turntables. I hugged my friends, who expressed their condolences for my cousin. We were ready for a good night together.

That was one of only two shows where I didn't watch the film. The merch tables in the other room, and tickets sold so well that it was standing room only for the last dozen people. When I did peek in the room, it happened to be my scene. I couldn't help but smile when the crowd cheered at my appearance. It was going to be a good show.

Since my table was in the other room, I also missed every other act on the show. I popped in for a song now and then, but I just wore too many hats to wander around.

My family had gathered in the park that day to release balloons for Hayden. My parents texted me a video during the

---

*Most people are uncomfortable when I get that mad. Terrell was in my corner and walked me through it like I was giving birth or something.

**Eventually dubldragon. would tour with Maxx as well.

screening. It was hard to watch, knowing that I chose to be away from my family.

My set was *especially* emotional that night.* I gave my best performance of "Hay Fever," and tears welled up in my eyes. When I performed "Other Desert Cities," I choked up so much I had to stop. Fortunately, the next line saved me.

> *I hope you notice when it's really genuine*
> *Folks 'll notice when they see me in the venue and*
> *I'm spilling my guts, tears running down my face*
> *You can feel it even drowning out the pounding of the bass*

There was a lot of love in the room. I was falling apart, and it was perfectly ok. The audience was right there with me. I completely lost it during "Vacant Eyes." I was full-on crying; tears, slobber, and all of it. I did not attempt to compose myself, just muttered a meek "thank you" and rushed offstage.

My friends were all waiting in the wings. They piled on a glorious group hug and I let it all out. I don't have the words to describe the feeling, but I'm grateful for it.

Later that night, a beautiful girl came to the table and talked to me about the set. She wanted to buy *Famous Last Words*, and I sold her my very last copy. I had officially sold out of every album since *Death of a Salesman.* Amazing.

She messaged me a couple weeks later, saying that the disc was defective. I remembered seeing one at a record store, so I bought it and shipped it as a replacement. I had signed her first one, saying something like THANK YOU—MY LAST COPY! so I signed the new one saying THE <u>REAL</u> LAST COPY! I had no

---

*I wrote about this in the studio version of "Other Desert Cities."

idea, until he mentioned the defective disc, that she was Chad's ex-girlfriend. Small world.

It's common to share your own music in the van. Often it'll be some new, unreleased project that you're working on. I was sitting on an untitled EP at the time, and wanted to play it for Terrell.

When the first song came on, Maxx—who generally ignored our music discussions from the back seat—said "that's dope! Who made this beat?"

Crosby!

The project consisted of me, Sarx, and Crozz on the beats. A few minutes later, a different song came on and Maxx chimed in again.

"This is *dope!* Who is this?"

Still Crosby!

It felt good that my friend was getting props from a master beatmaker.

I love sharing my music with Terrell because he's a great listener, and his technical ability enables him to catch damn near every nuance in the rapping, no matter how dense it is. Perhaps more importantly, he's still a genuine fan of music.*

Terrell reacts to beats, laughs at punchlines, and will ask you to rewind a cool pattern so he can analyze it. About half way through, I told him that I wasn't going to release it until I found a DJ to scratch on it.

He got a smile on his face. "Can I join your group?" This absolute *monster* of an artist just humbled himself to ask if he could be part of *my* project. "I can beatbox the scratches, no problem."

*Sadly, a lot of artists get lost in their own worlds and stop seeking, or appreciating music outside of their bubble.

I told him "fuck yeah, *of course!* But you've gotta rap on the posse cut. People will be mad if they see your name and don't hear at least *one* verse from you."

The deal was done. I texted the other guys without asking for their input. I knew they'd be stoked.

"What's the name of the group?" he asked. It was a fully mixed project with completed artwork, but we didn't have a name. I told him I was trying use the word "amalgamation" in some way. It was a departure for everyone involved, and we all brought a different style to the table.

We brainstormed for a while, trading words and phrases, trying to put a finger on the sound. Terrell said he'd been wanting to use the word "arcane" for a title. It only took a few seconds before he said it. "What about Arcane Amalgam?"

It was eight months before we'd have a chance to record, but that conversation wasn't just bullshit. The self-titled *Arcane Amalgam* dropped the following summer.

On that same drive, Terrell kept bringing up Gabe. He would say "you've gotta hear this beat that Web sent me," and we'd crank it up. *Good shit*. But then he'd make a comment like "it's too bad you guys can't make amends, man. You had something good together."

I knew he was right, but we had been on such bad terms—on and off since *DOAS*—that we hadn't even spoken in a year. We'd patch things up and then any small success I had would trigger an explosion of resentment from Gabe. Last I heard, he had been hospitalized for mental health issues. I knew he didn't want to see me, but I asked a mutual friend to keep me informed. When Gabe got out, the first thing he did was text me.

Please stay out of my life. You and Evan are extremely toxic. Take a hard look at how you treat people. Good riddance!

That message was actually kind of freeing. We had been up and down so many times, through the most brutal arguments, that it was nice to just have some closure. I missed him, and I appreciated the times we had. I wanted him to get better, but I knew that I couldn't be part of that process anymore. I finally sat down and wrote the song that I was always too afraid to write.

Take everything and waste it
Nothing if you're not complacent
in this self-destructive cycle of deception that you're facing

Say I used you for the music
What you used me for's apparent
But I'm not your therapist
We're not your fucking parents

Hate me for what I say
Don't blame me for your mistakes, though
Hate me but what you say won't
Make me your fucking scapegoat

The opposite of "do or die"
I talked you out of suicide
You bragged as if you built this
While I kill for it, you fucking hide

Cripplingly unreliable
Clinically certifiable
Predictably vindictive
and you know it's undeniable

It was the most viscous thing I'd ever written about a friend, but that resentment had built up for *years*. Every time I was attacked, I'd swallow my feelings and try to talk him down. But I finally didn't have to censor myself. It was healing to speak those words. I was done.

When we got to Eugene, I was telling Evan about all the crazy shit that had gone down. Just then, Gabe walks in. Ev and I looked at each other like *what the fuck*. I felt ambushed.

Gabe walked straight toward Terrell and gave him a hug. T was buttering me up because he had planned to get the two of us in a room again. I continued setting up for soundcheck when Gabe came over and gave me a big hug. "I'm so sorry," he said. "I'm proud of you."

We spent the rest of the night talking about the hell he'd been through with doctors and misdiagnoses and bad medication. We also discussed new boundaries. He honestly looked happier and healthier than ever. He said that another "new Gabe" speech wasn't going to change anything, and he had waited to reach out until he got his life together. His actions would do the talking.

I was cautiously optimistic. I worried that I was opening myself to the same old hurt again, but I couldn't deny how good it was to see him. Our relationship is complicated, but we've actually been on good terms ever since!

KI Design manages a popular "barcade" called Level Up. They're not a music venue, but on occasion, they've held events for Abilities, Mixmaster Mike (of Beastie Boys), Blueprint, and others. I reached out to him from Vegas, and put together a last minute show.

Being an arcade, they have TVs all over the place. But the games were so loud that it didn't make for an ideal screening.

On the plus side, it was a free show and people had been asking if the tour was coming to Eugene. I also had a fair amount of friends and family who wanted to support me because of Hayden. I hadn't seen any of them since it happened.

I knew that Jason was coming, so I had asked my shirt guy, Ryan Casad (Rage & Sail Screen Printing), to make something special. The premise of *Break The Bank* had been along the lines of *Cats, Pajamas* or *Original Recipe*.* Doug and I were going to smash a kid's piggy bank in front of him. Hayden was too tough to pull off the crying tantrum that I had envisioned, so we went another direction.

He laughed at every take, looking at his sister between shots. At one point, he flipped the bird and it gave me an idea. I directed him to put up the middle finger at me, and make a long *ffffffff* sound with his mouth. From the camera, it looked like he was going to say "fuck you."

Jason was supervising and told us to go for it. Hayden got a huge kick out of it, going *fffff* and trying not to giggle. I had one more idea. I got him to scrunch his forehead like he was squinting at the sun. This gave his brow just enough of an arch to look mad.

His photo was so good that we used his solo image—along with our album title—as the disc art. I pulled up the original artwork, changed the title to *Hayden*, and sent it to Rage & Sail. Ryan came through just in time, and I wore my new shirt to the show. He was even nice enough to make extras for the family.

It was another emotional set, but I felt more positive than before. I was home. People everywhere love Abilities and

---

*Originally we were going to be Photoshopped into a giant KFC bucket, but we couldn't get Sarx for the photo shoot. We settled on the 70's KFC style.

Carnage, but man, we love these guys in Eugene. With only a few days notice, we still had a really good crowd. My friend Emily helped me at the merch table, wearing an *EYEDEA IS DEAD** shirt that she bought from him in 2010.

Andy was filming every Carnage set, and he started recording mine as well. The footage in Eugene was some of the best, and we were going to edit angles from all the shows into a live DVD. I saw a rough cut on my laptop and it looked great. He had even filmed some interviews with me at SXSW (2016).

Unfortunately, the audio not good enough to sell. We later salvaged footage from my new song "Lesions," and used it for a music video.

We finished the tour in Seattle. For all the times I'd played in Fremont, I never got to play their nicest venue, Nectar. I had seen shows there before, like Sadistik** and Open Mike Eagle. The room wasn't huge, but the balcony made it a larger capacity than I'm used to. It was a perfect room for the film.

I actually played *before* for our local support that night, because we got Onry Ozzborn on the bill. Everything was perfect that night; the venue, screening, attendance, performances, you name it. Funny how there's little to say when shit isn't falling apart all around me.

Being the last night, I got a movie poster from Brandon and had everybody sign it. I have all my tour posters framed, but that one was special.

---

*Crushkill currently sells shirts that read *EYEDEA IS ALIVE*, but there was a time when Micheal wanted to try other styles of music and distance himself from any fans' expectations. Kathy supports any fan who wears the original design, because Mike would've sold it to them himself.

**Graves opened, infamously breaking the end of their bar while rapping on it.

We stayed at a house around the corner. We had been in separate rooms the whole time, so Maxx lost his mind when I walked out of the bathroom in my Batman pajamas (with matching Batman toiletry bag). I hadn't even got both feet past the threshold and he was laughing his ass off. "I forgot that about you," he said. I imagine his mind recalled the floor-to-ceiling Batman memorabilia in my studio.* "You're the Batman guy."

The next day was a solo drive, five hours home. I reflected on my memories of Micheal; seeing him for the first time on HBO, having my mind blown by *The Many Faces of Oliver Hart* (in Chris Wilson's high school bedroom), seeing three different E&A shows in high school, blowing people's minds with the *E&A* album in my first car, Micheal introducing himself after our sound check, my sister in-law's birthday dinner where Gabe called and told me Mike had recorded new vocals for his first remix, seeing him jump out of the van and hug me and Gabe that last night we met, and walking back to my car feeling childlike excitement.

I remembered dropping the phone on the day I got the news. I remembered crying on the drive to Gabe's house to tell him, and our embrace in the driveway. I remembered my parting words that day. "You know what this means? We have to go *harder*. He saw something in us, and we have to honor that. We have to carry the torch."

As the memories came rushing in, an old lyric came to mind.

If someone grew up in a cubicle as Plato once suggested
They would only know the cubicle and not the world outside it
And they wouldn't view the cubicle as something geometric
We only know it's a cubicle because we live outside it

At the DOAS release, we had to unplug my neon Bat-symbol so he could sleep.

> *Now the one inside the cubicle can't comprehend his measurements*
> *Because measurements are models made up for and by observers*
> *Relative to their position on the outside of the cubicle*
> *To understand objectively so they can study further*
>
> *If I grew up in a cubicle the walls limit my universe*
> *I have no knowledge of the entirety like the outsiders do*
> *If you follow what I say and can swallow the powdered water*
> *Close your eyes and open your minds, this one's for you*

That shit was game-changing in 2001, and it's a great example of why Eyedea is such an amazing artist. But when it popped into my head that day, it had my own words.

> *If someone grew up in the studio as records had suggested*
> *They would only know the studio and not the world outside*
> *And anyone outside the studio interprets information*
> *as the art is a reflection of the artist deep inside*
>
> *If you're the one inside the studio, then you know that we're learning*
> *and observing and repurposing a different point of view*
> *Whether you grew up in the studio or cooped up in a cubicle*
> *This one's for you*
> *(This one's for you)*

I had the first few lines in my head, and grabbed my voice recorder. I remembered that Durazzo had given me a beat on the *Rare Form* tour. I cued it up and it worked perfectly. I wrote the rest of it before stopping for lunch in Portland. Funny how the tour began and ended exactly the same way.

When I recorded the song, I couldn't tell if it was a clever homage or a corny imitation. I texted Blueprint and asked if he'd listen and give me his first impression. Micheal and Print were both Rhymesayers artists and had a ton of history together. I knew that if Print liked it, then I was on the right track.

To my relief, the song was a success. Print even helped me finish the song, recording a verse of his own. It was a great way to end an incredible journey.

R. Eye. P.

Micheal David Larsen

Great Eyedeas Never Die

Eyedea & Abilities, the night we met
(Left to right:) Maxx, Micheal
WOW Hall (Eugene, OR) 2010

(Left to right:) Kathy, me
Soundset (Saint Paul, MN) 2017

Sold out in LA
Photo credit: Stephanie Gonzalez
Los Globos (Los Angeles, CA) 2016

(Left to right:) me, Maxx
Unknown, 2016

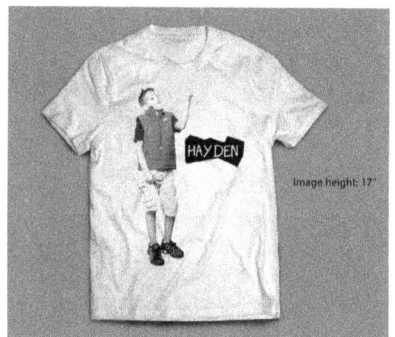

Art proof, Hayden's shirt
Rage & Sail Screen Printing (Junction City, OR) 2016

Squalor (2017)

Lineup: Dead Fucking Serious, Streetlight Cardiacs

Best show: Sacramento, CA

Worst show: Olympia, WA

Record store find: Berzerk – *This Silence Kills*

I'd been rapping for more than a decade. It was an unexpected turn in my life, and I'm glad that it happened. Life as a solo artist had afforded me many freedoms, but it wasn't my first love. It was never the plan. I didn't dream of touring the world with my laptop; I dreamed of touring with my band.

In 2012, The ILLusionists recorded our punk songs and retired the live band. All five songs were only three minutes combined, so Dead Fucking Serious reunited from a four year hiatus. We filled the other "side" with three old songs, one new one, and a cover. From that moment on, DFS was always in the back of my mind. The ILL was going hard, but I was ready to pick up my guitar again.

In 2014, I released *Stolen Songs 3*. Instead of acoustic covers, it was all punk. Even the Elton John song was punk. Then I recorded eight different albums called *Stolen Songs Sessions*. With a rotating cast of band members, I produced 30 minute tributes to Nirvana, Sublime, Foo Fighters, and five others. Rap had dulled my musical dexterity, and *Stolen Songs* reacquainted me with my instrument.

One by one, often months apart, I would write and record songs for DFS. There was no plan, and no deadline. My drummer Kellen would listen to those demos and then we'd record a proper version together. I filled in on bass because Chris Wilson had moved to Portland while we were apart.

After three years of baby steps, I had written the best punk album of my entire life. DFS was back.

That said, we didn't think anyone else would give a shit. DFS wasn't a big deal in 2007, so there was no reason that we would be in 2017. We were just doing it for *us*.

Now that I think like a label owner, I make more strategic moves. First of all, I aimed to make it my best recording quality yet. Every sound was just right. Every take was just right. It had balls, and it had energy.

The mix itself was clean and mean. I wanted to hire the Descendents-owned Blasting Room Studios for mastering,* and somehow we pulled it off.

Secondly, I wanted the artwork to be awesome. On a whim, I contacted long-time Dead Kennedys/Jello Biafra collaborator, Winston Smith. He specializes in collage art that's synonymous with punk rock. His contribution to *SQUALOR* was invaluable, both as a fan of his work, and as the label pushing the record.

The third step was promotion. I had zero contacts in the punk press circles, but I knew how to make an EPK and shop it around. We filmed a music video, got professional photos, and booked a tour. I pitched our album to dozens of websites.

*Producers Bill Stevenson and Jason Livermore are my biggest influence. Jason had also mastered *This Day's End* (2005).

With hip hop, you can email 10 different sites and *maybe* get one reply. They get so many bullshit links every day that it's impossible to keep up. Given our years of obscurity, my expectations were exceedingly low.

But it wasn't long before one of the biggest sites picked up on our video. *Punk News* published a short piece on the "Pulse" video, promoted our tour dates, and linked to the Crushkill preorder page. Within days, the other sites jumped on the bandwagon. *Punk News* followed with an exclusive stream of our song "Pacified," and a third article which reviewed the whole album. Our comeback was legitimized.

Evan and I first met playing punk. His band Streetlight Cardiacs had also reunited, though mostly behind closed doors. I had produced their 2006 and 2007 releases, so I knew everyone pretty well. We invited them to hit the road, just like old times.

Chris had been our bassist from the very beginning (2006), but starting a family in Portland had estranged us. Kellen and I recorded *SQUALOR* alone; I took over bass duties myself.

For six months, we rehearsed a brand new set with a "live" bassist, Justin Ryan. We had a natural chemistry, having been friends for many years. He was so into playing with us that we included him in the press photos and videos, even crediting him in the liner notes of the album.

It had been a long time since either Justin or I had played punk like that. If you play it right, you're moving your whole body. It's a fucking workout. Kellen was playing grindcore in my absence, so we were technically his "slow" band.

I watched some videos of DFS in 2007. They were terrible. Our songs are really fast and really short; often less than a minute long. On those old tapes, we'd play a song and then talk to the audience for three minutes. Probably half the show was just talking.

SQUALOR crammed 16 tracks into a 19 minute run time. I wanted that for our live show. The next song starts before you know the last one had finished. *BAM. BAM. BAM.*

To achieve this, we rehearsed the songs in medleys that I referred to as blocks. We were playing five songs straight—without stopping for a *second*—before we ever relented or spoke to the audience. Even then, I'd hardly say anything. It was the polar opposite of my interactive, confessional rap show. We let the music speak for itself.

It was important to me that we were road-ready before the tour started. We couldn't promote a big comeback show right before the tour kickoff,* so I booked us as "special guest." We didn't promote until the day of the show, simply posting *SECRET SHOW TONIGHT* online. People started texting us for the address, and it seemed like we might actually pull it off.

The secret show was packed, and we had a non-stop circle pit from the moment we started. The new set *killed*. Every expectation was exceeded, from ours to the audience. The headliner was another Eugene band who introduced themselves by saying "oh my god—we should be opening for *you!*"

SQUALOR was scheduled to drop on January 13th, 2017. The tour was set to kick off the same day. Around that time, however, I was offered an opening slot for RA The Rugged Man. He's one of my favorite rappers, and I'd wanted to work with him for a long time.** Since DFS was uncharted water, my rap career took priority.

*I've already spoken about playing too often and its effect on turnout
**So long, in fact, that "Blood in the Water" was written with him in mind. He gave me his email when we first met, but I never heard back about the song.

We all agreed that it was an opportunity worth taking, and rescheduled the first DFS show. I could've just taken the slot for myself, but we were promoting *Rare Form*, so it made the most sense to book the group.

Doug and I fucking destroyed. It was an especially *hip hop* crowd—and a solid turnout—who wanted nothing more than hard beats and clever bars. We hit 'em with bars from start to finish. Being the release date of *SQUALOR*, I actually sold quite a bit of DFS stuff, too.

The rest of the show didn't go quite as smoothly. When we got to soundcheck, neither RA, nor his tourmate AFRO were in sight. I asked the house manager if we should set up or wait for them to go first. RA texted him to say they were going to hang at the hotel until AFRO's set.

Cool.

That stung a little, since I'd been looking forward to playing with him. He's also really outgoing with his fans and brings some his openers up onstage at the end (including friends of mine). I've gotten respect from many artists on the WOW Hall stage, whether Fashawn, Myka 9, or Eyedea. But no matter how great we played that night, RA wasn't even in the building.

We were feeling good after our set. But as the night went on, I felt more and more bitter. I was at the merch table when someone brought two huge piles of loose shirts (no boxes), dropped them on the table, and walked away. For the next hour and a half, people came up to me (no one was working their side) and asked "how much for a shirt?"

RA opened with the namesake of the tour, "Definition of a Rap Flow." That song put him back on the map* after years of

---

*I had even recorded my *own* version, for a "Definition of a Rap Flow" contest, from which AFRO was discovered. My version was remixed by Web, renamed "Redefine the Flow," and re-recorded with Casual (of Hieroglyphics). It appears on *Vacant Eyes*.

relative obscurity. But there was nothing to boast about that night. I sat on the side of the stage, watching RA struggle through the first verse, feeling embarrassed for him. By the second verse, he fucked up so bad that he told the DJ to start over. They literally played the song again. I've never seen a professional rapper do that before. Even if you fuck up, cut the beat and do it a cappella. We've all done it.

It only got worse from there. RA introduced a song, and when the beat dropped, it was a different song. I hesitate to call it the *wrong* song, because I don't know whose mistake it was; the DJ or the emcee. RA made a big deal about it, cussing at the DJ *on the mic* and pacing the stage like a lunatic.

The crowd actually seemed to like it. RA's reputation affords him the freedom to do whatever he wants, even to the detriment of the show.* A few minutes later, the DJ played another "wrong" song, and RA fucking lost it. He grabbed the heavy, six-foot wooden DJ table and flipped it like The Incredible Hulk.** He stormed offstage, while the DJ shamefully picked up his equipment.

Ironically, RA used this time to take the mic and fire him—in front of the audience—for being unprofessional. After the soundcheck, the restart, and the tantrums, I couldn't believe it. I only talked to him briefly, because my brother asked for a photo with all three of us. My other rap heroes had spoiled me. I was disappointed to say the least.

The *SQUALOR* tour kicked off the next day. With Phil (from Streetlight) and Chris both based in Portland, we knew there would be a lot of interest. I kept that in mind as shit hit the fan.

---

*If he wrote a book, it would be much more interesting. Call it *How to Ruin Your Career!*

**Bill Bixby, not Ang Lee

I avoided booking Portland for much of my twenties, simply because I didn't have the contacts. Familiar places like Satyricon and the Paris Theater had closed,* so it was either house shows or nothing. That changed when I met Zoe at the Hawthorne, but she moved to the Panic Room, and we fell out of touch when it closed.**

We played at a bar called The Watertrough. They didn't have a PA, so I had to rent one again. Streetlight wasn't quite stage-ready, so we shared equipment. It was actually really handy because we could seamlessly change sets on tour. But with all our gear *and* a rented PA, the van was packed to the ceiling.

Earlier that week, Eugene had some pretty heavy snowfall. It was such a rare moment, waking up to that sight, that I grabbed my camera and filmed a rap video on the porch. I knew Portland would be twice as bad, so I asked Doug if we could film his verses before the show.

The streets in Portland were completely frozen. People were calling in sick to work, shows were being cancelled, and it didn't look good for our once-promising turnout.

We planned to meet Doug at a cemetery, but it was closed for the season. We met at a park instead. The view was perfect, but snow wasn't pouring from the sky anymore. Kellen and Justin stood offscreen, shaking tree branches to compensate.

Tire tracks had formed deep grooves in the streets. They were probably six inches deep and hard as a rock. Most cars could fit, but my oversized van shook violently.

It was just as hard on foot. Three-inch sheets of ice blanketed the sidewalk. It was like walking on a hockey rink. We killed time at record stores and the famed Powell's Books.

*The Paris has since reopened
**Panic Room later reopened under its original name, The Tonic Lounge

I gently pulled a U-turn in front of the venue. It worked beautifully until I applied the brakes. We started to slide *against* the turn, toward a streetlight on the corner. I babied the brake and stopped within an inch or two of a pole. We nearly made it all the way there, just to crash into the venue.

The Watertrough didn't have a stage, but we packed quite a few friends in a tight space. I was so excited to see Streetlight Cardiacs that I was up front, moshing and singing along. When I realized how much energy I'd wasted, I sat down at the merch table. I've lost my voice before just *talking* too much—I didn't want to lose it from screaming other people's songs!

We came out of the gate with absolute fury. The bands progressively got faster and louder through the night; a consistent trait of the tour. Chris even played a couple old songs with us, since he never had a proper send off. Justin was happy to oblige. We may have been out of shape, but we made up for it with heart.

We burned through 17 songs so quickly that the crowd wanted more. We had rehearsed "Something More"—the most melodic song on the album—but cut it to spare my voice. We pounded it out so sloppily that our exhaustion started to show. Nobody cared, but it was a lesson learned: Stick to the Script.

Kellen and I shared a celebratory hug, and went off to greet our friends. Crozz had gravitated away from punk over the years, flat out dismissing it in his mid-twenties. He made a point to say that he was proud of me. Earning his respect for *SQUALOR* was monumental. It defied our expectations right out of the gate. Friends, old bandmates, and new fans were all down with DFS.

Between the new album, video, press, and a secret show, we had a lot of buzz in Eugene. We played an all-ages venue called

The Boreal. I hadn't been part of that scene for so long that I didn't know many bands who were still around. I had produced Black Delany in 2014, so I asked them to open.

My contact at the venue was an old friend from middle school. I had produced one of his earlier bands and we played a lot of shows together. His new band had a lot of buzz as well. The audience was so packed for them that I worried nobody was there for us.

It was so good to see Streetlight Cardiacs, and for so many reasons. First off all, I love those guys. They're good people. It was a blast of nostalgia—complete with a hometown crowd—but also just cool to see my friends cutting loose onstage again.

It's also a special thing seeing a Take 92 band onstage. Much like Black Delany, I had produced two Streetlight albums in the past. I watched those songs come to life in my house. It's a surreal experience when I catch little changes that I made during the recordings. Maybe that's narcissism, but it reminds me of the times we shared in the studio.

But the biggest reason that I enjoyed their set that night? They're fucking great. Those songs were fun ten years earlier, and they only got better with age. Ev had toured so much that his stage presence was considerably more evolved. People were singing and clapping along with his simplest gestures. He was no longer just a vocalist;* he was the *frontman*.

The crowd was overwhelming. That room was so packed that I could hardly push my way to the front. I saw friends from all different eras in my life; some hadn't been to a show years, and others had come to see me at the WOW Hall two nights earlier. It was a special night.

*Ev and Phil share vocal duties in Streetlight Cardiacs

That said, we almost didn't play the show. I remembered hearing a rumor, years earlier, about my friend from The Boreal. At first, I couldn't see him in that light. But later, I saw his alleged victim with some mutual friends. I had to clear the air.

"If you don't mind me bringing it up," I asked, "I'm an old friend of his, and I was shocked to hear what he did to you." Undaunted, she told me, at great length, about their dysfunctional relationship, and his sexual coercion tactics. She felt unsafe, trapped, and abused.

I was stunned, recalling the many times he'd greeted me with a warm hug and a smile; all the laughs we'd shared over the years... But I realized that our interactions were always when it was *just the guys*. Then I recalled being on the receiving end of his temper. Her story began to resonate almost immediately.

It wasn't until we booked the show that I remembered that revelation. I reached out to her on social media and asked if we could speak on the phone. I wanted her opinion.

Our secret show was at a punk bar called Old Nick's. It was important to us that the kickoff was more inclusive. Eugene has a long history of singular, all-ages punk venues. One pops up, and loses steam after a year or two. Another would pop up, but almost never at the same time. The Boreal was the only game in town. The question was: *should we associate with them?*

I asked a couple more female friends in the scene. *Did they feel safe at shows? Had they heard these stories? Had they any stories of their own?* The answer was yes and no. There was a story circulating about Old Nick's, but it sounded like an issue between patrons, not employees.

When I called her to talk, she shared another troubling detail: there were others. A few young women had reached out to her with similar stories. At that point, I was livid. I said that we should tell the venue staff and get him fired.

But they already *had* informed the venue, and it was met with indifference (or at the very least, inaction). She said that they felt unwelcome after speaking up. It wasn't just hostility in the air. She said they would slam into her and her friends, even well outside the mosh pit.

I was floored. There were too many dots for it not to connect. Out of options, I thought *what if we boycott The Boreal?* I told her we would cosign any statement they wanted to make, but not every victim was comfortable going public. On top of that, we hadn't played a show* in a decade. What social capital did we really have?

Kellen was equally upset. We didn't want to turn a blind eye and be part of the problem. We decided that the best move was to confirm the show, and address it onstage.

To my surprise, our former friend's set began with a proclamation about safe spaces and equality. But it was part of the act. I wanted to speak off the cuff. Without getting into the nuances of subgenres, hardcore bands can be preachy and pretentious, while punks let the songs speak for themselves. Readers might disagree, but having played in both kinds of bands, that's my take on it.

When it was our turn, I didn't speak a word besides "we're Dead Fucking Serious." The crowd was amazing, but I was surprised that people weren't moving as much as they were for the other bands. What I noticed was that they were *listening*. We had their full attention.

*Secret show excluded

Five songs later, we paused for a break. I began by saying what a long time it had been; that DFS—and my previous band, This Day's End—had evicted ourselves from the scene after enduring years of toxic behavior.

"People started fights. They vandalized bathrooms. They caused our venues to close."

"Here we are," I explained, "ten years later. And before we played a single show, we've already heard stories of violence and sexual harassment. We're not gonna stand for that shit. All those tough-guy dinosaurs can get the fuck out of here. They have *no place* at our shows. And if you're one of those assholes pounding your chest, trying to intimidate people; trying to take advantage of the young women here... this one's for you."

One of our "blocks" began with a song called "Go Fuck Yourself." It was written about Task1ne, but at The Boreal, it didn't matter who it was about. What mattered was the message:
GO FUCK YOURSELF!

I employed a similar tactic, years earlier, when a radio station had badmouthed The ILLusionists. I can't say whether my friend ever got the message. For fear of fanning the flames, I never confronted him about it in person. The potential satisfaction wasn't worth making the victims suffer another sleight. There was nothing to do but play nice and hope that he was listening.

Ev and I had played 100-plus ILLusionists shows. The punk tour was different. It was the old dream.

We left The Boreal on top of the world. Until then, I hadn't realized that I was so musically unfulfilled. *SQUALOR* was about my depression and grief. That stuff didn't go away because I picked up a guitar. Perhaps some combination of losing loved ones—particularly Hayden's suicide—putting out some of the best work of my career, and touring with my *band*... maybe those things added up to a change. I felt euphoric. No local show had been so rewarding since the first tour.

After the show, Phil and his wife Rebekah invited me to join them at a bar called The Jackalope. They had listened to *SQUALOR* on the way to Eugene, and were absolutely gushing with praise. I admire Phil as a songwriter, so it meant a lot coming from him.

Streetlight couldn't join us for all the dates. Olympia was billed as *O'Malley's at Westside Lanes*. I asked Chad "did you book us at a fucking bowling alley?" He assured us that it was a separate bar, *connected* to the bowling alley.

Fuck it.

As we brought our gear inside, we passed several flyers for other shows. One of them is seared into my memory. I am terrified of spiders, and there was an 11x17 poster with a blue tarantula. When we played our set, one of those posters was *right next to my mic*. Justin took it down, so I wouldn't have to look at it. Even now as I type this, I can't un-see it.

I wasn't used to hauling all that equipment anymore, so it was nice to be headlining. Playing last meant we could backline our amps, and other bands would set up in front of ours. It not only saved time, but spared us from having to lug heavy amps right before a strenuous set.

Medford was just DFS, too. I told Evan they were sorely missed. The venue was called The Bamboo Room at King Wah's. *A bowling alley and a Chinese restaurant?!* We couldn't help but laugh.

On the plus side, they offered us a free buffet. After years of touring on one meal a day, food is the best accommodation—*especially* buffet-style, since I'm so fucking picky!

When *SQUALOR* was finished, I thought there was no topping it. I made the greatest punk album of my life. But once we hit the road, I was getting new ideas like crazy. It wasn't the end. It was a new chapter.

I worked on some new riffs after dinner. Kellen helped with the arrangement while I paced around the room playing. Then I remembered a riff that Justin wrote at practice. He taught me how to play it, and in an hour, we had a finished song. To show my gratitude, I called it "And Justins For All."

I set up the merch table right by the door, so we'd have the best visibility. When I bent over to remove the lid, that fucking blue spider poster was right in my face. Justin laughed his ass off, saying "I'm so glad I was here to see it!" *Fucker.*

It was another weird bill: a surf rock band and a nu-metal band (Phake). It was odd seeing that again. I genuinely thought nu-metal was dead. The only song I remember was an ode to their favorite kitchen utensil. I just remember them chanting *SPATULA! SPATULA!* like it was "Master of Puppets."

Medford could've been a town where we didn't draw any fans, but all three of us brought people that night. Some people bought merch before we even played, just because our name was cool. Others were intrigued, and then shocked by our intensity.

The Phake guys were really nice, and wanted to do a merch trade. I looked around their table and spotted a crudely engraved spatula. It was a no-brainer.*

---

*Now I use that thing almost daily.

I had a good feeling about Sacramento. The flyer was a detailed illustration of a guy puking and shitting at the same time! It was one of the greatest flyers I'd ever seen. But after two weird venues—three if you count The Watertrough—I wasn't expecting much.

Cafe Colonial became one of my favorite venues on the West Coast. It wasn't a cafe, but a dingy, stickered-up, punk club with old Nintendo consoles at the bar.

Our contact was a band called Pisscat. By then, I had quietly signed all my projects to Deep Thinka Records; Chad was my full-time agent. Since he wasn't there, I made sure to introduce myself as much as possible and get to know our hosts.

I immediately brought up the shit/barf flyer. Their bassist, Dustin, was the artist! There were tons of great bands that night, and the crowd not only showed up, but *stayed* the whole time. As an out-of-town headliner, that makes a big difference.*

The first band was on some old school, Suicidal Tendencies shit. Then a kickass Mexican group called Jesus and the Dinosaurs. They had an erratic style, alternating between English and Spanish songs.

The Roughies reminded me of Off With Their Heads; one of my favorite bands in recent years. Their album cover was a distant photo of the singer... fucking a girl on the hood of his car.

Streetlight commanded everyone's attention. Their style is at once so unique, and so universally appealing that it just works everywhere.** That time, I learned my lesson, and stayed in my seat as much as possible. We had an especially good set that night. There was even a photographer who got some good shots of the band.***

*It's hard to sell CDs to people who leave before we've started.
**Ok, we get it. I'm a fan.
***One of those photos became our next tour flyer

It felt good to be back in our natural habitat (with actual punk fans). I started a pit during "Fuck Yourself," with my guitar still in hand. During "Control," Justin did a pick scrape on *my* strings while I was singing. It cracked me up, but we didn't miss a beat. I remember having so much fun that I pulled Justin aside and said "thank you for saving my band."

We stayed at the same Motel 6 where we had the sexy photo shoot on the *Show Stoppers* tour. The Roughies were there, too. I got the feeling that they were hard-partying types, so Kellen and I declined an invitation to their room. Justin told us the next day that it didn't take long before people threatened to call the cops about the noise. It only made me more content with my decision to get a good night's sleep.

Berkeley is one of my favorite cities. One stretch of Telegraph Avenue has Amoeba Records *and* Rasputin Records, plus all the food you could ever want. Kellen and I loved to double up on those record stores, but I sensed that Justin wasn't as interested.

A 14 year-old kid was in the hip hop section at Amoeba. When we were next to each other, in the C section,* he called to his mom: "look, they've got Casual! From Hieroglyphics!" It's easy to feel like *kids these days* don't listen to good hip hop, so it was nice to be proven wrong.

I checked the Sammy Warm Hands section to see if it needed to be restocked. *Vacant Eyes* had a sticker on it: *FEATURING CASUAL (HIEROGLYPHICS)*, complete with a little Hiero logo next to it. The kid walked by and I couldn't help but say "hey, if you like Casual, he's on my CD, too!"

*Ha

A few minutes later, someone tapped my shoulder on the street. It was that kid from the store.

"Hey man, are you on Spotify?" I said yes, and handed him a *Rare Form* business card. I appreciated that he cared enough to look me up. There's still hope for the youth!

Kellen dug through Rasputin while I went to lunch with Justin. I was raving about how good it was to play punk rock again. It felt great to get so much love as an unknown band. But I wasn't sure if he felt the same.

When we got our food, I asked what he thought of the band. Justin was enthusiastic about the songs, and the shows—he was no stranger to the road, by the way—but I still felt like he was holding out on me. I decided not to push it and just enjoy the day. It was a significant one.

I had played at Gilman before, but that was hip hop. It was an even greater honor for Dead Fucking Serious.

I don't remember all of the local bands,* but one of them *definitely* stood out. Fat Lizzy was a three-piece band whose *drummer* was the lead singer. They were just 12 and 13 years old. They were a little shy when I introduced myself, but I was impressed. It was just three-chord punk, but they had an entire set list of original songs and played together like a cohesive unit. It reminded me so much of my first band EPD, with Crozz, Chris, and our drummer Chase. I wanted to encourage them.

"Playing shows at your age gives you a head start. All you have to do is stick together and *you'll* become the new veterans in the scene."

---

*I'd been planning to write this book for a long time, but Crozz suggested that I do it before I forget this stuff. After *Rare Form,* the memories have started to blur together.

I was glad to share that experience with Streetlight. Rancid was a monumental influence, so they respected the Gilman like I did. They killed. We killed. We earned their respect.

I jumped in the pit again and pushed the Fat Lizzy kids to mosh. It was during a 45-second song; I didn't have much time to get back onstage. It was a lot taller than Cafe Colonial, but I leapt back up didn't miss a beat. Lauren—Streetlight's drummer—was impressed, saying that he didn't think I'd make it in time!

I also had a habit of throwing my guitar. I had fixed up my 1997 Strat copy from EPD. The idea was that we could play rowdier shows without worry. (I've broken an expensive guitar before—it isn't fun!)

There was a note on our set list to switch guitars* for the Standard Tuning Block. Then I could jump into the crowd and flail around a little more. Afterward, I'd unplug and throw it over my shoulder. It was sort of a "move," but I had been doing it since band class in high school.

When we unlocked our instruments, I'd grab that guitar and throw it 25 feet toward the amplifier. I did that daily and it always bounced back. It was my beater.

That night was like any other night, but one of the Fat Lizzy kids yelled *THEATRICAL!!!* and we all laughed. Maybe it *was* gimmicky if I did it every day. I didn't care. I was having fun. We took a photo with our tourmates and called it a night.

Like Maxx, Justin preferred the back seat. On the long drive home, Kellen and I reflected on our impossible resurrection from obscurity. I still can't believe it.

Streetlight wasn't able to do a longer tour, but I wanted to get back on the road while the record was new. Kellen didn't want to

---

*I forgot to change tunings at a few practices. Switching guitars made it easier to remember.

live on the road and I didn't want that for us either. Just another taste... I was going to make physical press kits and send *SQUALOR* to a few labels. We had Crushkill, but if we could get on the road with *established* bands, it would be huge. We brainstormed and fantasized, listening to our latest demos.

This is not the end.

Two days later, Justin sent me an email. "I'm writing this out because I prefer to get all my thoughts out on paper when making a big decision..." *Fuck.* That explains it. He wanted out.

The letter said that he loved the band, but his job as a [successful] tattoo artist wasn't conducive to a full-time band. I tried to explain that the last six months were just stressful because we started from scratch: new lineup, new songs. We were about to take six months off to plan a new tour, but I could hear in his voice that it wasn't negotiable. I had one last question:

"Can we keep your riff? I really like that song."

(Left to right:) Lauren, Phil, Ev, Justin, me, Jesse, Kellen
924 Gilman (Berkeley, CA) 2017

(Left to right:) Justin, Kellen
Photo credit: G's Phrames
Cafe Colonial (Sacramento, CA) 2017

Cafe Colonial (Sacramento, CA) 2017

(Left to right:) Justin, me, Kellen
Photo credit: Kai Weybright
Take 92 (Eugene, OR) 2016

Rare Form 2 (2017)

Lineup: Sammy Warm Hands & Ogar Burl, dubldragon., N.I.C.

Best show: Berkeley, CA

Worst show: Denver, CO

Record store find: AFRO & Marco Polo – *AFRO Polo*

A week and a half later, I was back on the road. Doug took the train to his parents' house in Eugene, and I picked him up in the morning. On our way out of town, we stopped at the vet.

My 12 year-old cat, Devo, had been underweight for a few weeks, and Ang had scheduled a checkup. I walked in right as the nurse finished up and sent for the doctor. The vet is scary for pets, so Devo was relieved to see me. We had a very rare connection, that I cannot adequately describe. He was most comfortable in my arms, so I scooped him up while we waited.

We did our best to calm him while the doctor assessed his condition. It seemed that his appetite was normal, but he was four pounds underweight. They ran some blood tests and said that it would be a few days before we knew any more. I kissed my kitty and my lady, and hopped back into the van.

The tour started in Fremont—we ditched the van at Chad's. I had warmed up to the RV a bit. It's nice having a bed, and the fridge allowed me to store juice and milk for cereal. Gradient was unavailable during the school year, so we looked for a replacement. I had just produced the new Cerebral Coretext (of The Architex) album, *Polarities*, but he also had a newborn.

Danny had produced a new record as well; for a member of the Lobetrotters Collective, N.I.C. (Notha Instant Classic). I knew him as Nic, but the guys called him Class.

Doug and I weren't fazed by Fremont, knowing the barflies would make way for the rap crowd eventually. The bartender greeted me by name, which is always nice, and I recognized quite a few people from the last show.

The only problem that time was *me*. I was still infatuated with DFS, having tapped into such primal emotions on that tour. A solo tour *might* have challenged me enough, but a duo tour is so much less demanding that I just couldn't *feel* it onstage.

I found myself half-assing the verses, making stupid voices, and sauntering across the stage with indifference. I was on the road, supporting the best rap album of my life, and I just didn't care. I felt bad for Doug, but I couldn't get into it.

I was surprised in L.A., when *SQUALOR* outsold *Rare Form* at the table. It was the first of many times, which only affirmed my disenchantment.

The best part was a surprise visit from Gradient. He was in town for the weekend, working with a rapper called The Jokerr. It was cool to see another tourmate for a while. He joined us for "Amateur Hour" at the end of the show.

We stayed with Ill2lectual again, and Thomas tagged along. We ordered some pizzas, which I very cautiously accepted,* and

---

*I tripled my probiotics that day. Diarrhea crisis averted!

hung out in the studio. There was a lot of pot smoking, so I spent my time on the patio by the fire.

After a while, I noticed that Thomas was nowhere to be found. I checked the studio, the patio, the living room—even outside to see if his car was still there. I asked around, but no one had seen him. A few minutes later, he appeared in the hallway, completely soaked. Evidently the guys had gotten him so stoned that he wandered off and took a shower without asking.

Thomas couldn't drive in that condition, so he tried to sleep it off. He was so hilariously sprawled out in the living room that we just slept in the RV. He was gone before I woke up.

Devo wasn't doing well at home. Ang said that he had gone to the studio and wouldn't leave my chair. He hadn't eaten in four days; the night before I left. Ang found sores in his mouth, which surely made him less willing to try.

Then the vet diagnosed him with kidney disease. He said that it was severe, but not hopeless. "A human—or another animal," he said, "would've died from this already." Cats are more resilient.

He recommended daily fluid injections and anti-nausea medicine. Ang took him in for his first round, and it seemed to bring back his personality. They gave her the syringes and everything needed to do it at home. She was scared, and I wasn't there to help,* but my parents had been through it before. They came over every night while to administer his fluids while I was gone. It was a huge relief that they were able to help.

---

*Aside from comforting him, I would've been zero help with the injections. I don't fuck with needles!

After last time in Flagstaff,* we booked a different venue. At least they knew that we were coming. Sort of. We were informed that our sets had to be finished by 10:00, because it was karaoke night.

We performed to the backs of people's heads, who were happier at the bar than in front of the stage. Even worse, those people had the *time of their lives* when karaoke started. Danny sang one before we left, and I felt bad. We had made a reference to "Hotel California" that day, so he chose the song as an in-joke. But he underestimated the key of the song, because his typically strong voice couldn't keep up. It seemed nothing could save our spirits that night.

One fun thing was playing the Anal Game (not what you're thinking). Doug's girlfriend Kelly Rae told us about a driving game where you look for RVs and campers. They all have visual names, so when you add the word "anal," it's pretty funny. For example, Chad drove an Anal Four Winds. Perfect! Who doesn't love a good fart joke?

The following is a record of our *entire* game, compiled from texts and group messages with Doug and Kelly Rae. I'll provide photographic evidence at the end of this chapter.

Anal Cougar
Anal Swinger
Anal Fun Time
Anal Vista
Anal Big Horn
Anal Cruiser
Anal Catalina

*The coffee shop gig that never happened

Anal Windsport
Anal Minnie Winnie
Anal Leisure Craft
Anal Sundancer
Anal Hurricane
Anal Zinger
Anal Eagle
Anal Tracker
Anal Cyclone
Anal Komfort
Anal Intruder
Anal Momentum
Anal Ace
Anal Rage'n
Anal Weekend Warrior
Anal Supreme
Anal Wolf Pup
Anal Wild Wood (courtesy of Ill2lectual)
Anal Born Free
Anal Residency
Anal Chateau
Anal Ellipse...
Anal Cardinal
Anal Kate the Great
Anal Renegade
Anal Lazy Daze
Anal Triumph
Anal Fun Runner
Anal Wanderer
Anal Reflection
Anal Imagine
Anal Fiesta

Anal Brave
Anal Swinger
Anal Nomad
Anal Adventurer
Anal Jackpot
Anal Air Stream
Anal Advantage
Anal Challenger
Anal Infinity
Anal Holiday Rambler
Anal Open Range
Anal Beaver
Anal Cruise Master
Anal Unity
Anal Sportsman
Anal Residency
Anal Designer
Anal Solitude
Anal View
Anal Attitude
Anal Bigfoot
Anal Phantom
Anal Viewfinder
Anal Next Level
Anal Lifestyle
Anal Shockwave
Anal Workforce
Anal Spree
Anal Savvy
Anal Silver Fox
Anal Surveyor
Anal Tail-gator

Anal Pulse
Anal Fun Finder X

Some of these are so fucking funny that we suspect the manufacturers are in on it. At least somebody in their marketing department must be. I mean, Anal Intruder?! Come on. Why else would a family camping vehicle be called the Intruder?

When I sent that pic to Kelly Rae, she said "Sweet holy Jesus. FUCK YES!" I declared myself the winner of the game.

It was only a couple hours to The Juggernaut. Doug was ready to skate, while I tried out some DFS riffs on a P-Bass.

Chad approached me with caution, so I knew it was bad news: somehow, Ernie just *forgot*. It was the first date confirmed, so we probably set it up around Halloween. By February, it had completely slipped his mind.

Ernie offered to let us play, but there was no point. We walked to the only open restaurant—a ridiculous sports bar with celebrity autographs on the walls—and stuffed our sad faces. Doug denied a beer, because Oregon IDs use a sticker for address changes and it looks super illegitimate. Doug usually cheered me up, but we were all down that night. A pattern was forming.

Burt's Tiki Lounge had closed, so we tried a new spot in Albuquerque. When we arrived, it seemed really... out of the way. There wasn't another business in sight.

Inside, there was a flyer next to ours for a big metal band called Darkest Hour. I considered that maybe I had rushed to judgement.

I hadn't. The only person who came was Omen20012's grandma. Expectedly, she left after his set. We played the whole show for each other and walked away with a $10 bill.

During dubldragon.'s set, I came across a green room behind the stage. Doug was already there. We began to commiserate and then he dropped a bombshell:
"After this tour, I'm out."

Things were so shitty that I didn't blame him. He went from being a spectator at shows to doing five tours in a row. He went from freestyling in the basement to writing and recording two albums—not to mention all the videos and extra bullshit that came with it.

Doug was also in a serious relationship, missing both Valentine's Day and their *first* anniversary on the road. Was it necessary? Were the shows even worth it? At least *The World Has No Eyedea* was justifiable, given the reason behind it, and the sold-out crowds on top of that.

I accepted his decision. All that I planned for *Rare Form* was right on schedule. We did the Northwest/Midwest tour in the summer, and the Southwest leg was in progress. Five music videos were released along the way. We gave it a real push. It was over.

We stopped in Roswell, NM for Egg McMuffins. I called Ang and Devo had gotten worse. His sores were protruding from his mouth, and he was so weak that he pissed himself in lieu of leaving my chair.

The fluids were only temporary relief. He was suffering. On past tours, I had FaceTime conversations with Devo.* *Now he*

---

*Yes, my cat talks.

can barely speak. I stepped outside and called the vet. The last time we spoke, he said that Devo would live long enough to see my return. I no longer felt that it would be kind to wait.

The vet shared my concern. I took a long, deep breath and asked if we should make an appointment to put him down. It was Thursday. We scheduled the deed for 11:30am on Saturday—less than 48 hours away. I lost my composure and thanked him for his help. I crumbled.

I called Ang and told her about the appointment. She knew it was time. I walked into the RV to see Doug and Chad.

"I have to leave," I said. "I'm going home. Can you hold it down while I'm gone?" Without hesitation, Doug assured me there was *nothing* to worry about. All he would need is my laptop, and it was out of my hair.

My next thought was *how the fuck am I gonna get home?* I usually don't have any money, given how much it costs to release multiple albums each year, and I lose wages while I'm on tour.* It's pretty typical that I hit the road with $100 to my name and live off merch money.

Unfortunately, I had burned through all that money and was down to my credit card. Our shows had underperformed every night. I decided to ask for help.

It was going to cost a couple hundred each way, and the vet bills were already piling up. I created a *GoFundMe* account and posted a link on Facebook. There was a picture of me and Devo, titled *Devo's Goodbye Fund.*

It was a devastating thing to write, so I took a nap on the drive. I woke up to go to the bathroom and the guys were like "have you looked at the numbers?!" Still groggy, I reached for my phone. People had already donated more than $300! My first

---

*I never had paid time off

flight was already paid for. It was a warm feeling, knowing that my friends and family cared so much.

My emotions were all over the place, so I went back to sleep. It was going to be a long night. The next time I woke up, it was over $500. We were at a truck stop McDonald's when my mom called. She said that Rise Against and Thrice were touring together, asking if I wanted to go. I thought it was cool that my whole family wanted to see two of my favorite bands, but my finances were obviously in a bad state. After tour, she gave me tickets to cheer me up. Everyone wanted to help.

We drove from Albuquerque to the Austin airport. It was so fucking weird leaving the tour but they were very supportive. It was sometime after 4am. My flight was at 7:30.

11 hours later, two time zones away, I arrived in Portland. Ang and my brother and my parents were all at work. Luckly, Evan worked half days on Friday, and agreed to drive me home.

I was really glad to see him. I had been crying alone on the plane. He helped me decompress from the stress of it all. I was already low after those horrible shows. It only made me more vulnerable when everything came crashing down.

When we got there, Ev came in to say goodbye. Devo and Louie (our dog) had been with us since the beginning of Take 92, so Evan had spent nearly a decade with those boys in his lap.

Devo looked sickly and frail. His mouth was so swollen that it made him drool. Ang had thrown out the chair after he peed on it, but he still refused to leave the studio. She scooped him up and I held him in my arms, like I had a thousand times before. I sat down on the couch and wrapped us up in blankets.

Evan was petting him, in my arms, and saying his goodbyes. It was unbelievably sweet and I was grateful to have such an amazing friend. I started crying so hard that I couldn't even say anything when he left. Tears are welling up as I write this today.

My parents came over that night, for one last round of fluids. Finally, I could see the light in his eyes again. He purred and purred, even talking a little. Most cats meow for food, but he was remarkably smart. We talked all the time. The proof is on my voicemail. He's even on a few of my albums.

We didn't leave the couch for 12 hours. He stayed in my arms all day and night. We had our time together. My parents said their goodbyes and I thanked them for making him comfortable; and everything they did for Ang while I was gone.

Ang got up for work around 8am. I wasn't sleeping well in an upright position, so I figured I'd just stay up. I had cereal and watched my favorite movie, *Batman*. I held Devo in my arms the entire time.

Ang got home a couple hours later and we all spent some time together. I tried to show Louie that his brother was very sick, but he's not as intuitive as Devo.

Nothing going on up there...

Steve gave us a ride to the vet. I thought I'd be fine, having been to several funerals and deathbeds in recent years, but I couldn't have been more wrong. I let Ang hold the kitty for a while, 'cause I had been hogging him since I got home. I thanked the doctor for guiding us in my absence. He made it as easy as something so difficult could be.

The doctor said there would be two shots: one to relax him, and one to stop his heart. I held him and rubbed my face on the top of his head, like I had every day of his life. I told him he was going to get a shot, but that he'd feel better soon. I kissed his head.

The first shot made him wince and howl and I felt terrible. He calmed down after a few seconds. I kept petting him and talking to him. The doctor left the room for a minute and soon Devo's face was frozen. I didn't know the first shot was going to make him unconscious. I felt robbed of our final moments.

The doctor wouldn't allow me to hold him during the last shot. It had to be precise. We gently laid him on a towel and I held his paw 'til the end. When the doctor said "he's gone," my strength went with him. All those walls crumbled, and I collapsed in a sobbing heap on the floor. I clung to Ang's leg like a child. I couldn't be there for her. It was too much. My boy was gone.

The house felt empty with the three of us. The puppy didn't seem to notice anything was different, but every now and then he'd sniff the places where Devo used to sleep.

Ang and I took the weekend to comfort each other and regroup. The *GoFundMe* had raised an astonishing $1,460. We had enough for both flights, the vet bills, and then some. We used the remainder to order a painting of Devo, from a site called *Pop Your Pup*. I hung the canvas by my nightstand—where he often slept—with his ashes, and a mold of his paw.

On Monday morning, Ang had dozens of texts and missed calls from her family. Her grandpa died.

She woke me crying and we rushed to her grandma's house, where the family had already gathered. It was weird being there without Gene's friendly presence. Even as his memory faded, he always remembered me and asked about my travels.

In a way, we were lucky I was even *there* when we got the news. We couldn't believe the timing. Two devastating blows in two days. We spent the rest of the day in bed.

I left Tuesday morning, on Valentine's Day. It was surreal. Nothing felt right about leaving, but that's what I promised the guys—and all the donors. *The show must go on.*

When the RV pulled up to the terminal, my friends cheered: *yay, Sam's here!* They were really happy to see me; even more than I expected. I was starving after two flights, so we stopped at a Chipotle on the way to town. Ang was having the same thing in Eugene. I felt connected to her. I needed to be. I brought Devo's collar and wore it like a bracelet. It made me feel close to home.

I asked how the shows had been.

Silence.

Austin was ok, but they had Saturday off and found out *that day* that Denton was cancelled. The promoter fucked us over. Needless to say, our spirits were low. On top of that, the septic tank was leaking. It smelled like piss in the parking lot. Doug said the guys kept using it after it was full, which caused the leak. Then they started pissing in bottles. Doug, like me, was already unhappy with the Walmart parking lot routine. That crossed the line.

On the first *Rare Form* tour, we hit a couple RV parks and dumped the sewage for a very small fee. But when I returned, they were content leaving a pee trail from Texas to Colorado. Doug tried to stop them, but his pleas were ignored.

It irritated me that Doug wasn't respected as the headliner, or even as an equal, in my absence. "This shit needs to stop," I said. "If you guys keep this up, I'll leave again and take him with me."

There seemed to be some weight to my return, because the guys responded immediately. It wasn't who they were. But the tour was a disappointment, we were losing money, and I left them behind. They had given up. It was time to get the tour back to normal.

When we got to Denver, I walked straight to the back and set up our merch table. Les One walked in and gave me a hug. He also brought a gift.

Les had asked Ang for a picture of Devo, so he could paint us together. I was speechless. It was so thoughtful, and to receive it the first moment of my first show back... that was touching.

The good times didn't last long. As Chad and Danny unpacked, we got more bad news: the show was double booked. The best part? It was ANOTHER FUCKING KARAOKE NIGHT! All I could do was laugh. *I should've stayed at home.*

Instead of playing before or after the karaoke acts, we were mixed in. We each had three songs, in between people who just rolled in off the street to sing George Jones. It was humiliating.

When Class was onstage, Doug witnessed one of the regulars complain to the host that "he's already done *three songs*," as if he was singing too many karaoke tracks. They were completely oblivious.

Chad was fighting an uphill battle at the door, because *karaoke night is free!* Our poster was hanging at the door, so at least he could point to the cover charge, but most people ignored him and the host would let them in without paying. *Great.*

I've expressed my desire to add more connecting cities between major markets... but I would've rather played a third karaoke night than a weed store. If you're a rapper, I don't expect you to understand my point of view. I grew up hardly seeing my dad, who was a drug addict and an alcoholic. My mom and Steve raised me, and their support made me the person I am today. My mom had an absentee, alcoholic father as well. Steve had spent earlier years as a drug addict and alcoholic, and went through treatment to get clean. They both understood what my dad was going through and guided me through it. So from an early age, I've had a complete disgust for drugs and alcohol.

Even the RV—not being my vehicle (my rules)—was uncomfortable. Chad and Doug were either vaping or rolling joints the whole time. I fucking hate being at bars every night, but alcohol goes straight into your body and not mine. Weed is so aromatic that even when it's not being smoked, I'm breathing it in. Most smokers don't even realize it because they're so used to the smell. I can't escape it.

For most of my life, close friends would hide that side of themselves. Sometimes they'd unknowingly wear the stench in their clothes, but I didn't have to watch them light up the bong right in front of me. Little by little, my travels exposed to more of that culture. Strangers don't know me or give a fuck about my preferences. So I leave the room a lot.

I agreed to play the "cannabis club" on the condition that I would only enter the building at the time of my set, and I would leave immediately after. Additionally, we modified the set so that I had fewer songs. I brought my inhaler, in case the smoke affected my asthma. It did. I hated every moment; from waiting in the cold, dark RV for three hours, to the smoke-filled room* that we performed in. I wouldn't make that mistake again.

We booked Twin Falls on a Friday. Eddy fed us a fancy meal at the Brickhouse, and offered his sincerest sympathies.

"Most people don't know what you're going through," he said. "But they've never had that special relationship with a pet. I've been there, man." That was nice. Maybe I misjudged him the first time. He struck me as a genuinely compassionate person.

*Ironically, my *Freewrites* EP (2014) was written over a Graves 33 project called *Smoke Filled Rooms.*

As promised, the club was packed for Friday night. Unfortunately, it was packed for dancing. People were dressed to impress—even the bartenders were showing skin. *This must be what it's like "in the club."*

We were *again* relegated to three-song sets in between DJs. People were generally receptive to us. I filmed Class playing for the massive crowd. There were go-go dancers on both sides of the room. One was awkwardly placed on our VIP-booth-turned-merch-table.

Eddy introduced us and got the crowd cheering. It felt like they were placating us, but a lot of people came over to us after the set. I shook so many hands on the way to our booth that didn't even notice I lost Devo's collar.

A few minutes later, I panicked and started searching. I only walked about 25 feet from the stage to the merch table, so I used my phone's flashlight to search the area. It wasn't there.

Doug helped me look behind the DJ booth. The dance floor was so packed that I thought it must've been kicked around. It was another hour before last call, and I covered every inch of that place when it cleared out. When the house lights came on, Eddy asked what I was doing. He in the staff to help. I was embarrassed for causing such a scene. My tourmates and the bar staff scoured the area, but we left empty-handed.

The next day, I noticed the dubldragon. merch box next to mine. I had gone through every crack in those VIP couches and dug through my own bins, but never theirs. I reached in and found it immediately. I felt like an idiot, but it was also a huge relief. I wrapped the quick-release collar with tape so it wouldn't come off again. Today it's wrapped around his urn.

The last show was at 924 Gilman. It was amazing to have played there three times that year, but the turnouts weren't improving. That said, it was fun until one of the other acts got their window smashed and a bunch of equipment stolen. A fitting end to a shitty trip.

One month later, we played two shows in Austin, TX. It was the third annual Crushkill Recordings showcase at SXSW. It was nice to make up for our shit tour with an encore. At least then we'd part ways on a high note.

First, there was a screening of *The World Has No Eyedea*. We met up with Tytuus, the latest Crushkill artist, and Kathy took us to the theater. The guys wanted to see it (for the first time), so I tagged along.

Kathy hosted a Q&A for a modest audience. It had sold out the previous time, but it seemed people were preoccupied at the festival. We performed at the afterparty, along with Ecid, Les One, and Slop Musket.

That night, Kathy made enchiladas and the whole crew ate together. We wound up on the patio for much of the night, where many great rap debates have taken place. In this particular case, Tytuus was name-dropping modern day "mumble" rappers, arguing that they deserved our respect alongside Golden Era greats. He was single-handedly defending that position against every rapper in the house. That's when I turned from spectator to lecturer.

I'm overly passionate about music. It often puts me in the position of defending artists that I admire. That time, it set me on the offensive. I ran through a laundry list of reasons why the merits of the Golden Age obliterate the current trends. Sample laws have crippled creativity, so people use the same cookie-cutter drums time and again.

By the time we were discussing beats, it was 4am. I thanked him for being a good sport and went to bed. But my mind was racing, and I never fell asleep. An hour later, the guys trickled in to go to sleep. The conversation had been running through my head, so I got up and finished the debate in my Captain America pajamas.

The problem with "trap" drums, to me, is that they lack musicality. It feels robotic; more of a regression than an evolution. The chosen drum machines are often staples of hip hop, like the Roland TR-808. But if you listen to "Run's House" (Run DMC) or "She's Crafty" (Beastie Boys), you'll hear that those samplers were actually *played* like a drummer.

There was more nuance and funk in 1987 beats than there are today. How is that possible? Because even when those producers weren't sampling classic drum breaks, they aspired to *feel* like those great drummers. On my *kids these days* soapbox, I said *that's the difference* when I say new rap beats aren't musical. They laughed at me for having formed this argument in my sleep, and we all went to bed for real.

The next day, we had our annual brunch at the world-famous Franklin Barbecue, complete with Brady's traditional ass-handing of *Goldeneye.* *

The showcase was no longer on Sixth Street, but at Stomping Grounds North. Coincidentally, it was the same venue that the *Rare Form* tour had appeared without me. It was like a make up show.

Carnage joined us that night, and Michelle made a rare

---

*We used to play it at Doug's in the 90's, and now I enjoy losing to both of them.

appearance onstage as well. The whole bill was on fire, in a little room with a couch instead of a dance floor. During Ecid's set, the girl next to me fell asleep. Michelle took some pictures of us and she woke up for a split second. Then her head found itself on the shoulder of one of the Slop Musket wives. She was *out of it.*

Kathy wanted the show to end with an all-star cypher. I still don't freestyle, but if it's in honor of Micheal, then I'll make an exception. *Kathy gets what she wants.* Slop Musket jammed and we all took turns on the mic. Eventually, Carnage started cranking up the tempo and doing some crazy shit. No stranger to a cypher, Ogar took the other mic and kept up until it was just the two of them, trading *insanely* fast bars. It was one of the best freestyles I'd ever seen. I was proud of him for coming so far on that journey with me; seeing him become a seasoned veteran. It was a great time to say goodbye.

Devo Kittyman
2004-2017

(Left to right:) me, Doug
Photo credit: Chad Porras
The Green Room (Flagstaff, AZ) 2017

(Left to right:) me, Chad
Motel 6 (Unknown) 2015

(Left to right:) Doug, me
Photo credit: E. Ville
Downtown (Hood River, OR) 2016

Blank Check (2017)

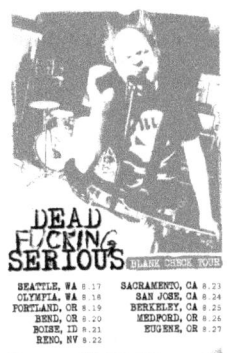

Lineup: Dead Fucking Serious

Best show: Reno, NV

Worst show: San Jose, CA

Record store find: Tony Sly – *12 Song Program*, Much The Same – *Survive*, Illogic – *Unforeseen Shadows*

In the following months, I started writing again. Kellen and I made 13 new demos, and I also started a follow up to *Vacant Eyes*. Durazzo had gone into retirement again, so I collected beats from friends, and made quite a few of my own.

It was a conscious decision to *not* write a solo album until I absolutely needed to. *Rare Form* was a new level of songwriting, but I didn't want to crank out the same kind of album. I needed time to grow. And by spring of 2017, there were so many ideas in my head that I couldn't wait any longer.

At the same time, DFS was looking for a new "live" bassist. We had accepted our fate as a two-piece, but couldn't tour without a third member. There was some interest, but nothing solid—and then it dawned on me: the answer was right in front of us the whole time.

Crozz hadn't played punk in an eternity, but his reaction to *SQUALOR* made me think that he'd come around. Sure enough, he said yes without hesitation. We played one local show to get comfortable, and there was instant chemistry. Our friends ICED kicked it off, and it was their singer Elle's 20th birthday. I joked that she was the same age as my guitar.

We didn't just do it for practice. All of our promo materials featured Justin instead of Crosby. We needed footage from the show to make a music video for "Blank Check." After one more show (in Olympia),* we set up another tour for August.

A few days before we left, there was a white pride march in Charlottesville, VA. It was a shit potpourri of human garbage; from run-of-the-mill Trump supporters to card-carrying neo-Nazis. One person was killed when a car rammed a crowd of anti-racist protestors. A VICE documentary publicized the group who organized the event, armed to the teeth, and their intentions weren't exactly open to interpretation. They were fucking Nazis. They were fucking Klansmen. It was for real.

The event was called *Unite the Right*, so naturally, many people on the Right defended it. I couldn't understand how literal white supremacists were becoming politicized—no one would dare align with them in my lifetime—but somehow, the flag-waving Republicans forgot about their grandparents; the ones who fought *against* the Nazis the first time.

It was a national debate at the time. Seriously. It was unbelievable that there was so much evidence and yet we were unable to come together and say *nope!* That should've been some post-9/11 unity shit. *What's that? Nazis are back? Fuck that!* And then the NRA motherfuckers mobilize in their American flag diesel trucks and send the Enemy retreating back to their mothers' basements. Right?

*I only mentioned the Olympia show because it was the only time I've ever seen someone smash a watermelon in a circle pit.

Well none of that happened and we were pissed the fuck off. People were *so* pissed off that the Nazi on the VICE documentary asked police protection because he feared for his life. It occurred just days after his cocksure remark that "people die every day" and "a whole lot more are gonna die before we're done."

When I sat down to collect my thoughts on the matter, I wrote 72 bars in one sitting. It was the longest song I'd ever written, covering American racism from the Civil War to the *Unite the Right* march. But I wasn't satisfied. It was the night before tour, and my eyelids were heavy. I didn't even record a demo. It could wait.

When we got to Seattle, one of the local bands commended my *Nazi Punks Fuck Off!* shirt. It was a good time for a punk tour. We could blow off some steam onstage and in the pit. We could heal together.

But when that band hit the stage, I became skeptical of their politics. The singer was in full army fatigues and military garb. He mentioned the neo-Nazis, but we couldn't fully understand his comment over the guitars. Jori was there and we both looked at each other like *what did he just say?*

By the end of the set, it was abundantly clear that they were on our side. I had a good talk with the singer and got the feeling he was an Iraq or Afghanistan veteran. It turned out that he was. He agreed with my point about our grandparents' generation. He said that the Alt-Right was disrespecting his fellow servicemen by flying the Nazi flag beside the Stars and Stripes. As a staunch pacifist, I had never felt so connected to a soldier as I did that night. We probably disagreed on a million other things, but our respect for history—and disdain for, you know, pure evil—brought us together.

DFS was gloriously pissed that night. We updated the setlist with two new songs,* and Kellen started doing backup vocals in Justin's absence. For anyone who had seen us in January, *Blank Check* stood on its own. Eric and Jori said that it was the best set they'd seen from me *in any genre*. We spent the rest of the night at their house, laughing and playing Nintendo.

McCoy's was the coolest venue in Olympia,** but they made us push back the show while the barflies watched a football game. *Cool.*

Yesterday's Enemas sounded like early Nirvana (*Incesticide*). We were super into it. I didn't even know they were from Kurt Cobain's hometown (Aberdeen, WA). We played our hearts out, but most of the fans were outside until the next local band. It was our third Olympia show that year, but I guess we weren't catching on. *Fuck 'em.*

I thanked the promoter when we settled up. "No, thank *you*," he said, emphatically. "These punk shows are doing *so much* better than the rap shows lately!"

For the whole first week, we were fighting tourist traffic. There was a historic eclipse, and people had come from around the world to find the best view: Oregon. The Interstate was completely stop-and-go during the day, so we drove by night.

We found ourselves at a Les Schwab Tire Center (Portland) and I'm glad we did. The inner seams of my front tires were cracked and leaking badly. They almost split apart. The mechanic was adamant that we replaced them before leaving.

*One of which was about losing Justin: *one step forward / two steps back.*
**Strangely, most of the music venues in Olympia are on the same block of 4th avenue.

Unsurprisingly, I didn't have $270 to make it happen. I had to borrow the money from my parents. I felt terrible, but it was the only way to ensure we didn't break down the next day.

As usual, Portland was fucked up. By the time we found out our promoter had flaked, the venue had already filled the date. Doug and I had played a great place called the Ash Street Saloon. Lucky for us, their booker remembered me!

Ash Street was a great room and great lineup. Tons of old friends attended—it was probably our biggest show of the tour. From the stage, I saw members Streetlight Cardiacs, Compact 56, True Form, and even DFS (Chris)! Crozz made a point to mention that Compact had booked* our first punk show in 2001. It meant a lot that they still had our backs.

Our next show was canceled, too—the booker had a family emergency—but we had a place to stay with our friend Ryan Kojan. Bend was in the heart of Eclipse Fever, claiming the *best view* in Oregon. With all those night drives, we joked about renaming it the *Totality* tour, since everyone was talking about the "path to totality."** There were hundreds of people in tents on the side of the highway. Fields were filled—as far as the eye could see—with campers and their cars.

Instead of enjoying our day off, we headed straight to Boise. The eclipse was the next morning, so everyone would be headed *in* to Bend while we were headed *out*. It was a pretty good bet.

Most drivers say that a long, straight drive is less interesting than one with turns and scenery. I completely disagree. I like to set the cruise control, put on a good album, and relax. Small

---

*EPD, our first band

**Meaning visibility of the total eclipse, as opposed to places where it would be seen as a partial eclipse.

highways often have little towns that pop up and lower the speed limit. In no time at all, it'll go from 60 to 30mph. Eastern Oregon is full of those roads. Halfway to Boise, I slowed to 40 and then sped up again without realizing it. I didn't even notice until I saw the flashing lights behind me.

The cop looked at the Take 92 Music van, my purple hair, Kellen's beard and flannel, and Crozz—who actually had his headphones on, making a beat on his Macbook. It was clear that he believed who we were, but I was like 20 miles over the limit. The ticket was unavoidable.

We stayed with Kellen's aunt in Vale, OR. It was a tiny, country town like you'd see in old western movies. Not a single restaurant was open, so we bought some Cup Noodles at a gas station.

The house was too quiet to sleep. I downloaded a white noise app to drown the ringing in my ears. The sun woke me up in the morning. But when I closed my eyes, the sunlight faded away. *Wait, what?* I opened my eyes and it was nearly dark outside. I looked at my phone and it was 10:30am. *This must be the eclipse.*

Kellen and his aunt were in the yard outside my window. I figured we should beat the traffic while everyone else was staring at the sun. I stumbled out there and asked, "can I use your shower?" I glanced up for a quick second and headed back inside. I laughed at myself in the shower, likening it to Beavis and Butt-head at the Grand Canyon or the Hoover Dam:

"Is this a god-dam?"

The Shredder was another casualty of the eclipse. Both the opening band *and* the sound guy were stuck in tourist traffic. Justin, the owner, didn't seem confident that we could even *have* a show. He scrolled through Facebook and came across four hardcore bands, playing a house show in Nampa. It was 30 minutes away, and 30 minutes to showtime. Justin messaged the promoter and got us on the bill.

Rose House was named after the dog who lived there. We pulled up as the first band was starting. Ayla, the booker, thought we were coming *the next day*, but she was cool enough to let us stay. The order of the show remained the same, but we could play afterward if people could stay. We did our best to spread the word throughout the night.

Worm Nest and State of Suffering, were right up our alley; fast, hardcore punk. The room was packed so tightly that we had to watch from the kitchen. The touring band, Impalers, were heavier, east coast hardcore. They put on an awesome show. We were lucky that the Shredder show got cancelled.

We brought in our equipment before Impalers even finished tearing down. Most everyone had seen us selling merch, but we didn't take any chances. That crowd was so fucking cool. They stayed all the way to the end and made us feel like we were the band they came to see. I've never had a show moved to another venue on 30 minutes notice. We were blown away.

Reno was a house show, too. It was an early show, so we started driving as soon as we finished at Rose House. There were no hotels in Boise, so we'd have to stop on the way.

I started getting tired after three hours. Kellen checked every hotel we could find. They were still full of tourists. Keep in mind, there is fucking *nothing* in northern Nevada. It's rare to come across a *streetlight*, let alone a city. We got so desperate that I just took any exit with a hotel sign. We drove by countless NO VACANCY signs and bloated parking lots.

When we finally saw a VACANCY sign, the front desk guy said it was full. The owner wouldn't let him take down the sign. After that, we stopped at every hotel and casino we could find. No luck. Not a single fucking room. It was hopeless.

I was adamant about not sleeping in the van, but I just couldn't another three hours. We landed at a Flying J truck stop. After rearranging every fucking piece of gear in the van, we had enough space to lie down. I was disappointed, having not slept in the van since about *12 tours ago!*

It had been a long time since one of my tourmates showed *me* a cool record store, but Recycled Records blew my fucking mind. It wasn't one of those clean, fluorescent light-washed stores. It was more of a shop. Didn't look like much from the outside. But *goddamn* did they have the goods.

Kellen bought some rare European black metal CDs, and I found all kinds of shit that you just never see: indie rap CDs that my friends were featured on, underground punk bands that have been out of circulation for years... I went a little overboard with the CD shopping. I usually have an iPod in the van for long drives, but it had long since died. Recycled Records was *exactly* what I needed.

The Reno house was called Clark Lane Maul. It was a legit basement show. There was plenty of space for the band, and plenty of space for the pit. Perfect.

At bar shows, people wander around and drink, or step outside to smoke. Sometimes they'll only come to the stage when their friends are playing, and leave right afterward. *This is not a bar show.* The air was thick with August heat, so the basement cleared out after every band, but they came rushing back when the next act turned on their amps. DIY shows are so much more rewarding, just because people are *only* there for the music. Nobody's trying to pick up a one-night stand. They just want some good songs.

Though we weren't the fastest band that night, we were still the tightest. That grueling setlist really made the difference. The energy was palpable, the circle pit was on point, and we played fucking hard.

In Sacramento, we returned to Cafe Colonial. I misunderstood that when Pisscat set up the show, they were unable to play themselves. Captain Cutiepie opened the show. I recognized two of them from the crowd at our last show. Jesus & the Dinosaurs did their damn thing again. They're just an inherently interesting band to see. The drummer is a monster, and the frontman is totally unique. After watching them, I was ready to fucking play! Dead is Better was oldschool thrash metal. We don't play with a lot of metal bands, but *that* shit is right up my alley. Their guitar riffs were infectious.

We had a good set, but my voice was getting rough. The first tour was not only shorter, but we had three days off in the middle. *Blank Check* was every damn day (except Bend). We practiced the best we could for *Blank Check*—even as a two-piece—but my throat wasn't nearly in *SQUALOR* shape. I used my raspier register more often, and screamed less and less. In some cases, I thought it made the songs better.

We were flying high after three great shows in a row. We crashed with Pisscat, and I immediately noticed the *Teenage Mutant Ninja Turtles* (and *TMNT 2*) posters in the living room—plus the handbill from our last show with the puke/diarrhea drawing. We were in good company.

I don't know how I'd never been to Streetlight Records,* a behemoth independent store in San Jose, but I'm glad we stumbled upon it. Kellen and I had already spent *way* too much money, and Crozz didn't come in at all. He made beats on his laptop while we spent the last of our money inside. I picked up *Band on the Run*—which is harder to find than you'd think—and an original pressing** of *Bedtime for Democracy* by Dead Kennedys.

I had planned for *Blank Check* to take us to L.A. So many of our influences are from San Francisco and Los Angeles that it made sense to play there. But the offers in L.A. were not great, so we opted for shorter drives.

I've lost count of how many times I've played at Back Bar, but that was my first time as a rock show. They always had security guards, but I didn't expect them to to go all TSA on our shit. When they opened the doors, I had to get a full pat-down just to walk in the door. Afterward, the guy goes "oh, you've been here before." I widened my eyes and said "MANY TIMES" as I walked past. They stopped us with every trip: armloads and hand-trucks full of gear. I'm like *my face is on the fucking flyer, I'm not trying to burn the place down!*

TSA guy lectured me on where and when to move and what the other bands needed to do before and after their sets. I told him that I wasn't running the show, and that Dru would let people know what to do.

Kellen was hassled for setting up his own drum stands, and Crozz got shit when he went to use his laptop. I'm glad they watched the gear, but *we were the ones who carried it in.* After a few times, TSA guy said "you're a pretty serious guy, huh?"

"The band's called Dead Fucking Serious," I deadpanned.

When I did see Dru, he walked me to the mixer and described it like I would be engineering. I asked who was the sound guy. There wasn't one. I requested a mic stand for Kellen. He went to look for it, and never came back. After all the times we'd worked together, I wondered if I had I done something to offend him. I'm still not sure why we were treated like that.

Chad texted me to check in on the tour. When I mentioned the [missing] engineer, he said that there wasn't even a door person last time. *Red flag!* I tracked down Dru and got the same story: no door person.

I started to get really pissed. *There's two people checking anal cavities at the door—surely* one of them *could take the money!* Chad wasn't happy, either. He instantly hopped in the car (an hour away) and drove all the way down to bail us out. I couldn't believe it. He came all that way just to work the door!

I. Love. Chad.

Stay Out was a three-piece band who reminded me of early Green Day. Catchy stuff. I tried to give them a decent mix, but the reflective surfaces onstage didn't help much. (That, and most of the gear wasn't mic'd.)*

Shark Punch, had a million members on that little stage. I couldn't remember the last time I played with a ska band, so it was a welcome change of pace. They reminded me a bit of Less Than Jake. I was a fan. They were good performers, and brought a good crowd, too. There weren't enough mics for the horns, so the vocalist would hold his own mic over his shoulder between

---

*I may have mentioned in my previous book that the term *mike* is not a proper abbreviation for *microphone*. I used the apostrophe to clarify that I'm not talking about rodents.

verses. They really made the most of it. At one point, they covered The Mighty Mighty Bosstones. It didn't bother me that it was their biggest radio hit, because again, I can't tell you the last time we even played with a ska band. Bosstones covers are rare. I was into it. We were all into it.

Since no one was running the show, there wasn't an official schedule or anything. But I could swear they were pushing 40 minutes already. As the out of town band, we needed to get onstage before people went home.

One song later, they thanked the crowd and started packing up. It was clearly their crowd, and fans called for an encore. That's always a good feeling, but as the middle band, *you don't fucking do an encore.*

So, of course they went for it.

It wasn't a 40 second DFS song. They played "Killing in the Name" by Rage Against the Machine. Having performed that song myself, I knew it was more than five minutes long. *Goddamn it.* But they did bring the energy even higher, and more aggressive than the ska tunes.

Maybe it was a better segue after all.

It's common to trade niceties with the other bands when you cross paths. Many times it's genuine; other times, it's just polite. When I don't have anything nice to say, I'll just say thanks for being part of the show. That's from the heart. Sometimes I'll comment on a particular song or band member that stood out. That night, I complimented their music *and* their ill-timed encore, and remarked that it was a smart song choice, given that we were up next.

Everyone seemed super cool, but the room was fucking *empty* when we started. I think there were two people left, plus two members of Stay Out, and Dru at the end of the bar. That's it.

We played anyway. After a few minutes, the bassist of Shark Punch came in to watch the rest of our set. It was disheartening that the show was going so well, but no one even wanted to hear out of town band was any good or not. They just came to see their friends, and bail.

To my surprise, the nicer security guard bought a *SQUALOR* CD and a shirt. He said it had been years since he bought a band's stuff on the clock, but we blew him away. We actually sold a few things that night. It just goes to show why I always play my heart out, no matter how pointless it feels.

Fat Wreck Chords (records) is home to many of my favorite punk bands, like NOFX, Good Riddance, and No Use For a Name. I can comfortably say that Fat changed my life. NOFX was the first punk band I ever heard, and I was hooked from the opening bassline of "Hobophobic."

I say that because Fat was holding an open house in San Francisco. I found out by chance, Googling when the next Fat pop-up store would be. We were in Berkeley, just a few minutes away. Being a huge fan of Fat and NOFX, I slipped a DFS CD in my pocket. *Maybe Fat Mike will be there. Who knows...*

I grabbed my guitar while we waited for them to open. Crozz and Kellen took a walk while I worked on some new riffs. Kellen came back gave me some ideas for the arrangement. When the song was finished, there were a few people in line.

Inside, it was an enormous warehouse. The staff led us to a bedroom-sized "record store" with shirts, vinyl, CDs, and stickers.

I have a shitload of Fat CDs, but I was hoping to find something from the late Tony Sly (of No Use For a Name). His solo albums are pretty hard to find, and I didn't even see any at Fat. I asked the woman working if they had any, and she brought some out from the back. That was cool. *Mission accomplished.* I added some stickers to my beater guitar, too.

We didn't meet anyone from NOFX, but I was elated to reconnect with Tony Sly's music (whose last No Use album was out in 2008). I told a couple people to come see us at Gilman, and we hit the road. It was Friday rush hour, but I thought it was worth it.

We ended up playing with Pisscat after all. Everybody wants to play Gilman, so Chad offered it as a trade for Sacramento. Jake broke a string almost right away. I quickly tuned up my own guitar and handed it to him the next time they stopped.

I restrung his guitar—on top of our merch table—in record time. When the song was over, I handed it back to Jake, tuned up and ready to go. Betsy Streeter, one of the Fat Lizzy moms, even made a cartoon about it after the show.

It was also cool to watch Fat Lizzy with Crozz, adding to the nostalgic vibe. All in all, I think it was my favorite Gilman show.

But wasn't our last stop.

I popped in a Tony Sly CD. The songs were so vulnerable and sad that I started crying at the wheel. It caught me by surprise. I remembered sharing "funeral songs" in the van, just a day earlier. Crozz had some great Sam Cooke tracks that I had never heard. I played him my own funeral pick, "The Curtain Falls" by Bobby Darin. As we passed the aux cord, I cued up "There Will Never Be Another You" by Frank Sinatra... the 1940's version that I had used for my grandma's funeral in January. My eyes welled up instantaneously. That was the end of the game. We drove in silence for the last few miles.

24 hours later, it was still just under the surface. When we stopped for gas, I gave Crozz a big hug. I don't run from grief,

but I don't always take enough time to process, and it caught up with me.

We drove by Willows, CA and I pointed to the gas station where Crozz and I had that flat tire with Doug. We saw the Shell, the AM/PM across the street, and the Motel 6 where Crozz made the beat for "Break The Mold."

A while later, we passed a semi at 70mph. Without warning, the accelerator failed. The dash lights came on. It was just like *The World Has No Eyedea* tour. We were fucked.

Since we were in the passing lane, I pulled into the center median. It wasn't the safest place, but still safer than coasting across the right lane. It was 104-degrees and there wasn't a tow truck nearby. Clothes were coming off as we dumped water on our heads. It was nearly the end of tour, so we barely had any water left at all. I nursed the remains of a fountain drink and chewed the ice. It was unbearable.

Once again, we broke down on a weekend and nobody was open. A Highway Patrolman was giving the tow truck driver a hard time. He said to drop us at a truck stop, where they have a mechanic on duty. Well that mechanic only works on semis, so we were screwed. I told Chad to notify The Bamboo Room in Medford. We would be very late, to say the least.

Neither State Farm or I could find an open shop. The tow truck driver called in a favor, and eventually dropped us off at California Transmissions in Redding, CA. The shop was closed, but the owner, Frank, was still hard at work. He promised to look at it as soon as he got caught up.

I told Chad to cancel the show. Aside from my emergency flight in Austin, I can't think of another time that I cancelled a show of my own volition. It wasn't a good feeling. We lost the guarantee *and* the free meal that night. Plus, we had to pay for a room. The tour earning, but that was a major blow. We were going to lose money after all.

We had practically sweat *gallons* on the side of the road, so the first thing I did was jump in the pool at Motel 6. I probably hadn't done that since middle school. The shade from the building made it bearable enough. I floated and swam laps for about a half hour. Paired with a shower, it was good stress relief.

We walked to a nearby Denny's, where I became jealous of Kellen's bottomless pancakes. He snuck a couple onto my plate and I regretted my entire order. I don't even remember what it was.

Frank never called. Crozz showed us a series called *Hot Ones,* where the host interviews celebrities over a plate of hot wings. The twist is that each wing is progressively hotter, so it always ends with a lot of sweat and cursing. In that regard, it wasn't that different from *our* day.

We woke up early, calling both the shop and Frank's cell, to no avail. It was Sunday morning, so there wasn't much I could do. He did us a favor by even taking it. We refused to cancel our homecoming show, so I ordered a rental car online. The only problem was that our gear was still in the van. If we couldn't reach Frank, we would have to borrow every single piece of equipment for the show... and we wouldn't have anything to sell!

Waiting for the cab was tense. I didn't know if we'd be able to get our stuff or not. On top of that, I called my boss and told him that I wouldn't be back to work on Tuesday. If the van was fixed in a day, I'd still have to come all the way back to get it. Even if it *wasn't* fixed, I had to return the rental car on Monday.

After 45 minutes in the sun, I got a call from Frank. He diagnosed the problem, but couldn't get the parts until Monday. Fortunately, he was willing to stay until we got the rental car.

I had never rented a car before. I paid for everything online, so I figured I'd sign a couple forms and get the car. Unbeknownst to me, they required a deposit: $107. The employee said that I wouldn't be charged; she just needed a card. None of my cards had any money on them, but I gave it to her anyway. *Declined.* Hertz needed to *hold* the funds; they just wouldn't *take* anything unless I fucked up the car. I pulled the gas fund out of my pocket —$500 in cash. Nope, no cash deposits. *Fuck!*

Finally, Crozz stepped up and handed over his card. It was embarassing, but I was out of options. She swiped the card and asked him to sign the receipt... for $325.

I asked how the fuck that could be, since she just said $107 to my face. Evidently, there were other fees that I was expected to know. She must've communicated telepathically. The price of my favor just tripled. Crozz reluctantly signed and we were on our way.

I had only heard of a Toyota Yaris because Hannibal Buress made fun of it on a Mike Eagle song. It was the cheapest car on the lot, but it could practically fit in the back of my van. We could only take the absolute *essentials*.

Frank said there were two ways to fix the van: replace the fuel pump, or replace the whole assembly. It was $300 for the pump alone, so we took the cheaper option. There were no guarantees that it would take.

The van was on a lift, so Kellen climbed into it. He handed down our luggage from the side door. I climbed into the back and pulled the guitars, drumsticks, and cables. Amps had to stay.

We toured with Kellen's drums, so my DW kit was waiting at home. Steve offered to use his truck, and we borrowed some amps from The Dimly Lit.

It was the most uncomfortable drive of my life. The Yaris was unbelievably cramped, and didn't have cruise control. On top of that, we drove straight through a cloud of smoke the whole time. Hundreds of wildfires had formed in the dry August heat, and though we first saw it in northern California, it was even worse in Oregon.

The air was dense, like winter fog in summertime. I breathed through my shirt to filter the ash. The sun was bright red, like a Tatooine sunset.

Between waiting for the cab, getting fucked over at Hertz, picking up the gear from Frank, and driving to another state, we only had a few minutes to stop by my house for the drums. I pet Louie and Tucker (our new cat) before quickly loading the drums into Steve's truck. I also grabbed the Dual Rectifier—my signature amp head—which was still at home because of a ground hum. All we had to borrow was a speaker cabinet and bass amp. Not too bad, given the circumstances.

They say laughter is the best medicine, but DFS is pretty fucking good, too. There's nothing like a good hometown show. We played a cathartic, fiery set. The past 24 hours were so stressful that screaming my heart out was transcendent. Not to mention, we had *all* suffered through it together. Crozz had only signed on for one tour, so we didn't know if it would ever happen again. It might've been our last hurrah....

After the set, I sold quite a few things at the table. We actually sold out of *SQUALOR* CDs! It was the last day of our last tour* and we did it. It was almost the highest earning show of the tour! It couldn't have come at a better time.

Crozz and I relate on a level that most people do not. We're connected by 25 years of friendship. We're connected by an unshakable drive to create. We're connected by hardship, both shared and individually. We celebrate together; we grieve together. He's a true friend.

That night, I felt a tremendous sense of gratitude. Crozz put in months of work to rehearse songs that he didn't even write. He's a brilliant producer and songwriter, but DFS wasn't his baby. He jumped at the chance to bring *my* songs to life.

What a gesture.

I told him that the punk tours had awakened something in me. It filled a void that I *thought* had been filled by hip hop. It wasn't. The *SQUALOR* tour was magical because it reminded me of that. But *Blank Check* was more significant. I've been chasing this dream since childhood. I want to make music, and tour every place on the map. But I never imagined doing it alone. The band *was* the dream. And though our first band didn't make it, we were on the road again. The dream felt real with Crozz by my side. *That* is what I pictured when we were kids.

"No," he said. "Thank *you* for taking me!" Maybe it awakened something in him, too. We shared a good hug and parted ways. The next day would require me to be well-rested.

After a few hours in my own bed, it was time to hit the road. I didn't even know if the fuel pump had been ordered, but the Yaris was due back in Redding. (If I dropped it off after hours, it would've been charged to Crosby's card.)

As I waited for Frank, I plugged in my phone and scrolled through Facebook. Danny G was on tour with his other band,

Full Moon Freakz... and they were headed for Redding. I texted him to see if we could meet up for dinner.

Frank had worked through the weekend and still gave me a good deal. The cheaper, pump-only repair worked after all. $350 felt like a lot of money, but it could've been much worse.

The van felt like home. I cranked up a rap record and pushed the subs. After 600 miles in the Yaris, it felt surprisingly clunky, but I was back in my comfort zone.

I met Full Moon Freakz at Denny's. It was the same Denny's from Saturday night. That time I got the pancakes. Having just driven six hours alone, it was great to break bread with Danny and his crew.

I'm a confident driver, but alone, there was no one to talk to and keep me awake. Six hours might not seem like a lot, but round trip was 12 hours in a day; and *18 hours* since the day before.

I texted Doug. I texted Evan. I wanted someone to tell me to get a room and sleep it off. I took my sweet ass time leaving the parking lot, hoping that my phone would vibrate.

It didn't.

I arrived in smoky Eugene around 2am. I was too tired to unload the equipment from tour. The nightmare was over.

(Left to right:) Crozz, Kellen, me
Photo credit: P Chill
Cafe Colonial (Sacramento, CA) 2017

(Left to right:) Danny, me
Denny's (Redding, CA) 2017

(Left to right:) Jori, Eric, me, Crozz, Kellen
Heartwise Recordings (Seattle, WA) 2017

Les Schwab Tire Center (Portland, OR) 2017

Fall Children (2017)

Lineup: Sammy Warm Hands, Lisa Vazquez, Gradient

Best show: Hood River, OR

Worst show: Iowa City, IA

Record store find: Various Artists – *All the Breaks* (sample pack)

After *The World Has No Eyedea* tour, there was supposed to be a midwest leg in the fall. The second tour amounted to only two dates in South Dakota. It was way too far to drive for free, so I decided to book a solo tour on the way.

I reached out to Pat Jensen, who had painted the *Rare Form* cover, and hired him to illustrate an homage to AFI's *All Hallows* EP. He loved the idea, but it was only a week away from his wedding. I told him not to worry about it, that family is more important than a flyer.

The first track on *All Hallows* is "Fall Children." Being October, I wanted to call it the *Fall Children* tour. The original art (by Alan Forbes) featured a scarecrow and a smattering of Jack-O-Lanterns. I wanted to be the scarecrow.

Pat was so inspired by the original art that he started sending me sketches that night. Wedding planning be damned. He was in.*

*The final version was signed *Pat Jensen, with apologies to Alan Forbes.*

The World Has No Eyedea tour had been in September. I had less than a month to secure enough shows to pay for the trip, there and back. Chad started immediately, while I started looking for a tourmate.

Doug already committed to the *Rare Form* winter tour, so I looked elsewhere. At the top of my list was Lisa Vazquez, a friend and former coworker from Portland. She was enthusiastic, but eventually declined. The late notice turned out to be a huge problem. It wasn't like I could call people and they'd say yes or no, right on the spot. Most had to check with their employers. Over two or three weeks, I spoke with The Bad Tenants, Cerebral Coretext, KI Design, ThatKidCry, and Les One. Not one of them was able to leave that soon.

Chad secured a couple of dates, but it just wasn't enough. I backed out of the South Dakota premieres and we cancelled the solo dates. The *Fall Children* tour was dead on arrival.

The following year, I told Chad that we needed to make *Fall Children* a reality. With four months of preparation, we'd have plenty of time to get it right. The flyer was already done and paid for. *Let's do this!*

I wanted to start looking at home: first, I reached out to Lisa Vazquez. She wanted me to produce her solo debut. Perfect timing. I hadn't featured hometown tour support since *Bears Repeating.**

Cerebral released his *Polarities* (2017) album in May, but he had his first child in the midst of post-production. I also produced *Move On* (2017) for Ebb One. He was excited, but couldn't get the time off.

*Streetlight Cardiacs excluded,—I'm referring to rap tours!

Then I considered a person who had been previously off-limits: Gradient. Our first tour together was weird, being in the RV and having so many people on the roster. It put me in a bad mood from the start, and it left him without any way to contribute offstage. I always wanted to make up for it with a *van* tour.

Thomas agreed right away. He had just graduated college and bought a Toyota Prius, which is incredibly gas-efficient. He suggested taking his car instead of the van. Being consistently impoverished by my career, I strongly considered his offer.

It wouldn't be comfortable, and I would not be the one in control... I also don't like driving other people's vehicles, so I'd leave that up to him. Lisa owned a Prius herself, but didn't think it would be comfortable for three weeks of travel. We agreed to keep an open mind, but it wasn't likely.

It was my first solo tour since *The World Has No Eyedea*. I incorporated some *Arcane Amalgam* songs, but they were only fragments without Sarx and Carnage. I had also finished a singer-songwriter album called *Daydream*.

It wasn't that much of a departure; I'd been performing one acoustic song, "Hay Fever," since the very first tour. But a headlining solo set is much more taxing than an opening set. I had to carefully pick the acoustic songs, not just to fit the show, but to make sure I could sing them without comfortably.

On top of that, I finished the Hayden tribute, "Other Desert Cities," and the anti-Nazi song, "Wildfire." I had nearly finished a double album that summer, and wanted to lead with some fresh material. After *Blank Check*, I spent an entire month learning four new rap songs, two *Daydream* songs, and two more from *Arcane Amalgam*. I loaded it with familiar tracks like "Famous Last Words" and "Heart and Soul," so my fans would get what they paid for. But I was confident that the new set was special; above and beyond what preceded it.

Though the tour was supporting *Daydream*, I was especially proud of "Wildfire." I finished it the day after my Yaris adventure in Redding. We talked a lot about white supremacy on *Blank Check*, and I discussed the song with Chad when we stayed at his house. It just needed time to marinate.

When we got back, Gabe had the perfect beat, and I added another 50 lines to what was already my longest song ever. After a thorough revision,* I recorded it, and filmed it with a tripod.

That song was a tremendous accomplishment. It reminded me of *Inglorious Basterds*, when Brad Pitt says "I think this just might be my masterpiece."

But like many artists, I wasn't so sure about that. It could've been amazing, or it could've been a self-indulgent rant that overstayed its welcome.

I sent it to Doug and Chad, who had both praised "God Paparazzi" as a long-form takedown of organized religion. The consensus was positive. We couldn't say if it was *better*, but Chad said it was "on that level, *at least*." I just had to memorize 128 lines and hope my lungs could keep up.

The promotion was strong for *Fall Children*. I knew that people weren't as interested in *Daydream* as much as my rap and punk. I wanted to make sure people knew that it was a rap tour.

I premiered new songs—from both genres—five weeks in a row. I switched formats every week to keep it interesting: rock/rap, audio/video, animation/live, studio/on-location, personal/political, you name it.

*I always maintain that the rewrite is the most important part of the process: write it, *rewrite* it, record it, learn it, play it onstage, and record it again with nuance.

Since *Daydream* was my most radio-friendly music, I promoted it outside of my usual demographic. Both newspapers ignored my inquiries, but Skip's Records (AKA CD World) booked me for an in-store, and local TV personality Rick Dancer interviewed me on his popular web series. I answered questions, sang "Unconditional,"* and rapped "Lesions" at the end.

Sadly, all the promotion in the world couldn't help us. We booked a small metal bar called the Black Forest. I played there once every couple years and they always paid well. It's small enough that almost *any* crowd feels like a full house.

Just not our crowd, apparently.

An underwhelming release show is hard to swallow. I was proud of myself for performing "Wildfire" without any mistakes, but in the back of my mind, thought *what's the fucking point?* The impact of my accomplishment was neutered.

On top of that, the well-intentioned sound guy didn't know what he was doing. The subs weren't even *on* for Gradient. The "engineer" shrugged his shoulders, so I checked to see if the sub was plugged in (yes), turned on (yes), and turned up (yes).

When I checked the other sub, it was off. The power switch was engaged, but the power cable was duct taped in place. I grabbed some Gorilla Tape from the merch box and taped that fucker back in place. *Presto.* I told him they should get it serviced, and he said "yeah, we'll probably just leave it."

Cool.

Gradient's set featured a cameo from our friend Brian Steveson, and one from me as well. Our song "Can't Wait" is so old that I'm credited as "Sammy Warm Hands of The ILLusionists." By the grace of Joe Pesci, I remembered it at the last second and we pulled it off. It was actually a fun song, injecting some follow-your-dreams optimism into the tour.

Lisa was flying by the seat of her pants. We had abandoned the plan to record together when the songs weren't ready. We settled on mixing and mastering, but she still wasn't finished when I got home from *Blank Check*. With time in short supply, she self-produced the whole project. Her CDs arrived the day we left!

After the show, I talked with Lisa and Thomas about what to expect on the road. We had enough guarantees to cover all the gas, so all the merch money could go toward food and anything else we wanted to do. Me and Lisa weren't feeling the Prius, but Thomas was adamant that we try it. We packed all of our stuff inside and it just *barely* fit. When I opened the van doors to compare, it was a no-brainer. The van won. Sorry, Thomas!

Lisa skipped the in-store to get ready for tour. My goal was to catch anyone who didn't stay up late enough for the bar. At our age, my friends have kids and jobs that make them less likely to come out to see me at midnight.

CD World had featured us on their 5,000 person mailing list, and there were posters all over the store, but I couldn't shake the letdown from the night before.

There wasn't a great place for our merch, so I drove to Walmart and bought a six-foot folding table.* I slapped two Crushkill stickers on top, so I wouldn't leave it somewhere by mistake.

We played for a dozen people *at best*. Numbers aside, I was grateful to see aunts and uncles and cousins who aren't as familiar with my music. I modified the set, favoring the heartfelt songs instead of the "hits." My uncle Larry bought a book and a CD. It was the only thing I sold at both shows.

*Something I should've bought in 2011.

I didn't want to spend like I had on *Blank Check*, so I brought along plenty of music. Thomas picked the newest Metallica CD, *Hardwired to Self-Destruct*. Being my favorite band, I was excited for him to hear it.

We picked up Lisa in Portland. I knew there was trouble when the first thing she said was "can we listen to something other than Metallica?"

I fucking love hip hop, but punk rock* is the soundtrack to my life. When I'm listening to four or five rappers a night, I need something else for a while. I've never really had a tourmate object to a driver's choice of music. I requested *one* album on both RV tours. It wasn't up to me.

As a control freak, I was insulted. As a Metallica fan, I still wanted to hear the rest of it.

"Sure," I said. "Right after this album."

I knew Lisa for many years before and we'd never butted heads. Next it was the heat. I can drive 12 hours a day with the AC on, but I'm useless with the heat. My eyelids close in a hurry. I started driving without a sweatshirt to level the playing field.

When that masterpiece of an album was finished, we had 45 minutes left. My tourmates were under the impression that it was up for grabs, and started the "pass the aux cord" thing. I won't say that Doug or Terrell never *asked* to play something, but it was our first drive and I was already losing control.

I realize how crazy it sounds, but I hope you understand how out of character it is for me to travel, be social, be around alcohol, and everything that comes with the territory. My routine is my safety net: I'm behind the wheel, I'm listening to something that will keep me engaged on the drive, and I'm bringing my friends along for the ride. That's my perspective.

*and its neighboring genres

I think I have a psychological issue, whether it's OCD or being on "the spectrum."* If you take my parking spot at work (like the delivery guy on Thursdays), it can ruin my whole day. If someone staples two pages together, in a way that is misaligned, I have to stop myself from removing the staple and redoing it when no one is looking. If I miss a turn or get lost, I get a spike of anger so intense that I can't describe it. I count ice cubes. I have facial tics. I set the TV volume to specific numbers (16 is ok, but never 17; 21, but never 22).

Most of these outbursts don't happen at home, because I'm within my comfort zone. I'm far more susceptible in the real world. I don't go to your house; you come to my house. I don't ride with you; you ride with me.

I shed some layers** and turned on the heat for a minute here and there. Lisa put on J Dilla, who is one of the most influential rap producers of all time. But it was an instrumental album, which I also avoid while driving. I'm naturally drawn to vocals. If there's nothing to do but nod my head, it will lull me to sleep. That's basically what I said at the time, and it spiraled into *how can a hip hop head not like J Dilla?*

"Look," I said. "I'll listen to the shit while I'm cleaning the house. I'll listen to it driving around town. But I probably won't listen to it on a road trip."

I was on edge. Never before—on 14 other tours—did I have such a contentious relationship in the van. It felt like everything I did was being questioned, and I *really* don't like being told what to do.

*Retarded
**I always prefer wearing a hoodie and hat, sometimes with a second coat, because I feel insulated from the world. The crazy hair is just a Plan B to keep you at a distance.

At The Underground Music Station, we played Mario in the green room. It was nice just to hang out.

The three of us had enough range—from Gradient's self-aware Harry Potter raps, to Lisa's soul-infused relationship stories, to my confessional raps and acoustic interludes—that we had more diverse shows than usual.

The opener, Jenny Jahlee, was a folk singer. It was a welcome change of pace. Jenny's voice melted my heart. And then I realized the song was about weed. *Damn.* It's a testament to anyone's drug/booze/party track if I love it regardless. She was great.

Gradient's set was stronger each day. I really enjoyed his music every night. The crowd was both smaller than before, and sort of uninterested. Lisa started to wake them up. Her songs were still new, so she looked down at the MPC a lot. But it was lightyears ahead of her old set.

When I started, there were fewer people than before, and they were 15ft from the stage. It was my third time at UMS, but I didn't have Open Mike Eagle or Nocando. It was all on me.

I began every set by saying "my name is Sammy Warm Hands and I represent Crushkill Recordings." When the beat started, I said "if you're feeling this shit, I want to see your faces up here. Let's have some fun."

"Hands Down" was a new opener, with a slower flow. There are a lot of punchlines, and ample time to digest each one. "Heart and Soul" begins with a rapid-fire chorus, but the verses continue that *economy of words* style. I could see that people were listening carefully.

By "Famous Last Words," we were all in it together. Then it hit me. Between the participation and the eye contact and the general *focus* of the room, I realized that it was *my* crowd. After playing a handful of shows in Hood River, I was actually building a following.*

It put me at ease. My stress faded away. My obsession with turnout went away. People told me where they remembered me from, or what album they bought last time. The show almost didn't happen (due to security fees and alchohol licenses), so I was really glad that it did.

We stayed at Lisa's house in Portland. We made up in the morning. I explained that I'm used to guiding the ship, and that it keeps me sane.

"If I don't respond," I said, "it means that I'm biting my tongue." Lisa had been under a lot of stress herself, and we *both* relaxed when we left the house.

I'd always wanted to play at Kelly's Olympian. I had seen Ceschi and Ecid play there before, and most importantly, it was where Micheal introduced me and Gabe to Kristoff and Sadistik. It was the last time we ever saw him.

Each time I return, I meditate on what a great night that was. I remember standing on the sidewalk, when he hopped out of the van and gave us each a big hug. He introduced us eagerly and called us his friends. It felt so good to be included like that. Micheal played some acoustic songs in the audience that night, so I played one of mine down there as well.

Here's to the memories.

Kelly's is a popular bar with an adjoining concert hallIt's just the right size for underground shows. You can make 25 people feel like 50, and that's exactly what we did.

*Boise and Denver, take notes!

Ogar Burl opened the show, and he was phenomenal. His artistic growth is really unparalleled. I said to his brother Chris that there wouldn't be a better opener on the whole tour.* He commanded the stage with ease. I was proud of him.

It was great to see new and old friends having a good time together. Justin Britton (of 800 Octane) was there.** Octane had shared stages with EPD, Outreach, This Day's End, and DFS. We really looked up to them.

I decided to promote the tour on Facebook Live. I had never livestreamed a show, but that Rick Dancer interview must've planted a seed. The funny part was that my phone fell down several times, and Doug kept putting it back.

I noticed that the acoustic songs only had about 80% of people's attention. That isn't too bad, but when I'm singing softly, 20% is pretty disruptive. I talked to Doug about my perceived 80/20 ratio, and he had noticed the same thing. I cut my acoustic songs down to just two. *Give the people what they came for.*

I planned a lot of NW shows to make up for those long drives in Montana and Wyoming. So we returned to the bowling alley. I had just played there with Kristoff and Kill the Vultures.*** It was a little too soon, but I remembered a great restaurant around the corner.

The first two shows were home turf for me and Thomas, sleeping in our own beds and basically living separate. The second two shows were near Lisa, staying at her place. It was nice to break bread out of state like a real tour.

*There wasn't

**Shout out to Dave Chaney, their singer, who came to see me at The Hawthorne Theatre as well.

***Check out my interview with Crescent Moon on the Take 92 Podcast. We recorded it at the show.

Thomas devoured his pho—likely his favorite thing on Earth—and went back to the venue to catch the openers.* Lisa grabbed a to-go box and left as well. My little bonding fantasy wasn't going to happen yet.

I finished the meal in solitude and texted Ang at home. Nothing seemed right; not the booking, not the turnouts, and not the chemistry. Something was *off*.

Eric and Jori put us up for the night (in Seattle), which is always a good time. I love seeing people's faces when they look around the studio for the first time. Thomas—much like Kellen—focused on the Nintendo games, whereas Lisa was drawn to the keyboards. Eric let me play his late father's Fender Jazz Bass, which was a great honor. RIP Pierre Munch, you wonderful man.

The next day, I went to a teriyaki spot alone. Nobody wanted to go, but I couldn't risk playing on an empty stomach. I texted Thomas, a self-proclaimed Juggalo,** with a photo of their soda selection. It was nothing but Faygo root beer.

Your loss.

I sat in the parking lot and vented to Ang on FaceTime. I was baffled by the tour's dysfunction. Even simple things seemed difficult. I already wanted to go home.

The van smelled like weed. Lisa's house had absorbed the scent of her trimming business. I worried that it affected the luggage as well.

---

*I always watch every single act, even standing up front for *at least* one song. It's hard on my feet and my ears, but it's worth it to support my fellow artists. But I was going to enjoy my one meal that day.

**Insane Clown Posse has a *religious* following. They're called Juggalos, and for some reason, they love Faygo.

I savored my moment alone, enjoying *New Maps of Hell* without anyone asking me to turn it off. No one had complained since Metallica, but I was feeling paranoid. Ang and I shared a laugh over that. She said "I wouldn't be friends with someone who turns off Bad Religion!"

Our Seattle show was at a tiny biker bar in Tukwila. AlterEgoz was already there, enjoying what looked like a good-ass burger. I was glad to see him because he designed the *Daydream* album cover, and I got to show him the final product.

It started with a live band called First Hill. Their emcee, Deadmics, was particularly impressive. Apparently they all had other projects and First Hill was a new collaboration. I'd definitely check them out again if given the chance.

The stage was miniscule, with a low ceiling beam that almost took out Thomas a few times. AlterEgoz grabbed a seat right up front, and Eric and Jori showed up just as Gradient was getting started. He played well, but nothing could get the room's attention...

Until Lisa.

From the moment she fired up the MPC—creating live beats in front of the audience—people took notice. The beats on her *Gravity* EP are amazing; people just can't stay still. They left their stools and approached the stage. As she started singing, they hung on every word. The narrow space in front of her was about as full as it could be.

Thomas brought his camera—a Canon 5D Mark III—replacing Danny as our tour photographer. The Tukwila pics looked great, and from then on, he would edit them daily from the van.

I started my set immediately, to keep the momentum. As people gave her props, they slowly made their way back to their stools (or left altogether). Lisa won that night, for sure.

Eric and Jori were kind took us out for dinner. They're seriously the best friends a guy could ask for. We went to an all-night diner and shared more laughs than any other time on that tour. Eric's monster breakfast burrito looked so good that I don't remember what I even ordered.

Our check came at 2am, as the restaurant was flooded with hipsters. Around then, about a dozen firetrucks came screaming by. The van was surrounded with emergency vehicles. There was an apartment fire and everything was barricaded. Luckily, we were able to follow a firetruck on its way out.*

Lisa booked a last minute date in Spokane, WA. It filled our day off *and* gave me a new contact! Her friend Jaeda invited us over, playing a Beastie Boys mix and sharing stories about all the cool shows she'd hosted. We were definitely in the right place.

When the talk turned to smoking, that was my cue to go call home. In the back lot, I noticed a rusted behemoth that looked like the guts of a piano. Jaeda called it a dominion. I strummed the thick row of coiled steel, and it made a cacophonous sound. When I plucked the higher strings, it sounded like a John Carpenter film score. I pulled a guitar pick from my wallet and recorded a couple strums on my iPhone.**

My sampling session was cut short when Thomas staged an impromptu photoshoot. I was distracted and uncooperative,*** but he did a great job despite me.

*I forgot to check the news to see if anyone was harmed.
**I re-recorded it with my laptop interface and the sample appeared on "Milo," *Fighting Words (2020).*
***You can tell when you see the photos

The Red Room held a rap weekly with a house band, sort of like *Return of the Cypher* (San Francisco).* Brotha Nature was a great opener, mixing live beats and freestyles into his written songs with ease. His backstage harmonica beatbox was so funky that I couldn't help but rap some verses over it.

The venue was nice, but *really* big. Most people watched from their tables, or the bar. We did our best to reach them, even if their reciprocity wasn't evident from the stage. A guy pointed to my Carnage The Executioner shirt during "Lesions." He asked if it was my name, "because you are *executing* the fuck out of this stage right now!"

I hadn't edited the beat drops for "Wildfire." I was far too busy memorizing the lyrics before tour. The sound guy took it upon himself to *repeatedly* mute the track without warning. It almost fucked me up because I thought the PA malfunctioned!

We definitely ended on a high note. When my set concluded, the band resumed and we all joined them for a couple verses. Thomas even played guitar in the band! I was so glad we went to Spokane instead of a night off in Montana.

That night, sleep was paramount. Billings was eight hours away, which is nine hours of *actual travel*. What I didn't account for was the time zone—we actually had to leave *10 hours* early. Chad double checked with the promoter, and our load-in time was 7pm. Get up at 8am and out the door by 9. *Fuck.*

I was dreading it, but at least I got a shower and a room to myself at Jaeda's. Just when I toweled off, Thomas knocked on the bathroom door.

"Hey, man," he said, sheepishly. "I accidentally left my camera at the venue. They're holding it for me. I'm really sorry."

By then, I was mentally prepared to be pissed off the next day. It wasn't his fault, and my chance for a good night's sleep was already fucked. I traded my Captain America pajamas for jeans, and we headed outside.

Thomas was very apologetic. I know I can be cold when I'm angry, so I told him about when KI left his insulin in Arcata: *this might be annoying, but it won't add four hours to the drive!*

I'm a late sleeper. But, when it comes to tour, I put in the extra effort. It's important to be professional with venues and promoters. With apologies to my tourmates, some are better at this than others.

Chad and Danny often needed an assist from me or Doug. Terrell has a tendency to hop in the shower five or ten minutes before checkout time. Lisa* had a similar habit, so I texted everyone just to be safe: *see you in the van at 9.* The last thing I wanted to do was play Tour Dad** while I was half asleep.

The next morning, I brushed my teeth. I got dressed and put my stuff in the van. I ate a muffin. Waiting alone, I expressed my resentment with a lighthearted text: *now boarding flight Take 92 to Billings...*

It was my 18th anniversary with Ang, and I wanted to listen to something nostalgic. Thomas had *Pet Sounds* on his iPod. Then I put on *Act IV* by The Dear Hunter, which is one hell of a good album. Perhaps more importantly, it's 74 minutes long. Since I was bringing CDs, I chose double albums and anything with an excessively long run time. This led to *The White Album*, for example.

*I'm not picking on you, I swear!
**That's what Chad and Danny call me
***I bought the album a couple months later. I'm actually listening to it now.

I was unfamiliar with Lisa's favorite albums, aside from radio and television. I asked her to recommend some Stevie Wonder. She started with selections from *Songs in the Key of Life*, and then we listened to *Innervisions*.* I was blown away by the musicianship—especially his drumming, which was *unbelievably* funky!

It was good for a long drive. Lisa moved to the front while Thomas slept in the back. We talked about looking forward to Denver. A bunch of her family lived in the area, and some were going to visit from out of town. We had booked a new venue from the owner of Quixote's (*Rare Form*). It looked like a big show all around.

I asked if Lisa would be interested in listening to my new demos. I had enough new material for a double album. The first disc was upbeat, hard-rhyming tracks. With few exceptions, most of the introspective, storytelling songs were on the second disc. That half was slower and still needed a lot of work.

Lisa responded positively to the new tracks, and I was particularly proud that she liked the beats that I made myself. When it was finished, she "really liked it," before adding "especially the first disc." That gave me a push in the right direction: disconnect from my ego and scrap the double album concept. *Maybe it just needs more time...*

The Coffee Tavern was more of a cafe than a tavern, but I knew we could make it work. Lisa and Thomas walked to the door and it was locked. Immediately beside door were three-foot letters that said *24 HOURS*. There was another entrance around the corner. An older man was drinking coffee inside. That door was locked, too.

"The boss," he said, "will be right back."

*I bought it at CD World after the tour

It was a literal Mom and Pop shop, and neither of them was expecting us. I was especially pissed, given that I woke up at 8am and drove through one of the largest states in the U.S.

I knew that our contact was a third-party promoter named Anthony Harbolt. The owner bristled at the sound of his name. Apparently he had done it before.

Chad tried to reach Anthony, who was "on the way there." When Chad implied that we were onto him, the texts stopped coming. We got bamboozled, frens.

I went inside and spoke with the owner. It wasn't that he didn't know who we were. Their text conversations revealed that, for months, the venue was asking for promotional materials from Anthony. Chad had booked our show at the same time as Fake Four's Dope KNife, but Dope KNife cancelled. *Our* show was not cancelled. *I* knew that, *Anthony* knew that, and the *venue* knew that. It was all in the texts. The very last message requested flyers from Anthony "if" the show was still happening.

There was no response.

I don't blame the venue for making an assumption. The owners served us free coffee and tea, and even showed me around their mixing console, in case we still wanted to play.*

I kept my friend Jessica informed throughout. She had been our only spectator on the *Rare Form* stop, and she wanted to see a *real* show. Sadly, that wasn't going to happen.

We waited around for two hours and Anthony never showed. He had even *signed a contract* to pay us a guarantee! Chad told him he was blacklisted from every DTR artist, including Blueprint and Illogic. Still, no repsonse.

---

*Well, that, and the owner made a big deal about how he's toured with rock stars before and that we would "go a lot farther in the business without all the curse words." It just wasn't a good fit.

After a long, disappointing day, we relaxed with Jessica and her homemade tacos. When everyone went downstairs, I chatted with her husband, Adam, in the kitchen. We shared stories about lives, and our wives—joking that we had both "married up."*

Lisa and Thomas were going to watch *Magic Mike*, so I wasn't in any hurry to get down there. After enough laughter, I went down to see what was on, and it was Donald Glover's standup. Jessica came down around the same time and we all fucking loved it. We needed a night off more than we needed a wack show.

When I woke in the morning, Jessica had waffles waiting for us. She's so kind. I pointed out her life-size skeleton that was on display for Halloween. We brought him outside to the van, posing in the driver's seat. I took a photo to commemorate our 10-hour drive from the previous day.

The only bad thing about our relaxing night off was the timing. We had two scheduled days off. Thomas worked at the Hilton in Eugene, so he was able to get an employee discount anywhere in the country. It was super handy in North Dakota, getting a suite for the price of a Motel 6.

Thomas brought a foam bed for himself. Nocturnal habits, he said, did not make for good bedfellows. Sure enough, we were dozing off to *Family Guy* at 2:30am, while Thomas was suiting up to play *Pokemon Go* in the bitter cold. I cautioned him to be safe, walking a strange city at night with headphones on, and hoped that our friend would return safely.

When I awoke to pee, around 6am, he hadn't returned. It was slightly disconcerting, but I knew better than to worry.

*I didn't know it at the time, but it was the last time I would see Adam alive. He was a truly sweet man, and I'm grateful for his hospitality. RIP Adam Pelatt

It was crazy driving from Washington to Minnesota without a single show in between,* but we hadn't planned it that way. We got to stay with Brady again (and his soon-to-be-wife, Danae). Their dog Oliver hates my guts, but their cat Charlie is my friend. Brady shared his wealth of hip hop with Lisa and Thomas, who happily pillaged his collection. We caught up on life, and I showed him a new demo called "Tailspin." It was among my first attempts at rapping over my *own* beat** and its three verses were different than anything I'd written before.

Brady was encouraging, calling it surprisingly fresh. He said that my lyrics were often vulnerable, but rarely so full of regret. We discussed my plans for a double album, which was still an exciting prospect.

Brady's always been supportive, even when my projects *aren't* for Crushkill, like *SQUALOR*. When I told him that I'd be taking time off to focus on a punk album, he asked if they could put it out for me. It was probably their first rock release since Micheal's band Carbon Carousel.

When I was in high school, 2Pac was dead and the Beastie Boys were on hiatus. Rhymesayers was the label putting out Atmosphere and E&A, plus other Minneapolis artists like Brother Ali and POS. As far as I was concerned, hip hop had moved from the coasts. Hip hop lived in Minnesota.

MN was incredible on *I Quit*. Since then, it's been a mixed bag... far more raisins than M&Ms. In 2015, I flew out to the Soundset festival and played a show while I was in town. We put together a good bill on Friday, the official Soundset pre-show on Saturday, so nobody gave a fuck about my little "pre-show."

I played for like four people.

---

*Had I known in the beginning, we would've canceled the Midwest dates.
**Aside from "Slubberdegullion" on *Rare Form*

Later that year, Kathy booked a celebration of life for Micheal, five years after his passing. It was a sold-out crowd of 1,500 die-hard fans. The bill was jam-packed with Abilities, Carnage, Blueprint, Sadistik, and more. (Kathy flew me out for the all-star cypher at the end.) Because of Eyedea, I was playing the biggest show of my life, standing onstage with Murs and Brother Ali. I will *never* forget that moment.

Tons of people came up to me after the cypher, saying how much they liked my verse. I hoped that between that, and my annual appearances at the Crushkill booth (Soundset), that those people would show up to my future shows.

Spoiler alert: They did not.

In 2017, our usual contact (CMJ) was unavailable. Eventually, we booked a small venue called The Viking Bar.* When we arrived, the marquee said *HAPPY HOUR* instead of our names. There weren't any flyers, either. Inside, a single bartender cared for two or three customers. I went to the bathroom and noticed flyers for *other* shows. *Fuck.* I approached the bartender and, as expected, he didn't know there was a show.

We set up a merch table and the sound woman arrived. At least *somebody* knew there was a show that night! I asked when the door person would arrive, and they looked at me like I asked when the blow jobs would start. There *was* no door person.

Tired of surprises, I texted Chad. We were both too experienced for those rookie mistakes. Something had to change.

After soundcheck, I realized that our opener, Kat Fox, wasn't there. I texted Chad again. I was getting pissed. I wondered how it was possible to run the door and the merch table at the same time. Thomas' girlfriend Lillie was there, and they agreed to

---

*I did not realize this was a sports reference until now.

cover the door while I worked the merch table.

There were food advertisements on the wall, so I asked the bartender for a menu. He said the kitchen was closed. I walked next door for some Chinese takeout. While I waited for my food, my phone rang with an unfamiliar number. It was Kat Fox.

Kat was upset with Chad, saying that she didn't even know about the show. After talking for a couple minutes, I was able to deduce that she not only confirmed with Chad, but he sent her a completed flyer to help promote it. Then we went back and forth as to whether or not she wanted to even come. My expectations had dropped so low that I didn't even care anymore.

Luckily, Kat played a great set. I liked both the content of her songs, and the way she performed them. All bullshit aside, I was glad to meet another great Minneapolis artist. There's something in the water out there, I swear.

The only people who came through for me were Brady and Kathy. She even had friends in tow. Lisa later told me that she was embarrassed because the only thing said to Kathy was "it's a $5 cover." I *always* forget to introduce people. My bad.

The turnout could've been ok for that room, but the layout betrayed us. It was a narrow room and the stage overlooked a long, empty dance floor.* On top of that, you could throw a rock from the sidewalk and hit me on stage. It was the perfect vantage point for seeing every person who took a smoke break during my set.

Kathy and the gang went outside right after Lisa. I was going to open with "Hay Fever," but I wanted to dedicate it to her. I put away the guitar and started with "Hands Down," like usual. I figured I'd play it later, instead of a *Daydream* song. But after a minute or two, I felt overwhelmed by the void of her presence.

*Actually just a walkway between the barstools and the adjacent booths.

It reminds me of a comedy special by Greg Giraldo, where everyone was laughing but one guy, who was *sleeping* in the audience. You can't ignore it, so make it part of the show. Giraldo said "don't you think it's a weird choice to fall asleep in the third row of my big TV taping?"

I used the proximity of the stage to my advantage. The mic cable stretched long enough to get me outside, about four feet from the entrance. I rapped for everyone who was smoking on the sidewalk. The people inside couldn't see me, but it got a few laughs and everybody came back inside for the rest of the show.

The Chinese food gave me a gnarly stomachache before my last block of songs. I considered stopping right there—I had already played 30+ minutes—but "Wildfire" started before I could decide. I ended up doing the next six minutes with my butthole clenched, and ran straight offstage to blast a dook.*

Thomas packed up early, so he could get a room with Lillie. He swore that he'd be back at Brady's before I was even awake in the morning. *Fine by me.* Lisa and Kat joined me at the merch table, but I had to go to the bathroom again. Lisa texted that they were going to "walk to the Nomad around the corner [real] quick."

When I came out, the bar was fucking empty. For a Sunday night on campus, I expected the streets to be busy. I sold a few things between dumps, and the bartender closed early.

Lisa said "I'll be back in 5," so I grabbed the merch, the table, and all of my gear. I didn't know how to organize Lisa's stuff, so I stacked it all on a chair. The bartender finished cleaning and moved on to mopping the floor, so I took her merch to the stage. He kept asking me when she was coming back.

---

*My wife puts up with a lot, but she does not enjoy the phrase *blast a dook.*

15 minutes later, I had moved the van and loaded all of my stuff inside. The bartender was getting impatient. He called it unprofessional, and I couldn't really argue with that. It was my tour and the whole thing reflected poorly on us as a whole.

It was Sarx in Vegas all over again.

I told Lisa that "I'm just gonna start moving your stuff because this guy is trying to go home." I hopped onstage, unplugged all the cables, tried to discern if the power strip belonged to her or the venue, and started wrapping it up. She showed up right as I finished.

I said very little on the drive to Brady's. Eventually, we started talking about something else entirely. It was only 11pm so we decided to watch a movie.* Since Thomas was gone, we thought it'd be funny to watch his favorite movie, *8 Mile*.** Lisa and I took a picture with the box just to tease him. I figured if he was gonna go get his rocks off, he should still feel like he missed his tourmates.

We left Brady's right on time, and headed to Cherokee Park. I wanted to visit Micheal's memorial before leaving town. But to my surprise, there was a shitload of construction and we couldn't get through. I apologized for turning a brief stop into a 20 minute detour, but I wasn't going to leave without paying my respects.

It's always a mixture of emotions at Cherokee Park. I showed Lisa and Thomas where his memorial picnic table was, where Kathy had hosted many get-togethers. Then we walked to his bench, overlooking the horizon. I thought of the first tour, when it was so cold that we had to buy gloves from a convenience store on the way. I thought of Eyedea's music, and the memories attached to it. I thought of Micheal, and the person he was.

*Brady has a huge VHS collection
**I don't know if it's his #1 *favorite*, but he had suggested it several times already.

I thought of where I was when we met, and all the ways my life had changed in the meantime. It never ceases to amaze me, just much has happened since then.

On some level, I'll never be satisfied. In the moment, I'm always focused on the next goal. But every now and then, I'll step back enough to see how fortunate I really am. At those times, the gratitude is overwhelming.

Taiyamo Denku put us on at The Cactus Club in Milwaukiee, WI. The main entrance led to a small bar, and a double door led into the actual venue. It was like a hip-hop Cafe Colonial (Sacramento).

I was feeling pretty good after some $2 tacos from across the street. The Lady sent me some pictures, too. But it was Monday, and I expected another shitshow.

Fortunately, Denku was hosting. He destroyed the mic with a *monster* freestyle and then introduced the first act. The openers were unremarkable, either rapping over their own vocals, stroking their egos too much, or leaving immediately after their time was up. Even when I liked their songs, those lesser qualities lowered my estimation of them as artists.

Despite the lack of a turnout, we still sold a few things and had a warm reception. I specifically remember two guys being fixed in a trance during "Wildfire." One dude wandered in, looked at this phone the whole time, and then asked me about collabs after the set. He hadn't looked at me once, or applauded, but he wanted to work with me—right away. *Neat.*

Denku took us to a Mexican place for a post-show meal. It was some of the best food I've ever had on tour. Reminded me of my favorite place at home, Don Juan.*

*On that note, I'm gonna go to Don Juan tonight!

We got a good night's sleep, which was invaluable. We had no idea how hard the coming day would be. When I got up, Denku invited me upstairs to listen to his new collabs with Snoop Dogg and Busta Rhymes. While we were playing songs for each other, Thomas came upstairs with a fresh Gradient verse and they recorded a song right on the spot!

When we filled up for gas, I saw that my driver's side headlight was out. We drove to a mechanic across the street, and Lisa took it apart while we waited. It was one of those situations where you tell them the make and model, and they bring out something a quarter of the size. Upon *seeing* the light we needed, they sent us to two different AutoZones until we found one.

In the pouring rain, Lisa and I tag teamed that giant bulb back into place. I was glad to have her there, because I felt a bit of panic when the light went out. Thomas sensed my stress and bought me a bag of mini Kit Kats. I was relieved to be in the company of good friends.

We were behind schedule, and the rain didn't help, but Lisa showed us some great music that I'd never heard before (Nitty Scott). From the ashes of anger came relief. Thomas put on *The Slim Shady LP* and we sang along to together. It was funny because we knew all the lyrics, but were still surprised at the words coming out of our own mouths. The shock value didn't hold up as well as we'd thought. Somebody put on The Fugees to cleanse the palette.

We made it to Iowa City just in time. I hoped our second show at Gabe's would be bigger than my first. The venue's glass doors were completely covered with *giant* posters for the show. That Pat Jensen artwork was never more impressive than it was there.*

*I convinced the bar staff to let me take one home. I actually don't know where it is.

I snuck over to Teddy's Bigger Burgers next door. Thomas tagged along and we ate together. We both noticed that everyone on Facebook was talking about Eminem dissing Trump at the BET Cypher. Cell phones are obnoxious at restaurants, so we agreed to watch it that night at the hotel.

The first surprise of the night was back at Gabe's. They clearly invested in marketing, but there were NO LOCAL ACTS. That might work in places we've played a dozen times, but for our second appearance? Not smart. I consider that a mistake on both *our* end (Chad and I) as well as the venue. The barflies seemed to tolerate our intrusion, and the pool players seemed not to notice us at all. We walked away with $15. I was thoroughly embarrassed.

Feeling defeated, I *absolutely couldn't wait* to get to our room. Thomas had hooked us up at a brand-new Home 2 Suites, and it was only a five minute drive.

But the second surprise of the night came then: the accelerator stopped, just like in Redding. Lisa quickly grabbed her jump battery, which started us for a second. After that, all the dash lights were on. There was no clear shoulder, so we pushed it across the street. I knew we weren't leaving anytime soon.

I turned on my hazards and called State Farm. They used my GPS, but couldn't pinpoint our location. It was a dark, remote area without any street signs. I described a parking structure with smoke stacks and a skybridge.

It was the middle of the night, so it took *forever* just to find a tow. When State Farm finally found someone, they patched me through and I described the location. A few minutes later, they cancelled.

At that point, I walked to a vacant lot and let out a guttural scream. I was so fucking stressed. We were already defeated, after such a shitty show. We had also suffered that no-show cancellation in Billings. It felt like my old days in Guitar Center management: there was so much shit was going wrong that it wasn't surprising anymore. The rage spread through every cell of my body.

An hour later, I called State Farm asked for a supervisor. He was very apologetic, but none of the tow companies were responding. It was just too late at night. The supervisor vowed to personally man the phones and get someone as quickly as possible.

I told the guys to get an Uber back to the hotel. Few tow trucks can accommodate passengers, so there was no point to keep them waiting.

My phone rang and it was the owner of Off Campus Auto Repair.* He said they were having trouble with our location. He asked if we might be near a hospital. I had no idea, but there was a large building on the other side of the bend. It was across the street and facing the other way, so I jogged down the street to get a closer look.

Hospital. *Finally.*

The owner said he'd wake up his driver, but it might be a while. Lisa gave me a blanket—it was cold enough that I was shivering and my toes were numb—and I waited another 45 minutes alone. The time zone worked to my benefit, allowing me to text Ang for a while before she went to bed.

I asked the driver to drop me at the hotel. I didn't know where to get it fixed, and that was a problem for another day. At least then I could have a shower and a bed! The driver informed

---

*I edited this book with the Off Campus Auto Repair pen.

me that they could repair it—right down the street from our hotel. They would call first thing in the morning.

The suite was a goddamn miracle. Aside from the room that I shared with Terrell in Vegas, it was the nicest place I've ever stayed. We were stranded in luxury.

I got an early call from Off Campus Auto Repair. We discussed the new alternator, and the fuel pump that I *just* replaced. They also told me that my ball joint was near failure and needed to be replaced before driving home. I knew that part was true, because I was told it had about a year left on it... about a year earlier. Too bad they didn't catch it on my latest inspection. The estimate was $1,600.

I don't know what $1,600 is to you, dear reader. At the time, it was about three whole paychecks. I was down to my last $40. My credit cards were maxed, and the album wasn't selling. I had no choice but to ask for help.

I felt *terrible* making that call. Ang might've been able to cover it, but she had just bought our plane tickets to New York for my birthday. I already owed my parents for the tires, but I didn't have any other options. It's times like these that I regret cashing in my retirement funds after *I Quit My Job For This*.

Steve said that they'd cover it, but it would depend on both their savings *and* credit to pull it off. I would need to start making payments right away. I already planned to pick up some hours for the holidays and try to get back on my feet. I stayed true to my word and made my first payment on Christmas Day.*

Once I secured the money, I needed to see if we could lower the price. If that fuel pump was under warranty, then maybe I could save that $300. I called Frank at California Transmissions,

---

*Between the auto loans, and a sizable feature, I finally paid them off in early 2020

but he wasn't scheduled until noon. The time zone was working against me, because it was only 8am in IA.

After those stressful-ass calls, there was no going back to sleep. Thomas and Lisa had gone downstairs for breakfast and brought me some oatmeal. I told them I wanted to film "Wildfire" in bed, like some *I can do this in my sleep* shit. That got shot down quickly. Maybe they saw more potential in the video than I did. In any case, they suggested I give it a real take.

Thomas grabbed his camera, while I grabbed my hat and jacket. Lisa asked why I wasn't doing my hair. Thomas concurred. I reluctantly complied, haphazardly putting some gel in my hair. *Time to put on a show.*

Our hotel was across the street from two other hotels; one ahead, and one to our right. In the adjacent quadrant, was a big empty field. We stomped through the wet grass and filmed "Wildfire" a cappella in a single take. It was still *really* early for me, so I was impressed that I got through it. But there was a tiny mistake. I decided that, since this was supposed to be an impressive feat, I'd do another take and get it right.

Five takes later, we had it.* I could've edited the mistake, but I wanted to do it live. Part of the reason I'm so aggressive on the video is because I was pissed off, having to redo it. I had played it every night on tour without mistakes** but I was still waking up and couldn't get it right. That anger fueled the best take.

We went back upstairs and uploaded the video. Within minutes, I was getting notifications. In this digital age, it's hard to get people to listen to a three-minute song, let alone a six-minute one about politics... with no chorus. But none of that mattered. Or, perhaps *because* of that, people responded to what I was saying. Many people felt that Trump had emboldened

*Oh, fuck off. It's six minutes long!
**Except a minor one in Portland

white racists and that resurgence had become impossible to ignore. Add to that Eminem's video the night before, and all the sudden people wanted to listen to "Wildfire."

Lisa kicked back, while Thomas and I killed time at a nearby mall. Thomas chased digital Pokemon and I found a NECA Catwoman figure that I'd been wanting for a long time. Unfortunately, that shit costs $100 and I was in the midst of a financial crisis. But it was cool to finally see one in person.*

When we got to the food court, our eyes scanned the signs for something edible.

"THEY GOT A FUCKIN' ICE SKATING RINK?"

I didn't mean to say it that loudly, but it surprised me. It was out in the open like a basketball court. Wouldn't it require special temperature control? I quickly noticed someone who had stopped eating her lunch to give me the side eye like *calm down, asshole.*

Meanwhile, the video was already at 1,000 views. My original YouTube video had 400. And that was three weeks earlier. The Facebook algorithm worked to my benefit that time.

We were picking up some toiletries at Target when Frank called. He gave me his AutoZone account, which I provided to Off Campus Auto Repair. After some phone tag at Target, they secured a replacement. New estimate: $1,300.

OCAR had replaced the ball joint already, and the fuel pump was scheduled the next morning. We were almost out of Iowa.

When we got back to our room, I got a call from Terrell. The *Attack of the Show Stealer* tour was having setbacks as well. Chief amongst them was a no-show by a promoter in Billings.

*When I stopped touring as much, I got the whole NECA DC collection: Batman (Keaton, Bale, and Affleck), Superman, Wonder Woman, Joker, Catwoman, and Penguin!

Wait—did you say Billings?

Anthony had fucked over Terrell just a few days after he fucked me. Exact same story. I couldn't believe it. He was ok, though. For the *Show Stealer* tour, he put a tip jar onstage and asked people to donate for gas. It worked so well that he didn't have to come out of pocket for gas on the whole trip. It made me jealous, given my own situation. I'd try a tip jar on the next tour...

Later that evening, we realized that it would be impossible to make a 12 hour drive for our Denver show. I called Chad and we cancelled. Again. It bothered me intensely. That was the third show* that I cancelled in 2017. It was more than the previous decades combined. I was tarnishing my name.

It was a stressful day, but we had a good night. Thomas convinced us to play a game called *Quiplash,* which successfully lightened the mood. We watched *Family Guy* in bed and laughed hard. We needed it. On top of that, I checked my phone before bed: the video was up to 3,000 views.

OCAR called bright and early. Remember when I said there were two ways that Frank offered to repair the fuel pump? The pump itself or the whole assembly? Well the warranty was just for the pump itself. Guess which one we needed.

All that time on the phone was pointless. I got stuck with the whole bill. I napped another hour before their courtesy driver picked us up. We spent the next 12 hours cruising through rural states** and trying to keep our spirits up. There weren't enough mini Kit Kats in the world, but we did our best.

*Austin (*Rare Form*), Redding (*Blank Check*), and Denver (*Fall Children*).
**CORN!*

Kelly was kind enough to stay up late again, and let us in. We carried our luggage past the old Quixote's to her apartment. It felt like salt in the wound.* The three of us were so exhausted that we didn't stay up long. Lisa turned on *Rogue One,* but not even *Star Wars* could keep me from the imminent crash. I peeked at my phone one last time and closed my eyes. 10,000 views.

The next day was scheduled off—Wyoming and Utah are hard to book—but we had to get to Salt Lake if we were going to be on time for the last leg. We got up early, had Tokyo Joe's, and went to Twist & Shout. It took a little convincing, since I had avoided record stores the entire time,** but I'm glad we went.

I've established how little money I had, but I did buy something. The hip-hop section had a CD called *All the Breaks Vol. 1-3.* It had 99 tracks of classic drum loops, all sampled from vinyl. As soon as I popped it in, I realized that many of those 99 tracks had two or three breaks on each one. So I probably got 250 breaks for $10.99. Well worth it. Several of them would end up on my next solo album, *Figures of Speech.*

Thomas was losing it by about track 80, but we were so close to the end that he let me finish. I was in Breakbeat Heaven.

Not long after we entered Wyoming, there was a traffic warning: *ACCIDENT – 12 MILES.* Within minutes, we came to a complete stop; a nine-mile traffic jam.

It felt like an eternity. People were getting out of their cars and walking around. By the last mile, we could see a rest area. Bladders were full, and tensions were high. We stretched our legs and I let out a big DFS scream to blow off some steam. When I

We should be playing right now!
**It was the longest I'd *ever* gone without record shopping on tour.

got back in the van, the guys started making fun of me.* But pretty soon, they realized the healing power of a good scream. I plugged my ears and they wailed away. Lisa called it "primal screams." By the time we were finished, the lanes had cleared up again.

10 hours later, we were in Salt Lake Shitty. We knew that Home 2 Suites had spoiled us when the Hampton in Utah looked like a dump. We arrived so late that the pool was closed, and I had been looking forward to a hot tub all day. With Thomas' employee deal, we're Hilton Honors members. I decided to ask the desk if maybe we could have an afterhours key to the hot tub.

To my surprise, that was all it took. We changed upstairs and the maintenance man escorted us to the pool. A middle aged blonde woman was sitting in the hallway, reading a book on the floor. *I* noticed that *she* noticed our swim gear. Sure enough, a few minutes later, there was a knock at the door. She was waving at us through the window.

I thought we had accidentally opened the floodgates, and more people would be trying to get in. Thomas answered the door and she said the janitor invited her to join. Our silent, relaxing hot tub became a rountable interview: small talk questions were directed at each of us, until revealing that we were musicians on tour. *Ohhh, my son is a musician! He's been starting to make beats, but I don't understand that music...*

I felt like kind of an asshole, but I really just wanted to unwind. Quietly. It's never fun trying to describe your music to someone who has absolutely zero frame of reference. I just wasn't up for it. Then I noticed how she overemphasized the

*On long drives, especially when I'm tired, I'll get random bursts of energy that manifest as jibberish, screaming, and fart sounds. Lisa once asked if I have a quota for daily fart sounds. "Nope. Just bored!" [See also: Jonah Hill in *Get Him to The Greek*]

word *Black* when describing someone. Then I heard it again. It felt... off. She was trying to relate to the music, but just made me uncomfortable in the process.

Having been on the road for 12 hours, Thomas & I went to In & Out Burger and I went to bed with heartburn. 30,000 views.

I was the first one to the van in the morning. I ate my muffin and even had time to go back and use the lobby's bathroom before anyone came out. I opened the back doors for Thomas and observed that it no longer smelled like weed. I said that Lisa's bags must've aired out over time.

Thomas looked at me with hesitation and said "I'm not supposed to tell you this..." Apparently, I had unknowingly trafficked weed across state lines and Lisa delivered it to someone along the way. I was fucking furious, but we were almost home and it was already a shitshow. I never mentioned it.

There was snow on the ground in Idaho Falls. It had been two years since The Sickhouse. There were a number of punks at the show, who weren't familiar with rap shows, and I think they came to see what the green-haired Sammy Warm Hands guy was all about. I was their gateway drug to indie rap.

One of these guys, Jonny, started his own company: Riot Guys Productions. Riot Guys specialized in punk shows, but he remembered me from The Sickhouse, and Riot Guys hosted their very first rap show.

The Gem was a nice venue (a little big for us). It had a full kitchen and everything. That said, they had a great sound system and a sound man who was actually engaged in the show.*

*A lot of sound people will set you up and then go outside to smoke, or space out on their phones. Better not switch vocalists, or it'll stop the whole show!

The first opener sounded like every bad Soundcloud rapper. He looked at the floor the whole time, and talked about how original his [trend-riding, cookie-cutter] beats were. The second one was a good performer. His whole family showed up to support. It was borderline gospel music, but he was great live.

The last local act was Genuine Percussion. I recognized one of their emcees, Hard A, from the Sickhouse show. The other rapper was even more familiar. Prosper had opened the Sapient show on the *Bears Repeating* tour. I remember it because he drove from Idaho to Eugene for that *one* show.* Small world.

Genuine Percussion played a fantastic set. Their live drums and bass accented the beats, while Hard A and Prosper passed the mic with gusto. The first couple acts weren't quite my style, but these guys were energetic boom-bap; my favorite kind of hip-hop. They worked up the crowd to a fever pitch and we were ready to keep that energy going.

Whenever you have a popular local *before* you, it's urgent that you get onstage before their fans leave. Thomas and I walked on as they were walking off. He addressed the crowd while I waited for our cue from the sound man.

"Wow, the energy," he said. "Give it up for Genuine Percussion!" But then his self-deprication kicked in: "I hope you're ready for some *prerecorded* percussion!"

Knowing Thomas, and his sense of humor, it didn't register as significant. I was filming his set when I noticed that the drummer from Genuine Percussion was back onstage. He was tearing down his drum kit *during the Gradient set!* I focused on closeups and kept the camera moving away from the background. Most of the fans had left or sat down at the bar, but I still felt it was disrespectful to interrupt the show.

---

*Sapient is his favorite artist.

Lisa told me that GP was talking shit about Thomas and that's why everyone left. I was really confused. *Who in their right mind would hate Thomas?* I joined him onstage for "Can't Wait," as I did every night. It was lonely up there. I closed my eyes and tried to erase my surroundings.

The crowd was slightly more attentive to Lisa, and I didn't fare much better. When it was time for "Excuses," I asked the crowd to *welcome Gradient back to the stage.* But when he got onstage, he said "stop the beat!"

Thomas explained his comment about "prerecorded percussion" was a jab at himself. Apparently there had been some infighting about whether or not GP's drummer should have to play to the beat or just make it 100% live. Thomas' comment, though misinterpreted, triggered all that resentment. He insisted that GP was one of the best acts we'd seen on the whole tour.

All of the sudden, people were cheering and coming to the stage. Prosper and Hard A were right up front laughing about it. The drummer was so pissed that he had to "leave before someone gets punched in the face." I'm just glad it got cleared up before it came to blows!*

The second half of my set was met with more enthusiasm. I performed "Wildfire" mostly a cappella. People had been talking about the video, so I wanted to give them a recognizable version. It had a happy ending after all.

Unfortunately, Riot Guys didn't fare too well. I asked what Jonny thought of the show, and he said "it was fun... but never again." They paid our guarantee, but I didn't realize that he *rented* the venue. That's an unusually big expense. Normally places will just book you or not. Jonny's foray into rap was over.

*Just for laughs, picture me and Thomas in a fight.

Back at the hotel, my video had been played 40,000 times. It had tripled yesterday, from 10 to 30k, and today was another 10. It was incredibly exciting, but I knew it was the end of our little experiment. Overall, it showed up on people's feeds 90,000 times and about 50% of them actually watched the fucking thing. I gained 200 new followers that week alone. I might get 200 new followers a *year*. "Wildfire" was a success.

I was excited to play The Shredder again, since DFS had moved our last show to Rose House. When we loaded in, a stranger jokingly asked if we were the bus outside. Oblivious to the reference, I said "no, we're the van." Justin corrected me, saying that The Interrupters were parked around the corner. Instantly, my eyes widened.

The Interrupters (Hellcat Records)* are hands down my favorite band to emerge in recent years. Being on tour at the same time, I was bummed to missed them in Portland. But that night, they were playing two blocks away!

I might've waited around their bus for a few minutes... I met the band in Portland once before, and they were super cool, but I wasn't committed to lurk there all night.

Our show was mostly terrible, maxing out at maybe five non-performers in the room. Justin suggested that we cancel again and watch The Interrupters at the Knitting Factory. It was a tough call, but I told him that we should honor our commitment. I could've used the pick-me-up, though.

We finished early, around 10:45. Justin closed the venue and said he could probably get us in for the end of the show. By 11, some punks walked by, saying the show was over. So much for redemption.

*Owned by Tim Armstrong from Rancid

Lisa found an all-night restaurant and Thomas treated us to an amazing dinner. We listened to The Interrupters in the van. Sometimes it feels like I need *things* and distractions to be happy, but there's no substitute for friendship.

That would've been the end of the tour, but KI invited us to open for Carnage at Level Up. One last chance to end it right.

The drive through eastern Oregon is among my least favorite. It's narrow, rough, and almost complete wilderness. We passed the place where I got my *Blank Check* ticket and I thought: *could be worse.*

Excited to be home, I cranked up some RUN DMC. We pulled up to the venue with "Run's House" blaring through the subs. I let out a huge sigh of relief. *We made it.*

It was our third Eugene show of the tour,* and it was better than the first two combined. We each played shorter to accommodate Terrell. He offered to let me headline, but I think his shows are best when he can just go off and not worry about time restraints.

Andy was filming the tour again, and it was great to see them both. There was a lot of love in the room. Each one of us had family there. Both Thomas and Lisa's moms thanked me for taking them on the road. We all shared hugs and went our separate ways. It was a hard tour, but we parted in good spirits.

I got home at 2am and left for the airport at 8. Ang and I spent the rest of the week in New York City for my birthday. We saw friends like Ecid, Zac HB, and Louis Logic. We went to The Comedy Cellar. We ate dinner at Tavern on the Green. In any other circumstances, I would've been depressed after that tour. For the millionth time, she pulled me through.

*Black Forest, CD World, and Level up! What the fuck, right?

(Left to right:) Thomas, me, Lisa
Photo credit: Thomas Hiura
Jaeda's house (Spokane, WA) 2017

Lisa's toilet (Portland, OR) 2017

(Left to right:) me, Ang
The Tonight Show (New York, New York) 2017

Ravenous (2018)

Lineup: Carnage The Executioner, Sammy Warm Hands, Mammoth

Best show: Seattle, WA

Worst show: Olympia, WA

Record store find: [N/A]

The financial tolls of *Blank Check* and *Fall Children* were too much to ignore. To be honest, it didn't inspire much confidence in myself, either. I told Chad that I'd some time off to get my money right.

I accepted a promotion at work, which was my first 40-hour position since we left for *I Quit* (2011). I made a few payments to my parents, and started overpaying every credit card bill. By the end of the summer, I had raised my credit score by 100 points.

Music has always dominated my spending: CDs, studio/band equipment, artwork, merchandise, etc. Since I started this path in middle school, it's consumed me. But for the last couple years, I had fantasized of changing priorities.

I've been a Batman fan since I was about two. I had accumulated some cool items over the years, but in 2018, I finally invested more in my Batman collection than I did in my music collection. I even started a new Instagram account, @BatFanAddict, so I wouldn't annoy my followers with toys.*

While my new priorities were enjoyable, I was still hard at work. I wrote this book in November and December 2017, immediately following *Fall Children*. (This chapter is my first real-time entry for the book.)

On New Year's Day, I was struck with the inspiration to finish my double solo album: *Figures of Speech*. It was my crowning achievement in hip hop.

Figures suffered some delays because of the features, so when Carnage asked me to do a fall tour, I turned him down. *Bears, Famous, Vacant Eyes,* and *Rare Form* were all sold out. I didn't know when *Figures* would be ready, and I wasn't about to rush it again.

Over 12 months, I refused all headlining offers. I wanted to grow my audience by opening bigger shows again... and try out my new material. I played with Epic Beard Men (Sage Francis & B. Dolan), DJ Abilities, Blueprint (in Eugene, Portland, and Seattle), Carnage (in St. Paul, MN), and played the Main Stage at a summer festival called the Whiteaker Block Party.

I changed my set list every time, trying 20 new songs altogether. Those shows informed my delivery on the final recordings, which had more intensity than previous albums.

By August, the last features rolled in, and *Figures of Speech* was ready. My manager title prevented me from taking extended vacation, so I joined Terrell for just a few shows instead.

On October 11th, a year after *Fall Children* ended, I flew to Spokane for the *Ravenous* tour. Terrell and his opener, Mammoth, had started in Minneapolis a week earlier. It made sense for me to meet them, ride along, and get dropped off in Eugene. It cost me nothing in gas, and $180 for the plane ticket. I packed my suitcase with as much merch as I could fit (19 copies of *Figures*, which wasn't even *out* yet, and a dozen *NOBODY GIVES A FUCK* shirts, from the Blueprint mini tour).

To be honest, I'm terrified of planes. I fly about twice a year; to SXSW (Austin, TX), and to Soundset (Minneapolis, MN). It gives me a week full of anxiety, dreading that I will not survive the trip—and wondering how to best compartmentalize my life before I die.

We've also established that I'm not as comfortable when someone else is running the show. I did my best to adjust expectations and just be down for the cause. It was only six shows. Fortunately, Terrell and I are very close. He's one of my favorite people to travel with.* I crammed myself in the back seat, with suitcases stacked to the ceiling. It was much more comfortable than it looked.

The first show was at Red Room, where I had played with Lisa and Thomas. I was a little worried because the lineup was bloated with four locals. Typically that means they'd play shorter, so the headliner isn't starting four hours into the show. That was not the case in Spokane. And as to be expected, the show was running on Rap Time (about 45 minutes late).

I liked every act on the bill, but having been awake since 8am—five flight delays and a rescheduled connection—I found myself nodding off at the merch table. The crowd was mostly at the bar, with their backs to the stage. It wasn't very promising.

Sara Bourland, one of my tourmates from *The World Has No Eyedea*, surprised us with her presence. Not only did I think she still lived in Denver, but she had been hospitalized with a collapsed lung. I couldn't believe she was there!

*I know that he feels the same, because he said it onstage in Olympia

Another surprise was Landon Wordswell. He appeared on my *Bears Repeating* album, back when he lived in Eugene. Our relationship has been strained recently. The primary delay for my album was over a deal that I made for a Gift of Gab feature... through Landon.

I typically only collaborate with artists who I have played with, or personally met. If we share a mutual respect at the show, then I'll ask for their contact info. When it comes to features, I do not like *or recommend* working with agents or middlemen.

Long story short, the fee that Crushkill paid did *not* go to Gab, who didn't even know my name until months later when I got his personal email address. It took months to get the money back from Landon, $100 at a time.* As of this writing, I've only received half of the money that we paid. Luckily, Gab honored the deal because I helped him recover some of that money.

I was texting Landon from Red Room, asking when I could expect another payment. Gab had done his part, but I didn't want to take advantage of his kindness. A couple hours later, Landon tapped on my shoulder. It turned out he was on tour as well and heard I was there. I was so taken off guard that we just exchanged niceties and he took off.

Mammoth began by beatboxing into a seashell, and the crowd took notice. By the time I started, a lot more people had showed up. Brotha Nature had offered to play last and give us his time slot. I really think he saved the show.

My new set was 90% new songs, so people were eager to check out *Figures of Speech*. I only brought 19 CDs, so I was pleased to sell about $75 in merch the first night. For a supporting act, it's not bad at all.

*Each payment was forwarded to Gift of Gab, hoping he'd record the verse for me.

It's worth mentioning that last time, the sound guy was muting my track during "Wildfire," without my knowledge or permission. I told that story when we were parking, and lo and behold, a *different* sound guy added weird, pitch-shifting effects to our voices that night. Thankfully, Terrell intervened.

Seattle was special. It was the album release for Sarx's new project, GunsGodsGhosts. Evan and Ambur drove all the way there from Springfield, and of course, Eric and Jori were there as well. Coincidentally, I had actually met Mammoth once before... on tour with Ev and Sarx!

DFS had played at the venue, Substation, for *Blank Check*. It was a good sounding room, and I was excited to see how it translated to hip hop. The subs were really prominent, as is true at a lot of rap shows, and I struggled to understand the opener's lyrics. I made a note to the sound man, that my lyrics are the most important part of my songs, even if the beat needed to be turned down. Sometimes a comment like that can be the difference between a *good* set that people can't fully appreciate, and a *great* set that people truly understand.

We were all stronger the second night. I wasn't fighting to be heard over the bass, so I had composure and control of the stage. Terrell's beatboxing was tighter and funkier than the night before. It makes a big difference when you can hear clearly.

GunsGodsGhosts headlined, and I was really proud of Sarx. Flanked by live bass and a DJ, it was one of his most memorable sets. The new material was strong, and people were excited for his return. Terrell couldn't believe that he hadn't played a show in five years. We were all in his corner.

Sarx also made a nice gesture to Mammoth, who was added to the tour last minute, and played a very early time slot. Sarx brought him back near the end of the show, to make sure he got to play in front of the whole crowd. Mammoth freestyled at such a fast pace that I remembered past times where I had been in awe of Minnesota rappers like Kristoff Krane or Zac HB. Their ability to improvise is a skill set that I do not possess.

I had nice conversations with Sarx and Ana, Eric and Jori, Evan and Ambur, and a number of fans who had been to my shows. It's the kind of night that reminds me why I spend all this time on the road.

After a hot shower, I slept for 11 hours. We had short drives and moved at a comfortable pace. Personally, I'm always happier to wake up naturally than to an alarm.

Mammoth played his new CD on the first drive, so Terrell played *Ravenous* on the way to Olympia. I had heard a few of the beats and live versions before. When he was writing the album, we would talk on the phone, discussing lyrics and arrangements. He even used my notes on one of the verses. I thought it was cool that he looked to me for feedback, making it even more exciting to hear the final product.

At first listen, I told him that *Ravenous* was his best album. We always strive to improve and experiment, but sometimes an artist will exemplify their growth by touching on their entire repertoire. It felt like one of those albums. A look ahead, but through the prism of his past work. Albums like that almost feel like a career retrospective. In any case, I'd call it his most restrained and *musical* effort to date. He sounds comfortable as he does confident; nothing to prove.

We hit up my usual Thai spot in Olympia, and walked over to O'Malley's. So far, all three shows had venues (and lineups) in common with the *Fall Children* tour. I was writing this chapter as Terrell displayed the merch, when we got another surprise: Kathy and her friend Netti.

Needless to say, we were thrilled. I knew that Kathy was on a trip, but she hadn't said where. The tour was proving to be a family affair from start to finish.

O'Malley's is not my favorite place to play—no stage, audience sits down, low turnouts—so I wasn't fully into it at first. My second song, "Rough Days," is one that I had only performed a few times. I made a minor mistake, saying *while I'm coming up with gimmicks, you're bumping the first Xzibit* instead of saying *while YOU'RE coming up with gimmicks, I'M bumping the first Xzibit*.

I stopped rapping and looked at Carnage saying "I just dissed myself! When have you ever seen me fuck up like that?" I should've just kept rhyming, but I was mad at myself. I jumped back in on the chorus and the rest of the set was fine.

But I didn't forget it.

A few minutes later, I was talking to Mammoth about my mistake, after he had just memorized a verse for Terrell's set. Sure enough, he forgot the lyrics, too! They stopped the song and started again. Same result.

Later, they tried to do the same song, over a beatbox instead of the studio track, and they tag-teamed the verse to make it through. After the chorus, TERRELL FORGOT HIS WORDS, TOO! I couldn't believe that all three of us were off that night! At least I wasn't beating myself up anymore.

The silver lining was that no matter what, people still looked me in the eye and told me they'd never seen anyone like me before. I wasn't coloring my hair or anything; they're talking about my lyrical content, the clarity and passion of my delivery, and the fast pace of the show. A woman named Amy had a long talk with me about these things and said it looked like I didn't even breathe. It means a lot to hear those things from people, but especially on bad nights.*

The Paris Theater (Portland) was a shitshow:
-Venue wasn't open for load-in
-Booker lived in Tacoma and did not come to the show
-No one was in charge, or had any information
-Most of the locals didn't appear for soundcheck
-Some locals didn't show up at all
-Attendance was low

There were maybe 10 people in the room when I went on. All but two members of the opening acts had fled. The sound man disappeared, so I couldn't adjust the deafening monitor mix. Ogar joined me for a song, but the other mics were both muted. The sound guy came back *seconds* before his verse began.

Once again, the quality of the people made up for the quantity. Qbala, the best opener to date, came up to me super excited, saying "man, you were on some MAMA SAID KNOCK. YOU. OUT! SHIT!"**

A few minutes later, I was talking to her partner Ariana, and she said "I have to ask about your Cool J cover!" I told her that my set was all original; that I just write old school styles. She was in disbelief that my song—I assume "Razor Tongue" or "Break of Dawn"—wasn't a Def Jam classic.

*It also throws me off when beautiful women love my music and give me hugs and stuff, because I'm so used to rap shows being 90% dudes. Spokane was like 50% female, and they still loved it!

**I only met Qbala that night, but she was wearing a Just Enough Food shirt (Josh from Travellers Music in Denver, CO) and we had a great talk about longevity in music; balancing ambition with self-care, etc. She had health issues that limited her ability to perform long term, which mirrored my own hearing problems, and I felt like we really understood each other. Her set was amazing, too.

Outside, a guy approached me who said "you are what we *all*—everyone who writes rhymes or makes hip hop music—you are what we all *aspire* to be." Whatever feelings I had about merch sales or turnout were all but erased. I texted Gabe about the LL comparisons. He said "Damn. That's high praise... that you deserve." Good times.

We had another free crash pad (fourth in a row!), and I wound up with my own room. For once, I wasn't disturbed by the morning sun or others who wake up before me. After my predictable stomach issues—I had Voodoo Doughnuts after the show—I got at least six hours of uninterrupted sleep.

On that note, I'd like to address my bathroom habits. It's fascinating to think that I could be a Johnny Crappleseed, shitting all across the country. I thought this short tour would be an opportunity to take inventory of these events.

I believe I've established my lactose intolerance, but my guts can also revolt from anxiety or lack of sleep; even just from eating too much greasy food. All of those things are common while traveling, so here is a typical amount of my suffering:

Eugene, OR – Eugene Airport
SeaTac, WA – SeaTac Airport
SeaTac, WA – SeaTac Airport
Spokane, WA – Red Room
Spokane, WA – NKNGS' house
Spokane, WA – NKNGS' house
Seattle, WA – Substation
Seattle, WA – Phil's house
Olympia, WA – O'Malley's bar
Portland, OR – Paris Theatre
Portland, OR – Paris Theatre

Portland, OR – Travis' house
Portland, OR – Travis' house

That's pretty much how I'm living on the road. And those are just the dumps! Fortunately I haven't been stuck with any rest areas or truck stops yet, which are often nastier than bars.* With my luck, it'll happen today, in the middle of eastern Oregon.

Terrell had lost something like 100 pounds after going vegan. Mammoth was on a similar diet, so I wound up at a vegan restaurant called Next Level Burgers. Now, I love animals. I really do. But my tastebuds are assholes. I don't like *anything but* meat.

In the past year, I had started eating meat substitutes like vegetarian burgers and breakfast sausages. Ang and I had those every week, so I was making a dent in my meat consumption. For years, we had also used ground turkey instead of beef, making baby steps in responsible eating.

Unfortunately, meat substitutes have a lot of wheat and soy products, which aren't really things that Ang can have. So while I'm making the effort, I don't believe we'll ever be fully vegetarian. That said, Next Level is the shit!

It was my turn to show off a new record, so we played *Figures of Speech* on the way to Bend. It's always great hearing people's reactions in real time, and they were both giving me a lot to be proud about. Terrell had already memorized a number of my lines (from playing them live), so he was singing along on the first listen!

"Local" was written after some lengthy conversations with Terrell, about the "hometown curse" that many touring artists

*The Paris Theater doesn't have a door to the bathroom or the stall!

have experienced. For some reason, people are objectively excited when they hear our music in other cities, but our own cities are often less receptive because we're "local." That isn't always the case, but many artists have felt this way after traveling enough.

Halfway through "Local," Terrell started it over. He asked who made the beat. *Danny G.* He said "man, I didn't know he could make beats like *that!*" We listened through it again and paused for a 20 minute talk on the subject. When it was time to resume, it had been so long that he started it over again, so that we didn't start cold on Track 3 (Disc 2).

In the end, they both gave me glowing reviews. When we unloaded the car, I asked Terrell about it on video, and he said "man, that shit is dope as hell!"

My lead single was "I Don't Care," which was directed by myself and Taylor Morden. He's a long-time collaborator and a good friend. We were scheduled to film "Hearts of Kyber," using Star Wars cosplayers, but most of them backed out at the last minute.* We had three days to change plans. Taylor was in town for one day only, interviewing the Cherry Poppin' Daddies for his ska documentary *Pick it Up!*

Since we couldn't reschedule, I chose a different song that I could perform alone (without features). "I Don't Care" was going to be a single anyway, so we filmed a bunch of performance scenes at Steve's warehouse.**

*Due to concerns about use of the characters outside of a non-profit capacity
**The same place where "Famous Last Words" was shot, but in an adjacent building. The property is so vast that I've filmed six videos there, without ever using the same room: "Re-Endtroducing," "pwnd," "Crisis of Conscience," "Famous Last Words," "I Don't Care," and "Break of Dawn."

Later, I wrote a video treatment and hired LA punk model/actress Erin Micklow to star. Gradient drove me and my equipment to Hollywood in his Prius. We stopped at Amoeba Records in Berkeley, because they sell my music there (Amoeba Hollywood does not). A short clip was used of the SAMMY WARM HANDS title card, and we spliced it with some shots of Erin browsing the S section in Hollywood.

Syd hooked us up with the lounge area of East West Studios, so that I could have a set for Erin's first scene. The rest was filmed on Sunset Blvd; a collaboration of my notes and Erin's knowledge of the neighborhood.

In the meantime, the *Pick it Up!* Kickstarter had broken $100,000 and Taylor was buried in work. He would not be able to edit "I Don't Care," but he did some color correction and let me chop it up. It made my LA footage look more professional than my own skills would've allowed.

The video quickly hit 1,000 views on YouTube, and I uploaded it again to Facebook for another 1,000. It was probably my best music video to date.

Taylor stopped by the Bend show to surprise me. I've been a fan of *Pick it Up!* since Day 1, and he's given me a peek behind the curtain along the way. I knew he had been working in LA, interviewing The Interrupters and quite possibly, Rancid frontman Tim Armstrong.

He told me a story that included Tim, The Interrupters, Aaron Barrett (Reel Big Fish), Corbett Redford (director of *Turn it Around: The Story of East Bay Punk*), and surprisingly, Flea (Red Hot Chili Peppers). Needless to say, my jaw was on the floor most of the time. He may have been working his ass off, but he was also living the dream.

Then Taylor dropped a bomb on me: he reached into his pocket and said, "oh, I brought you something." He extended his hand with a copy of Rancid's *...And Out Come the Wolves*. It had red Sharpie all over the cover:

TO MY BROTHER SAM
-TIM ARMSTRONG

I can't describe the elation that I felt at the time. There were a few curse words, and genuine tears of joy. Few things have rendered me so speechless, and for a moment, I just hugged Taylor and took it in. What a good friend.

Terrell was doing soundcheck while I caught up with Taylor. I had already finished, but Terrell called me back to the stage. He was playing a beatbox loop that sounded familiar, but I couldn't quite place it. He said "'Hands Down!' What do you think?"
The first track on my album features Carnage and our mutual friend Supastition. I had been using it as my set opener, but a shortened version that was just my parts. Terrell invented a way for us to play it *together*—and offered to put it in his set!

Galaxe* opened the show, playing live beats with an electronic xylophone. He used mallets, in a traditional style, but sounded like "Durazzo on crack," to quote Terrell.
It was a Monday night, so literally nobody was near the stage except me and T.* We were shouting out reactions to his set, which soon turned into a tutorial. Galaxe started breaking down his technique—much like Terrell does with beatbox looping—and collaborated with us on the spot. We were thrilled to have met him, and disappointed when he left immediately after his set.

*Mammoth tends to disappear for long periods of time

By the time I played, there were a *few* people, but all seated in the back of the room. I didn't sweat it, though. I could see their eyes light up, reacting to lines. Sometimes I'd catch them filming me, too. A Monday is just a Monday. Doesn't mean they don't like you. I sold merch to practically everyone in the room.

We tried "Hands Down" in Terrell's set, and it was great. In typical Carnage fashion, he stopped the beat at the end and we repeated our verses a cappella, making every punchline crystal clear. The crowd had grown in size, and they were loving it.

Though *I* played short, due to the low turnout,* Terrell was an hour into his set already. As the clock neared midnight, October 16th crept up like a familiar dark cloud. It was the eighth anniversary of Eyedea's death. For the first time on *Ravenous*, I watched Terrell play "Star Destroyer" for some elated fans in the front. Every single person came onstage for a hug afterward.

The show concluded with a freestyle cypher between my tourmates and a couple guys from the crowd. I'm always impressed with T's ability to control the cypher. It can get ugly really easily. People are thinking, so they're not always aware of their surroundings. (Not to mention all the egos involved!) But Terrell keeps people in check, and challenges them to think on their feet. One of the openers had not impressed us earlier, but held his own in the cypher like a champ. It reminded me of a Blueprint line: *[I'll] make a Kodak moment out of the most boring open mic.*

The promoter offered us a place to crash, but only until 10am. We opted for a Motel 6, so we could take our time. I requested a noon checkout, which was granted. Of course, that turned into a 1pm checkout, but they didn't give me any shit.

*It's a good idea to make sure your headliner goes on at a decent time.

Bend also had a Next Level Burger, so we filled our bellies and headed home. The guys did some laundry, and Ang joined us for Mod Pizza. My studio had the drums and mics set up for DFS, so I asked KI if they could crash at his place instead.

After dinner, we filmed a couple takes of "Hands Down" (beatbox version). I used it to promote the Eugene show, and sure enough, we got another 1,000 plays overnight. Something was going right with *Figures of Speech* and I was pretty happy about it.

Eugene can be tricky, and with *Daydream* still lingering in my mind, I had low expectations. Ev came to soundcheck and we played "The Show Stoppers" with Terrell. We'd only got to perform that a few times, so it was a treat to break it out again.

To my surprise, Eugene came through. The show was at Old Nick's Pub: home base for DFS, but relatively untested for rap shows. KI and Cerebral both played stellar sets. It feels good to bring tourmates to my city and show off the homegrown talent. Mammoth had never heard them before, calling them the best openers of the whole tour.

By then, Terrell had memorized a lot of my new songs. After moving "Hands Down" to his set, my opener that night was "Redefine the Flow pt. 2." After the chorus, Terrell started rapping Casual's part* from the audience, and I forgot my second verse. I laughed, stopped the beat, and performed it a cappella. He knows my shit better than I do!

"Hands Down" was even better the second time. People had seen the video that day, and when we did the a cappella recap, we actually traded lines the whole time. It was fucking awesome.

*As featured on the record

My set was great and I sold every CD that I packed for tour.*
But people were *really* feeling the new songs. That's a success in
my book, and this *is* my fucking book.

There's a great song on the *Ravenous* album called "Still
Work." The gist is summed up in the line:

This ain't a woe-is-me stress endorsement
Just know that running a music business
doesn't make my job less important

During the song, Mammoth stands onstage with an *Attack of the Show Stealer* bucket; the former home of some neapolitan ice cream. Terrell breaks down the daily grind of a touring artist and illustrates the value in what we do. Mammoth takes the bucket around the room and people put ones, fives, and twenties in the slot. That alone paid for the gas on his last four tours, leaving the guarantees for hotels, food, and—god forbid—*profit!*

Terrell didn't play quite as long, but still closed with an all-star cypher. Spirits were high and I think we parted ways at the right time. After *Fall Children*, I didn't want to be on the road at all. I dreaded leaving for *Ravenous*, but enjoyed it as I always do. But I am not in that headspace right now. Perhaps I'm not the road dog that I once was.

The show was on a Wednesday, and my birthday was on Friday.** *Figures* had some momentum after the tour, so I dropped it spontaneously on my birthday. At midnight, I uploaded it to Bandcamp*** and posted an Instagram story.

*Everything but the display copy
**I shouted out Steve when it turned midnight, as his birthday was Thursday
**The primary website that sells my music

I awoke on Friday to good news. There were plenty of well wishes from friends and family, and a handful of preorders. I did a proper announcement on all my social media pages, and the orders kept coming in. I made $300 in the first five days, which I happily sent to Brady. He never pressured me, but I wanted to start paying back my advance right away. If my retail promotion was paying off my credit cards, then the album sales needed to pay off the label.

Today, it's one week after the *Ravenous* tour. I'm in a much better place now than I was a year ago. I was able to take it slow because I had an ace up the sleeve. And with 24 songs, I can make a lot more singles over a longer period of time.

DFS is nearly finished writing *PERIL*, our follow up to *SQUALOR*, and I've started a new album with Gabe called *Demented Inventive Energy*.

All I know is that I've enjoyed spending more time at home,* and honestly, it feels good to watch this mountain of debt begin to erode. I've been so financially irresponsible since *Death Proof* (2010) that it's going to take a while to dig myself out. But it's a good start.

---

*In 2020, I took that even further, working from home during the pandemic.

Photo credit: Cerebral Coretext
Old Nick's Pub (Eugene, OR) 2018

Nobody Gives a Fuck
O'Malley's Lounge (Olympia, WA) 2018

(Left to right:) me, Eric
Nectar Lounge (Seattle, WA) 2018

PERIL (2019)

Lineup: Dead Fucking Serious

Best show: Berkeley, CA

Worst show: Santa Cruz, CA

Record store find: Batman *Knightsend,* Jel – *Greenball*, John Frusciante – *Enclosure*

Where do I even start? Figures of Speech satisfied me, creatively, in a way that few projects have. It felt like closing a chapter of my life. Without the typical workflow of three albums at once,* I was able to focus completely on DFS.

Listening back, *SQUALOR* was good. It captured the intensity of the band. But it lacked the ceaseless motion of our live shows. The momentary fade between songs seemed to kill any urgency that preceded it. I wondered if there was a way to record the album in medleys, imitating our tour set.

The challenge was sequencing. Normally, you can change the order of songs as you're mixing and mastering. But playing it live, bleeding one track into the next... the track list would have to be set in stone. While I tinkered with that idea, my amp began to lose its presence on our practice recordings. I immediately knew the culprit: tubes.**

---

*Admittedly, that's a lot easier when you're only working 24 hours a week.
**If you don't care about guitar stuff, you can skip the next five paragraphs.

I bought a Mesa/Boogie Dual Rectifier in 2004, and it was my baby. But times were tough after *I Quit*, and it seemed unlikely that I would need two monster guitar amps in the near future.*

The best that my Mesa ever sounded was when I replaced the original 6L6s (power tubes) with JJ EL34s. And by removing two of the four power tubes, the 100-watt head operated at 50w: better tone at a lower volume.

In 2014, I bought another Dual Rectifier. The 90s model was the sound I always wanted. Listen to those old Pennywise albums and you'll know what I'm going for. *SQUALOR* sounded great, but as my tone began to fade, I thought of those EL34s.

From the moment I plugged them in, I knew that I fucked up. The 90s version has a lot more midrange, and so do EL34s. What saved my first amp had neutered my current one.

I recorded test takes with new 6L6s, the old 6L6s, and the EL34s. They all sounded bad. Eventually I got a shiny new pair of Mesa 6L6s from Sweetwater, but it was still lacking some punch at 50w. I ordered a second pair and that big, fire-breathing motherfucker was back! It was time to record.

The most important part of recording was *actually* doing it live. I couldn't overdub the bass parts, so we invited Eric Munch to play on the record.

As confident as I am in Eric's abilities,** I booked us a show at Luckey's to rehearse. We all stopped learning the new album, and started practicing the set from *Blank Check*. And much like our first show as Jori & the PUSH, we had only practiced *once*, the night before the show. Still, we sounded great with him.

---

*I still have my VHT Deliverance, but I always use two amps to record.
**He's a *far* better player than I am!

The show was fucking *fire*. It was also Eric's birthday (almost), which really helped the turnout. We discussed adding him permanently, though I cautioned him that we were coming down from the high of a great show.

We recorded three weeks later. Bringing Eric from Seattle, and Kellen from Corvallis, we only had two days to record the instrumentation. It was ambitious, but attainable. Eric had played with us only two other times (one show and one practice), so Kellen and I would record each rehearsal and send them to Eric.

To my surprise, we recorded all 18 songs in a day! What sounded impossible had actually been easier. Playing nonstop was more comfortable than starting from scratch, 18 times in a row. The set was divided into six blocks and, for the most part, we sailed through on pure chemistry.

Since we only had a short time, I booked a photo shoot for the album and press kit. Given the lineup changes, we constantly need new photos. Cerebral Coretext had become quite skilled with a camera, so I hired him to set up in my living room while we recorded. After tracking three blocks, we went inside for an hour and that's what you see inside the CD.

Having spent two years on the demos, I was primed to make the best sonic recording of my career. And with a raise at work, I finally had the budget to take it further. I contacted Bill Stevenson at The Blasting Room. With only six medleys, recorded on one file, I suggested that the mix could be done in less time.* I presented a budget, knowing it was less than he quoted me before, but Bill said yes! After decades of dreaming, I finally have an album of my own that was mixed and mastered

*Essentially asking to bill me for six mixes instead of 18

at The Blasting Room.*

Eric was on board and Chad was already booking a summer tour when Kellen told me that his wife was pregnant. We talked to our friend Chase about filling in, but we settled on a shorter tour with Kellen.

With only 10 days to work with, I minimized our drive time. As much as I wanted to play the Northwest, we booked California exclusively. It was the smart move.

I still had Post-Tour-Stress-Disorder from *Blank Check* and *Fall Children,* so preparation was paramount. I wanted zero chance of breaking down again. The first step was completing the set of tires that I got on *Blank Check*. After that, my stereo froze on the same iPod playlist for weeks.** It was so bad that even the volume was stuck. What's worse, is it started when I put in a brand new CD.*** I couldn't even pry it out.

Three weeks later, the disc ejected itself. I celebrated until realizing that the hundreds of times I pushed the eject button were catching up to me. For the next two months, it tried to eject something that was no longer there. I knew that would be maddening on the road, so I replaced it before we left town.

State Farm cancelled my roadside assistance in 2017, so the next thing I needed was AAA. In addition to towing, they offered a battery service, so I played it safe and bought the upgrade.

Nothing's gonna fuck up the tour this time!

---

*Blasting Room engineer Jason Livermore wrote me to say that on his way home from the studio, he got pulled over while listening to our mixes. He later shared our video on Facebook and followed/friended us. I was really happy that a guy who's worked on ALL [pun intended] of my favorite albums was that stoked on DFS.

**Luckily, the playlist was A Wilhelm Scream, and I didn't really get tired of it.

***Clowns – *Nature/Nurture* (Fat Wreck)

Except there almost *wasn't* a trip.

Through the decades, I've learned that Eric and I communicate differently. My style, as you can tell from reading this motherfucker, is over the top. He prefers to be a little more off the grid. There's an ebb and flow to our friendship. We'll talk a lot, and then not again for a while. But he's always pulled through when it counts, and that's what I told Kellen.

We had prepared to record the long way if needed (song by song), but as promised, we heard from Eric the night before and the session went beautifully. Afterward, there were so many things going on (artwork, recording vocals, mixing, tour booking, press inquiries, etc.) that I was sending them daily updates on our progress. It was a lot.

Before long, we stopped getting replies from Eric. As time went on, and booking progress was made, I started reaching out to make sure we were good. I had almost lost Kellen to fatherhood, and with our history of temporary members, I was nervous about the tour. After six weeks of emails, texts, voicemails, and postal mail, we made a contingency plan.

Ben Polonsky had filled in for a few shows in 2018, so we asked him to play our release show before the tour. It was only three weeks away, and I just couldn't leave it to chance.

By week seven, I posted a music video for "Steps." The title comes from the closing line, *one step forward, two steps back.* I captioned the video, referencing our frustration with losing Justin after the *SQUALOR* tour. We finally had the band back and people loved the album, but we were quickly relinquished to a duo again. The shadow of Chris Wilson was everpresent. We had four different replacements (Justin, Crozz, Ben, and Eric), and as the release date crept up, our future was uncertain.

I wrote that the "rotating door" of bassists "affects us to this day." It was true. I desperately craved consistency. With two years of work, and $4,000 invested in the release, I worried that *PERIL* was on the line.

I was pleasantly surprised to receive an email from Eric that day. It said that he loved the record, but was offended by my comments online. After a couple days of correspondence, it was clear that we had both hurt each other and he was moving on.

Graciously, Eric texted me the day of the release show, saying "congrats on the album" and "wishing you guys a great show tonight." With that, I knew that we could work it out.

That resolved the lineup question, but it was really bad news for the tour. The release show was July 27th, and the tour started on August 17th. I asked every past member and a dozen other friends—even offering to fly them from out of state. No one could get the time off work.

Streetlight Cardiacs joined us on the 27th. Their bassist, Phil Roberson, was one of the first people I had asked, but his situation had changed. That Monday, Phil quit his job. He said that if we could get him back to Oregon after the last show, that he'd sleep in the van and go straight to his new job in morning. He fucking saved us.

Everything about the tour was difficult. We haven't even talked about the nightmare that was *booking* it. *SQUALOR* and *Blank Check* came together easily, and were profitable.* We assumed that DFS would continue that trajectory, but we didn't. The last three *PERIL* shows were confirmed just *days* before we left.**

*Before vehicle repairs anyway
**The Fullerton show didn't even have a flyer. I only had faith because the venue, Programme, liked my post about the tour.

We weren't able to confirm Chico or Medford, so we drove straight to San Francisco and stayed with Danny G. I love crashing with old tourmates. He and Kellen geeked out on video game music while Phil and I split some Chinese food.

I had eaten well on *Ravenous*, so I decided to give myself a $15 per diem, avoiding fast food at all costs. If I'm gonna eat one meal a day, it's gonna be something that *won't* make me feel like shit. I had Chinese, Thai, Mexican... really anything with rice or noodles.

Danny offered to do a photoshoot in the morning. We already needed new pics with Phil, so I was all for it. Afterward, we headed into town for the *real* reason we drove down early: Winston Smith.

Winston did the artwork for both *SQUALOR* and *PERIL*, but we had never met. I often wrote when passing through The Bay, but that was the first time our schedules aligned. Winston gave us a tour of his place, a basement-level art studio crammed with more artwork and memorabilia than you can imagine. It was located down an alley between busy San Francisco streets, so the best parking we could find had a 15 minute limit. The three of us took turns feeding the meter for about two hours.

Winston was great. He opened the door wearing our *PERIL* shirt with a smile. He was warm and welcoming, even giving us signed prints when we left. The only thing missing was the artwork for *PERIL*, which was missing at the time.

On the way out, we took some photos together, and Winston recommended a record store across the street. They were going out of business. At home, CD World had announced their closure as well. After 30 years, Skip locked the doors for good. That place had so many memories for me, and practically speaking, I still did *all* my Christmas shopping there and bought 90% of new releases there. They were also one of the only stores with a sizeable collection of Take 92 CDs.

It's troubling as an artist, too. People have been telling me for years that "nobody buys CDs anymore," and I usually respond by saying "then why do my CDs sell out every year?" People want something to take home with them after a good show. And for as much as people talk about vinyl, it's still only a fraction of the market share. We've come a long way from when Napster killed the chain stores. Now, even department stores (Target, Best Buy, Walmart, etc.) are drastically reducing their inventory.

I'm a fan of several artists who have already released their music exclusively digital, or vinyl, so I can never buy their album. There's shit that I fucking love, that I don't have, because they decided it's not worth it to print the most popular physical format available. It started with Apple making disc drives an add-on accessory, instead of a stock feature. Then car stereos went to touch screen and Bluetooth. Now with Spotify, there's practically no reason to actually pay an artist for their music.*

In any case, it wasn't that type of store. It was a heap of random electronics with barely enough walkway to browse one unobstructed aisle. Downstairs was a treasure trove of vinyl. I imagined the many times that DJ Shadow must've picked through that room. The shop owner had a much different disposition than Skip, who had last greeted me with a teary hug.

*Except it's fun to collect, the artwork is cooler than a thumbnail, you can READ THE LYRICS, the nostalgic smell of the paper, it's easier to decide what to play when it's not an endless digitized library, supporting artists allow them make more music, buying merch puts gas in the tank so you can see them in person, paying the artists instead of the distributor (Spotify, Apple, etc.), keeping local businesses alive (record stores), taking something off the shelf is a physical commitment so you're less likely to skip from song to song and actually listen to the whole fucking thing... but I guess I'm old fashioned.

"Oh, you're a punk band? Well we don't have any of the bands on your t-shirts." I made my way outside as he tried to close a sale with Phil. "I've got Conga Fury. Japanese punk. First pressing. Got five copies. How many you want?" He had some super cool shit in there, like an SP1200 sampler for one, but his bitterness was palpable.*

Fat Lizzy* booked us at a new (to us) venue called The Honey Hive. It was an artsy little room that fit about 20 people with no stage. Perfect!

I grabbed some beef and broccoli down the street, and when I got back, Evan and Ambur walked in. I was dumbstruck. Ambur and I had even texted that day, after she posted a pic of their dog at home. It was bait! I'm such a sucker for animals that she knew I'd respond! Those fuckers drove 500 miles just to surprise us. True friends.

The show was good from front to back. Fat Lizzy was much taller, faster, and more pissed off this time. I mentioned onstage that we had never actually played with Phil before that very moment, and people were blown away. He nailed it.

Most of our shows were all-ages, so we actually got out at like 11pm. Normally, I haven't *started* by 11. Ev and Ambur paid a fortune to stay in the city, but with our budget, we drove to a Motel 6 in Sacramento.

When loading up the van, Kellen found A SCREW IN MY NEW FUCKING TIRE. We weren't losing any pressure, so we decided to drive a little bit and keep an eye on it.

We didn't get far.

*That could've been the name of this book: His Bitterness Was Palpable

In the middle of the Bay Bridge, we heard the unmistakable sound of metal striking metal. It sounded too big to be a screw, but also *not* too big for a screw at 70mph. We lost traction on the left side pretty quickly. There was no exit, and no shoulder for a vehicle of our size.

The Bay Bridge is four miles long. At 45mph, with hazard lights flashing, it felt like an eternity. The first exit was on the left, and I couldn't cut across five lanes to get there. Eventually we pulled over at a bus exit. I called AAA. *It's ok. We're covered.*

But after 10 minutes searching for us, we were outside of their jurisdiction. I panicked, thinking that were going to spend a ton of money before we even *made* any. Luckily, CalTrans replaced the tire for free (with my spare) and the driver was a bassist who had "toured up and down the east coast in a van just like this." We gave him a CD, and he gave us an escort across six lanes of traffic.

I bought us a room for two nights (post-SF & Sac). After a good night's sleep, we went to Dimple Records, where "Blood in the Water" was filmed. I had seen an ad online: yet another Going Out of Business sale... a tour of record store funerals.

Dimple was flooded with vultures, picking through aisles with reckless abandon. Signs read *70% Off* and *Buy 2 Get 2 Free*. I walked away with eight CDs for $12. Normally I'd be excited, but it was just sad. As a fan *and* an artist, the future looks bleak.

The show was at a little dive called On The Y. It looked great until they wouldn't let us backline or even load in the gear. The sound guy had never worked there before and worried (aloud) that their equipment was inadequate. It was gonna be a shitshow.

I was laying down at the merch table, feeling sorry for myself, when a familiar voice startled me awake. Ev and Ambur surprised us again! We had a real good time, joking about stacking donuts on our dongs and other intelligent topics.

The next day, waiting for a new tire at Les Schwab, I counted my blessings. It's the friends that make this life bearable.

I could swear that I'd never been to Santa Cruz, but when we got to town, I realized I had played the *exact same venue* on *Vacant Eyes*. This shit is really becoming a blur.

We did some digging at a record store next door, and then Phil and I walked to Five Guys. We were nerding out about my SVT2-PRO (bass amp) when we came across a music shop. Surprisingly, they had a vintage SVT-II, which is pretty rare.

Stay Out was supposed to join us, but one of their members had a death in the family. That meant our only opener was Kinetic Radio, who wasn't even local. Needless to say, we played for ourselves again.*

The next day, we hit up two Streetlight Records and a comic shop. I found a super rare Mikah Nine** CD, and completed the Batman *Knightfall* trilogy that I started on the very first tour. Used books can be tricky because you have to track down the same versions of each volume. That one took eight years to find!

I got to see another good friend in San Jose. My *Daydream* and Judo Pony drummer, Ben Schaaff, came to the show and gave us a place to stay. It was great to catch up since he had moved to California right after *Daydream*.

Stay Out *did* show up that night, but their drummer was underage and they got kicked off the bill. I felt so bad that we

*Would've been more fun playing *with* ourselves, honestly
** now known as Myka 9 (Freestyle Fellowship)

couldn't work it out, especially given the circumstances. I also wanted to get their new album, but they split right away. The show was actually pretty good, reconnecting with The Roughies and Kinetic Radio.

The best surprise, however, was a photo text from Winston: he had *PERIL* in his hand. He offered to sell it to me, and we set up a meeting before the Gilman show on Saturday. I couldn't believe I was going to have the original on my wall.

Fullerton almost didn't happen. I had seen a thrash punk band called Skullcrack in Eugene, and told them I was looking for new punk venues in LA. They said Programme Skate & Sound was the place to be. I checked out their Instagram and it looked AWESOME. So many great bands had played there, all crammed into a little skate shop. I was stoked.

Except for the fact that I couldn't get a response. They had so many bands hitting them up that I was just one of many others knocking on their door. Later, I was talking with Erin Micklow, trying to schedule an interview for *Last Rockers TV*. She said "oh, my friend Efrem works there. Let me text him for you."

I said "wait, Efrem from Death By Stereo?!" Within minutes, I was texting one of my hardcore heroes. He was on the case.

Fast forward to the first day of tour. I called Efrem from Danny's kitchen. We still hadn't received 100% confirmation that a show was even happening. There was no time/lineup/details, and the venue hadn't posted about it. I was *concerned*. I left a voicemail, and we had confirmation a day later. It wasn't much notice, but I was just glad to get a foot in the door.

The drive to LA is grueling in the summertime, but the van made it in one piece. Programme was tucked around the corner of a strip mall. I walked in wearing my Skullcrack shirt, and was immediately greeted by Efrem and the shop's owner, Chris. DFS went to a Thai restaurant next door, and we then hung out with all the Programme guys. There was a copy of the then-new *Beastie Boys Book*, which I had just read at home. Chris and I geeked out about the Beasties and old school hip hop throughout the night. It was a good vibe.

The opener was a new punk band from LA called Raptors. They didn't have a record out yet, but their set was great. (They've recorded since then and you should check them out!)

The headliner was an Australian thrash metal band called Wolfpack, and the absolute *nicest* guys ever. They wanted us to fly out and tour Australia, which would've been amazing if we could afford it! It was the best hang of the whole tour. On top of that, one of the dudes hanging out turned out to be the drummer of Death By Stereo, Mike Cambra! We also hit it off, and kept in touch ever since.*

We started the day at Amoeba and Headline Records in Hollywood. What we didn't know is that The Rolling Stones were playing next door to our venue in Pasadena. Traffic was absolutely maddening. We circled downtown over and over, trying to find a spot big enough for the van to parallel park.

As I researched my flyers photos for this tour, I found a GIF dated August 22, 2019. Seeing Chris Farley's raging bus driver from Billy Madison, I immediately remembered what happened: stopped at a traffic light, I began to turn and heard a scrape with a loud honk. Somehow, a small car had crammed between me and a parked car *in the bike lane*, trying to pass me. I swiped them as I made my perfectly correct and legal right turn.

*Check out Episode #72 of The Take 92 Podcast to hear the Mike Cambra interview

We parked in front a thrift store and checked out the damage. It was minor, but noticeable. I decided to part ways with the guys and eat by myself. I needed to cool off, but just my luck, some fucking mouth breather started talking as I read the menu on the door, saying *tHeY dOn'T sErVe StOnEs FaNs HeRe*.

I was *not* having it.

My only photo from that show was with Kelly, who had recently moved to LA with her boyfriend. It was nice to see a familiar face, especially in an unexpected place!

We played with a skate punk band called CC Potato. They had classic 90's riffs and melodies that would be perfectly at home on Fat Wreck. They may have played a NOFX cover, if I remember correctly.

The highlight of the night was seeing Failing Up, who I had discovered through Programme's Instagram. They had an original sound and a powerful vocalist. I had missed out when they toured Oregon, but we got to share the stage instead. They seemed like a new band, and had a lot of excitement around them. Their bassist invited us to crash at his place, but we needed a head start if we were going to make it to Stockton.

Quick detour: before the tour, I took one of Ang's gold rings. It belonged to my late mother-in-law, Kathy, and Ang had always wanted to melt it down, into a new design. With our 20th anniversary approaching, I took it to a jeweler and did just that.

I got the call that it was ready when we were at a Barnes & Noble in Stockton. I don't lie, but when it comes to presents, I'm pretty tricky. I told Ang where I was, and said that I got her an anniversary present.

Weeks later, we were celebrating in Hawaii, and *that's* when I gave her the ring. Through tears of joy, she said "I thought you bought me a CD at the mall!" Mission accomplished.

Stockton was booked through one of our rap contacts, so I didn't know what to expect. We played at a grange, which was as nostalgic as it was terrible. The PA was a hodgepodge of inadequacy, and the first band was in high school. They played proggy hardcore that kinda reminded me of my friend Thomas Erak from Seattle. The guitarist was pretty incredible. Then they played a cover of Thomas' band, The Fall of Troy. I thought it was super cool, and sent him a video of the performance.

Someone gave me a big hug, and it turned out to be a girl named Kristin,* who I met on the first rap tour! She, along with her boyfriend Pedro, fed us Korean BBQ and came to our show in Riverside, CA. Eight years later, at a Stockton punk show, my band was on the bill with her little brother. Small world.

We returned to Winston's that day, and got our first look at the original, handmade artwork for *PERIL*. At 17 inches square, it was truly stunning to see all the detail that went into such a complicated piece. Seeing the collage in person reveals all the tiny layers of paper, and the insanely precise cuts, on the gun lettering especially. It's a true work of art.

Winston hung out with us again and shared a few laughs. The bathroom was equally fascinating. It was the size of a closet, covered from floor to ceiling with his art prints. One was a poster for a book I actually owned in high school, *The Best Democracy Money Can Buy* by Greg Palast.

*Pronounced Kristine

We had one last show after Gilman, at a skate park in Arcata. It was a two-day punk festival with two stages and a TON of bands. There was a food truck and several vendors outside, but we were told to put our merch in the loft overlooking the skate ramps. I hung out there for quite a while before realizing that *no one* was coming, and moved our table outside.

The lineup was packed with *10 acts*. It started with a feminist punk band called Sad Krotch, and had everything from jams to death metal by the end of the night. We were ideally placed at 8pm, just before the headliner, White Manna.

Since Phil had to start a new job in the morning, we packed the fuck up as soon as we finished. Our merch was damp from the humidity as we rolled up the shirts one last time. The food truck gave us some giant burritos to fuel the drive, and Phil slept as much as he could in the back seat.

After 300 miles and one Kamikaze bat on my windshield, we arrived at my house in Eugene. Phil's wife met us in the driveway and my bandmates returned to their cities. With my ambition waning, and Kellen's imminent fatherhood, I knew that it was our last tour for a while. We discussed bringing in Chase to fill in, but losing Eric on top of it was just too much. DFS isn't a solo act.

We agreed to a hiatus for 2020. What I didn't know, is that months later, a new coronavirus would end *all* touring worldwide. Our timing was actually pretty good.

Since *no one* could hit the road, it seemed appropriate to finish this fucking book. As mentioned, I wrote it before *Ravenous* and *PERIL*, but added these chapters when my original editor, Thomas, kept missing deadlines.* This is why I'm DIY.

---

*We would soon have a falling out as well, though for very different reasons

I did have one last show after *PERIL*. Terrell was coming back to Old Nick's on October 19th and asked if I wanted to play. I did not.

After Hawaii, I considered myself "semi-retired." It was the happiest I'd been in years, just working, spending nights with my Lady, recording The Take 92 Podcast, and expanding my Batman collection. I even flew out to meet Michael Keaton, which became the catalyst for The Bat Fan Addict Podcast (with Ben Polonsky and Evan).

So when Terrell asked if I wanted to play on my birthday, I said no. My idea of a nice 34th birthday was going to dinner with Ang and maybe seeing a movie. Low key.

But I couldn't leave him hanging. I quickly relented, and it was everything I expected it to be. Chris and Chase came; both former bandmates. That was rare. But as a fitting end to this story, it was a Birthday Party show. I played for a handful of friends and my immediate family. I was so unenthused, that at times I would lie on the ground or just stop rapping and talk until the chorus. In a way, I embarrassed myself in front of Terrell and all the people I loved. But my heart wasn't in it and I didn't care.

In January 2020, I received some shocking news: my greatest fear was coming true. For years, I had put music before my family, friends, and finances. I was living far beyond my means, but couldn't stop myself. The dream seemed just within reach.

Ang had started therapy a couple months earlier, to learn some coping and communication skills. To the best of my knowledge, there was some unresolved grief after the loss of her mom. What I didn't know came crashing down in an instant: "I haven't been happy in a long time," she said. "I've wanted to leave for years." *YEARS.*

I could see how devastating it was for her to say that, and how much she had been holding back to protect me. She believed that I could hurt myself if she came clean.

I was in shock. She was perplexed that I remained calm and unemotional, but my mind was reeling. Every insecurity I had was true. We sat on the bed for hours while I asked questions, trying to connect the dots. She did her best to articulate some very difficult truths.

I knew when Kathy died, in 2013, that I needed to be there for Ang. Instead, I waited until the day before the tour to cancel. I only took six months off the road, and resumed working harder than ever.

She put herself through school while working a full-time job... to supplement my part-time retail/full-time music life. She had supported me through half a dozen tours by then, and it was my turn to step up. I didn't.

Instead, I made a gesture by telling her success story on *Famous Last Words* (2015). It wasn't a love song, it was an empowerment song. I directed a music video that dramatized her story arc, and was disappointed by her positive-yet-passive reaction. It was one of the first red flags, but also not a total surprise. Exhibiting some level of self-awareness, I wrote another song on the same album:

> *I wanted to provide when she was going to college*
> *Now she's started a business and I can only acknowledge*
> *that she did it by herself, and I'm proud of her for it*
> *But when I'm handing her the bill, it's still hard to ignore it*

That was the same year I learned that we were behind on our bills. After the *Vacant Eyes* tour, I committed to put in more hours at work, and take back one of the bills that I had pawned off after *I Quit*. I began working four days a week (an astonishing half-measure), and didn't tour until the following summer. These gestures were sincere, but inadequate. She was trying to build a new career from scratch, and I was still leaning on her financially. We were no longer partners. I was her dependent.

After six more tours, I accepted a management position and resumed full-time work. I finally took back my fair share of the bills and no longer spent time on the road. It was the right thing to do, but in 2018, it was *too little, too late.*

All of these things ran through my head while I sat motionless, listening to my wife hyperventilate. I thought back to when we were 19, and had tearful sex for the "last time" before I left for Seattle with This Day's End.

I vividly recalled being 18, when my dad told me in detail about how his drug addiction led to their divorce. He concluded by saying how lucky I was with Ang: "don't fuck it up like I did." In spite of my straightedge defiance, I managed to ruin my own marriage with a much different addiction.

I went to Evan's house and talked it out. I was fully aware of my selfishness, and had long feared that a great cost would be paid. When Ang and I talked the next day, we were both unsure what to do next. In my mind it was over, but she hadn't gone anywhere yet. We needed to clear our heads. Together.

That weekend, we went to our honeymoon/anniversary spot in Lincoln City, OR. It was an awkward two and a half hour drive, and neither of us knew what to expect. The minute we got into our room, it was clear that our passion hadn't waned. That was a good sign. We ate at our favorite restaurant, Kyllo's, and then spent hours talking in the jacuzzi. It was the most unflinchingly honest conversation of our lives.

That confessional trip saved our marriage. Most of what we discussed had been rectified by incremental changes, but the years of imbalance had fostered deep resentment. I accepted full responsibility and apologized profusely. We both felt better with it all on the table, and vowed to communicate more openly.

I'm eternally grateful that we had that opportunity before the pandemic would keep us in close quarters for a very long time. I'm happy to report that we've lasted 21 years and counting. I may not have *fully* understood this before, but the true success of my life is our relationship.

After Lincoln City, I recorded a mixtape (*Fighting Words*), released the long lost Judo Pony album (*Paper Mountains*), and resumed writing a long-awaited new album with Gabe (*Demented Inventive Energy*).

Then, as my day job became "essential" and subsequently hazardous, all that creativity was drained. After months of severe anxiety, I quit my job of eight years and started working from home. Like the flick of a switch, my old self was back.

Today, I'm writing features, hosting two podcasts, chipping away at *D.I.E.* and recording demos for a third DFS album. So while many are missing the road, I'm writing this chapter *on the clock*, between two computers and a laptop, grateful that I may never have to leave this studio again.

(Left to right:) Kellen, Ben, me
Old Nick's Pub (Eugene, OR) 2019

Recording *PERIL* demos
Take 92 Music (Eugene, OR) 2019

(Left to right:) me, Winston, Kellen, Phil
Grant's Tomb (San Francisco, CA) 2019

Acknowledgements

To my Lady—for selflessly enduring these struggles behind the scenes. I would not be here without you.

To my family—for your unwavering support since Day One.

To Evan and Sarx—for changing my life with that first tour. Those days will stay with me forever.

To Chad and Brady—for being invaluable partners, allowing me to elevate my craft while you both did the real work.

And to Micheal—for renewing my faith in myself. If not for that gesture, I might still be wondering what could have been.

Artist Credits

How to Ruin Your Life (Pat Jensen)
I Quit My Job For This (Chris Rowlands)
Not So Bluish (Char Houweling)
Cats, Pajamas (Tucker Jackson, Tron Burgundy)
Bored with Buddha (Char Houweling)
Original Recipe (Char Houweling)
Attack of The Show Stoppers (Evan Vaught, Char Houweling)
Bears Repeating (Char Houweling)
Blood in The Water (Char Houweling)
Vacant Eyes (Tucker Jackson)
Rare Form 1&2 (Pat Jensen)
The World Has No Eyedea (Brandon Crowson)
SQUALOR (Winston Smith, Tucker Jackson)
Blank Check (Tucker Jackson)
Fall Children (Pat Jensen)
Ravenous (Pat Jensen)
PERIL (Pat Jensen)

Additional formatting and art direction by Sammy Warm Hands

www.ingramcontent.com/pod-product-compliance
Lightning Source LLC
Chambersburg PA
CBHW050851160426
43194CB00011B/2118